Under The Canopy

STUDIES IN
COMPARATIVE RELIGION

Frederick M. Denny, Series Editor

Under the Canopy

Ritual Process and Spiritual Resilience in South Africa

Linda E. Thomas

The University of South Carolina

Cloth edition published by the University of South Carolina Press, 1999
Paperback edition published in Columbia, South Carolina, by the University of South
    Carolina Press, 2007

Manufactured in the United States of America

The Library of Congress has cataloged the cloth edition as follows:

Thomas, Linda E. (Linda Elaine)
    Under the canopy : ritual process and spiritual resilience in South
Africa / Linda E. Thomas.
        p.   cm. — (Studies in comparative religion)
    Includes bibliographical references and index.

    ISBN 1-57003-311-0
    1. Spiritual healing.   2. Church and social problems—South Africa.
3. Independent churches—South Africa.   4. South Africa—Race relations.
5. Racism—South Africa.   6. South Africa—Social conditions.   7. St. John's
Apostolic Faith Mission Church (Guguletu, Cape Town, South Africa)   8.
Guguletu (Cape Town, South Africa)—Church history.   I. Title.   II. Series:
Studies in comparative religion (Columbia, S.C.)
BT732.5 .T473   1999   99-6132
289.9'3'0968735—ddc21

ISBN: 978-1-57003-752-8 (pbk)

To my parents, Henry and Mary,
whose example taught me
the tenacity to hope for, fight for, and live for the truth

To my spiritual parents, Reverend Leslie and Mrs. Antoinette Dyson,
whose love sustained me during my early years of ontological inquiry

To my siblings, George, Joyce, Beverly, Harriet, and Henry,
with whom I celebrate life in its fullest dimension

To the memory of
the Reverend Dr. Lydia August and Reverend and Mrs. Mjoli

To my newfound African parents, Reverend and Mrs. Xaba,
who embraced and claimed me as a daughter of South Africa.
Through them I received new life.
Amandla!

Contents

Illustrations   ix
Tables   xi
Series Editor's Preface   xiii
Preface   xv
Prologue   xix

Introduction   1
Chapter 1   An Inquiry into an African Indigenous Church   15
Chapter 2   The Setting   22
Chapter 3   Ethnographic Profile of St. John's Apostolic Faith Mission Church–Guguletu   33
Chapter 4   The Ritual and Theology of St. John's   62
Chapter 5   Symbols in St. John's Ritual   86
Chapter 6   St. John's Health Care System   95
Chapter 7   Conclusions   115

Appendix 1   Methodology   123
Appendix 2   Demographic Information   133
Appendix 3   Schedule of Questions   136
Notes   141
Bibliography   155
Index   171

Illustrations

following page 32

The baptism of two initiates in the ocean

A holy dance during the worship service

An usher washing a priest's hands

A member under the canopy

The removal of a cow's skin

The bishop and his assistant blessing the entrails of a cow and sheep

The burning of entrails to honor the ancestors

Members receiving communion

Map

Guguletu — Location of St. Johns Apostoloc Faith Mission   xxiv

Tables

following page 128

Table 1. Sex, Marital Status, Age, Place of Birth, Number of Surviving Children, Number of Deceased Children

Table 2. Education, Employment Status, Monthly Income, Current Residence Location, Number of Rooms in Residence

Table 3. Housing Conditions

Table 4. Sex, Language, Church Affiliation Prior to St. John's Membership

Series Editor's Preface

This book breaks new ground in this series's history. It takes us to South Africa, a richly diverse region of the world only recently delivered from the long ordeal of human deprivation and suffering under apartheid. This field based study provides both an ethnographic profile and an extensive ritological analysis of an African indigenous church, St. John's Apostolic Faith Mission Church, in Guguleto, a township outside Capetown. The central focus of this study is healing among the church's members in a world filled with suffering and its effects, both inherited and contemporary. Linda Thomas is aware of her own role as an outside investigator in a situation long accustomed to being victimized in one way or another by outsiders.

Although unique and valuable in itself, St. John's Church is representative of a widespread type of newer religious institution in South Africa. One witnesses in this church the creative combining of traditional, indigenous beliefs, practices, and values with the colonialist culture. The author's approach has been to combine theological, ethnographic, and hermeneutical perspectives and methods in a harmonized manner, thus capturing not only the external and quantifiable aspects of the congregation's life, but also its inner, intimate qualities and strengths through interviews with members and sensitive interpretation of their faith in a healing process that is rooted in profound spiritual experiences.

It is not usual to find an active theological dimension in today's academic study of religion. But in this case it is essential, because otherwise there would be no means of appreciating what actually propels and assures the congregation's life, both at the individual-personal and community levels. There is also a strong political dimension to Linda Thomas's study, because St. John's Church has provided its poverty-stricken people with a means of resistance to many threats—political, economic, and social—and empowered them to endure, whether during the period of apartheid or today, when South Africans are still faced with great challenges as they build a just and secure social order.

It is a pleasure to place *Under the Canopy* alongside an earlier book in this series, *Feeling the Spirit,* Frances Kostarelos's ethnographic study of an

African-American storefront church in Chicago. The two books provide valuable insights into the ways people at risk order and lead their lives by means of a faith system that enables them to find meaning and hope in difficult circumstances.

Frederick Mathewson Denny
Series Editor

Preface

Under the Canopy is about rituals of healing at St. John's Apostolic Faith Mission Church and the ways that members live their everyday lives at the close of the apartheid era in South Africa. St. John's is a Zionist/Apostolic Church of the Spirit that incorporates practices from various streams of African religion and Protestant Christianity to form a new religion that gives meaning to poor, oppressed people who struggle daily to have continuity with their precolonial past and to accept the signs and symbols of the religion of those who colonized their ancestors. The rituals of healing blend worldviews to form a cosmology that helps people live with everyday challenges. Just outside of Cape Town, in Guguletu, the township where St. John's is located, and in the surrounding black African townships where members live, ultrapoor people—those who earn less than 178 rand (R) (U.S.$51) a month—create meaning in their lives through rituals of healing. Because poverty, unemployment, and violence are social stresses affecting daily life, these experiences are gathered under St. John's cosmological rubric of sickness (*ukugula*). The rituals of healing, performed four times a day, seven days a week, are a way to resist the negative effects of social strain in a supportive community.

This book is the result of four years of writing and research. Twelve months of fieldwork were conducted during a period of rapid social change in South Africa (1991–1994). In 1996, I conducted twelve more months of research at St. John's as a Pew Charitable Trust Fellowship recipient. During my first six months of fieldwork, I lived with a family in Guguletu, attended and participated in rituals of healing, and interviewed members in Cape Town's black South African townships. During that six-month period, St. John's minister, Reverend Malinge Xaba, took me under his wing, taught me about the signs and symbols in the healing rituals, and granted me permission to interview members. In July 1992, Reverend Xaba died suddenly, and his widow, Mama Nosipho Xaba, communicated clearly in a mailgram and in telephone calls that as a "daughter" of the family I was expected to return to South Africa for the funeral. Reverend Xaba had given me a new Xhosa name, Fonica, meaning "we need you," and now the family into which I had been "adopted" wanted me to return. While I initially thought that it was impossible to fulfill Mama Xaba's expectation, I gathered my resources, managed to get a visa, and returned to South Africa in time for the funeral. If I had had any doubts about being a member of the Xaba family, my return to Guguletu laid those uncertainties to rest. I did not feel like an outsider, although I was unambiguously aware that I was. I learned about funeral rites of healing and continued to talk with members about their lives, the rituals, and Reverend Xaba.

Many people have read portions of the manuscript or heard me give lectures about its contents. I cannot begin to thank all of the people who have shown interest and offered encouragement. I gave lectures on African religion and independent African churches at Iliff School of Theology, where my students were acutely curious and asked candid questions about my research in ways that helped me reflect deeply upon my work. I have colleagues at Garrett Evangelical Theological Seminary and Iliff School of Theology, as well as at other institutions, who also asked probing questions, read the manuscript, and showed great interest. Tom Troeger read the text in its earliest draft and offered insightful comments. Jose Cabazon, David Himrod, Dwight N. Hopkins, Barbara Troxell, and Zolani Ngwane also read the manuscript and gave a helpful critique. I would like to thank the entire faculty at Iliff for the stimulating discussion of a portion of the text presented at a faculty colloquium. Likewise, I appreciate the Garrett community's invitation to give a lecture in December 1997, which permitted me to sharpen my analysis. At both Garrett and Iliff, I benefited from the participation of colleagues from diverse academic disciplines in colloquia on my manuscript.

I want to thank especially Karen McCarthy Brown, whose gentle spirit and rigorous mind offered encouragement and criticism. *Under the Canopy* is a better book because of the support of Barry Blose, my editor at the University of South Carolina Press, and the meticulous copyediting of Cheryl Hoffman. I also acknowledge and thank David Himrod of Garrett Evangelical Theological Seminary and Linda Adams of Brigham Young University for editorial assistance.

This project from its inception has been made possible because of people in Cape Town who supported me. University of Cape Town's Vice-Chancellor Mamphela Ramphele, having completed her fieldwork for her Ph.D. in social anthropology in 1991, told me about the skills of her research assistant, Barbara Manata. As a result, Barbara became my research assistant. She has been the backbone of this project as we traveled together finding shacks in Philipi, Khayelitsha, and Crossroads; houses in Langa, Guguletu, New Crossroads, and Nyanga; and festivals in the Transkei. Her research skills are superior, and she has been available at every turn throughout the duration of this project.

I cannot say enough about the members of St. John's who let me come into their homes time and time again to ask the same questions and sometimes new questions, but all the time questions. I am grateful for members who let me sit with them during moments of social distress when they were particularly vulnerable. For friends who told me their stories and offered a cup of tea, I am grateful. I am also eternally grateful to the Xaba family members, who were a steady harbor during the course of this journey. Mama Xaba always permitted me to videotape services and to be an invasive presence. When she became the pastor of the church after her husband's death, she increased my access to field materials. She opened doors to the hierarchy within the St. John's family. To her I am deeply indebted. Finally, I want to thank the Department of Religious Studies, the Department of Social Anthropology, and the Centre for African Studies at the University of Cape Town for offering a stimulating intellectual center and physical space for me to write and reflect upon my research throughout this project.

This research was funded by Iliff School of Theology's Louise Iliff Fund. I was able to attend Reverend Xaba's funeral in 1992 because Iliff's president, Donald Messer, generously granted resources from this fund. The Pew Charitable Trust Fund granted money that permitted me to take a year's research leave to write the manuscript. I also want to thank Jane Smith, formerly dean at Iliff School of Theology, for her encouragement. Gratitude is also expressed to Celia Walter, reference librarian par excellence, of the Jagger Library at the University of Cape Town. Her zealous tracking of sources was phenomenal. The technical assistance that I received from Margaret Manion, Shirley Kaaz, Annette Perenzee, and Laura Banks in transcribing interviews and preparing portions of the manuscript is gratefully acknowledged as is the support of various research assistants, particularly Tron Moller.

Finally, my deepest gratitude is extended to Dwight N. Hopkins, my best friend and husband, whose exuberant spirit and remarkable mind encouraged me in extraordinary ways. Our love and life of scholarship bring joy to our marriage. Moreover, our intellectual pursuits have motivated me to write this book's sequel.

Prologue

While growing up in a black neighborhood in Baltimore, Maryland, called Turner Station, I learned very early that race matters, because myriad signs, symbols, and practices around me demonstrated this to be so. I remember distinctly the railroad tracks that were across the street from the Methodist church I attended all my life. All members of the church, from the youngest child to the oldest adult, knew that we were not to cross those tracks because white folks lived on the other side.

When I was eight years old, a new highway was constructed not far from my house. The people in Turner Station were happy that a capital improvement was being made close to our community. While there were benefits in having the highway, the main drawback was that it created a physical barrier that further enforced racial segregation. I remember the sadness in my mother's voice when she said, "Black folks and white folks will be further apart now." I realized very early that black and white folks were not to live together.

Early in the summer of 1965, parents in my neighborhood had a series of meetings about the ramifications of elementary-school-aged children being bused to an all-white school in Dundalk, an adjacent, predominantly white neighborhood. I had just completed third grade and was excited about going into my fourth year at the all-black elementary school that was walking distance from home. My friends and I were also excited about the possibility of going to a new school, but our parents were cautious. My young mind kept wondering, "Why are our parents worried?" After all, I was excited about going to school on a bus and making new friends.

When September arrived and the first day of school approached, I could tell that my parents were both pleased and nervous. They believed that we would get a better education at the white school but were worried about the scars we might have to endure because of racism. Would I and others be treated with respect? Would we be encouraged and told that we were achievers? Would we have a positive experience with white teachers? Mama stayed home from work on our first day to help the three of us children prepare for school. Since I was the oldest, my father talked to me the night before about my responsibility to look after myself and the twins, Henry and Harriet, my younger brother and sister. The next morning, as we were about to leave the house to board the bus, Mama looked at me and said, "Linda, just remember that you're as good as any of those other children." I looked at Mama with feelings of bewilderment and encouragement. I knew that something felt strange, even dangerous, but at the same time I knew there was great opportunity.

I now know the terror that my mother and father felt in sending their children into an all-white environment at a time and in a nation where being black meant living with the threat of being harmed. During my first year at the new school, I had both positive and negative experiences. The lesson I learned about race during my first month at the new school, however, was something that has stayed with me all my life. That lesson was that racism is learned and passed down from generation to generation. While it is often practiced unconsciously, it is blatantly apparent to those who are negatively affected by it.

I was only nine years old when I had an experience related to the social construction of race. Debbie Smith, a white girl in my fourth-grade class, and I had earned the privilege of erasing the blackboard after school. Both of us worked hard at our task before Mrs. Roseberry, our teacher, stepped out of the room. However, the moment Mrs. Roseberry left, Debbie, who I thought was my friend, rushed over to me and said, "Linda, I want you to know that you are a nobody. And you aren't going to amount to anything good in life." I was shocked to be spoken to in this fashion and to receive such a message. Yet as I stood there, something within me pushed away the sting of those words. Even though I was only nine, my resolute mind said, "This is not about me. This is about Debbie." Moreover, I thought to myself, "Debbie's folks must be teaching her bad things." I didn't respond to her, but I felt great sadness. Now I understood why my mother told me on the first day of school to remember that I was as good as any other child. I now knew that she meant that I was as good as any of the white children. I pushed that story about Debbie Smith to the recesses of my mind and never told anyone about the incident until I was an adult and encountered South Africa in 1985.

I heard about apartheid when I was in college and noted its similarity to the racial discrimination that black people experienced in the United States. During my last year of college, I applied for a fellowship from the Fund for Theological Education to attend a seminary. One of the essay questions I responded to asked, "What is a critical issue that the world will have to deal with in the 1980s?" My response was that the world would have to deal with apartheid in South Africa. How did I know that this would be so? Had I experienced something in my life that taught me about the high costs of racism?

Was it because I was one of twenty-five black students who attended a predominantly white college in Maryland from 1974 to 1978 and experienced
what it meant to be black in America in a way that I never had before I left
home? What had happened in those four years?

During my college years, I was continually on the defensive with my professors and my peers. Not only did I constantly have to prove myself, but also
there was a level of support I did not get because a subtle system prevented me
and other black students from achieving our full potential. I understood why
my mother wanted me to go to Morgan State College, a predominantly black
school in Baltimore, and live at home. She knew that there would be more
support for me because I would be encouraged and affirmed simply because
there would be people who could affirm my worldview.

The essay question that the Fund for Theological Education asked permitted me to look outside my own experience and see that others suffered and
yet were strengthened because of their experience with racism. I realized that
South Africa's reality for black and white people was strikingly similar to, and
yet different from, my experiences in the United States. I knew that I would
fight for justice in South Africa just as I had fought for justice on my college
campus, despite sometimes feeling as if I were on the most-hated-person list
because of the questions I raised.

As a seminary student, I was active in the anti-apartheid movement. I and
other students asked the board of trustees at Union Theological Seminary in
New York City to divest from South Africa. Our goal was to bring an economic crisis to South Africa because we believed that threatening a material
base would send a message that the Reagan administration's policy of "constructive engagement" did not. We had learned many lessons from the civil
rights movement in the United States. For instance, during the 1955–56
Montgomery, Alabama bus boycott, one of the reasons the white establishment paid attention was because of their financial losses. We'd also learned
from the 1960s nonviolent resistance movement. In 1984, I was arrested for
demonstrating at the South African embassy in New York City along with others from the New York Annual Conference of the United Methodist Church
(UMC), including Bishop C. Dale White. I prepared my predominantly white
congregation in White Plains, New York, for my action on the Sunday before
I was detained. My church's membership included a significant number of
executives who worked for IBM, a company that antiapartheid activists had
targeted to pressure to divest from South Africa because its computer tech-
nology helped the South African Defense Force (SADF) enforce pass laws that
monitored the movement of black people and aided the South African state in
keeping apartheid in place. As a pastor, I believed that my arrest was a rare

opportunity to teach through action. I wondered what effect the arrest of U.S. citizens would have on ending apartheid and decided that if this action would give
a glimmer of hope to black South Africans, then it was worth it. Being arrested
seemed the least that I could do. My congregation supported my decision.

It was also in 1984 that I and a team of eight other United Methodists
planned a trip to Mozambique to assist people who were in the midst of war,
famine, and drought. At that time, the media focused on the famine in
Ethiopia, and international experts informed us that very few were responding
to the situation in Mozambique. Several team members met with the treasurer
of the United Methodist Church in Mozambique, Shadrack Uquelo, who urged
us to go to his country because there were problems with which the government needed outside assistance. For instance, South Africa was destabilizing
Mozambique, and medicine was urgently needed. My colleagues and I raised
donations from churches in the New York Annual Conference of the United
Methodist Church and filled our suitcases with a quarter of a million dollars'
worth of medicine for Mozambique. There we witnessed great devastation:
people were starving, many lived in refugee camps, and disease was rampant.
To gain a better understanding of the causes of the war in Mozambique, we
decided to travel to South Africa. Peter Storey, president of the Methodist
Church in South Africa, while passing through the Mozambican capital city of
Maputo, told us that President P. W. Botha had enforced a state of emergency
in South Africa. The black townships were hotbeds of unrest, and the state
feared an insurrection by black South Africans who had grown tired of the
tyranny of apartheid.

My white colleague Randy Day and I were asked by the team to enter
South Africa early and determine whether it was safe for others to come.
Randy and I arrived in Johannesburg on 15 July 1985. While I was annoyed
that I had been designated an honorary white person because of my U.S. pass-
port, I decided that it was more important for me to connect with people to
whose struggle I was committed than to be concerned about my pride. When
I entered Jan Smuts Airport in Johannesburg (renamed Johannesburg
International Airport on September 4, 1995 as a sign of a newly elected government [the African National Congress] and as an end to the apartheid era),
it seemed no different from arriving at New York's JFK International; people
were going in every direction and there seemed to be no apparent segregation.
Our hosts, members of the Methodist Church of South Africa, housed us with
members who lived in a Colored area of Johannesburg called Coronationville.
By the time the other team members arrived, I better understood the impact
of racial segregation and discrimination and was acutely aware of color in a
way that I had not been prior to entering the country. I wondered what it

would be like to travel as an integrated team of four blacks and four whites in a country where it was illegal for blacks and whites to worship, live, and eat together. The group's anxiety increased to the point that we had a major fight on the morning we were to go to Soweto. Our hosts told us that we were going to the township at an extremely tense time and that they could not guarantee our safety. The team had no disagreement about whether we would go into Soweto; the disagreement was about whether we would take camera equipment to document what we witnessed. Since we were illegally entering a township that was under heavy military surveillance, black team members were adamant that no camera equipment be taken. Two of our white colleagues agreed and two did not. As we argued about our safety, I was aware of my intensity about this issue. Not only was I afraid—somehow I was reminded of the danger I had experienced as a black woman at various times in my life in the United States. I knew that if we were stopped in Soweto, the black Americans would suffer more abuse than white Americans from the white SADF. We came to a consensus that no photos would be taken, and our hosts took us to Soweto.

Entering the township was like entering a Third World country in the midst of a war. While driving from central Johannesburg to Soweto, we noted a rapid deterioration in living conditions; there were dirt roads instead of paved roads, and huge military vehicles that looked like army tanks were everywhere. The streets were filled with people; I saw three white policemen throw a black man into one of the military vehicles as though he were a piece of paper. There was no respect for human life as white police held their AK47s ready to shoot. I was glad that I had made out my will before I left the United States.

I of course lived through my South African experience, but as I traveled to black townships and relocation camps throughout the country, a part of me died. The stories of people who had been tortured in ways too gross to write about were often overwhelming. I could not believe that human beings could treat other human beings so brutally. A part of me died because of the blows I saw people take upon their bodies and psyches. Unlike the suffering servant, Jesus, they screamed, shouted, and fought their executioners. At the same time, a part of me came to life with even more fervor, as I saw people who were full of life and determination; people determined to have freedom and dignity.

This book came to fruition because of the stories of people who claimed this freedom and dignity. I returned to South Africa in 1991 as an anthropologist, filled with compassion and commitment to write about the lives of some of the people who live there. I made a conscious decision to deal with a portion of the population whom I expected to be extremely marginalized—the poor, primarily women. Since the church has played a significant role in my life, I decided to focus on independent African churches, particularly the Zionist/Apostolics, because more often than not their members are part of the country's ultrapoor population.

This book brings me back home to the church that was across from the railroad tracks. That church, St. Matthew's UMC, nurtured and supported me and instilled in me the belief that I could and would be somebody in spite of the obstacles that the construction of race in America put in my path. The church that is the focus of this book, St. John's Apostolic Church, has given me a new sense of meaning as it relates to healing the wounds caused by the stress of apartheid. St. John's members and Reverend and Mama Xaba offered new meaning for ritual and life. For this, I am eternally grateful.

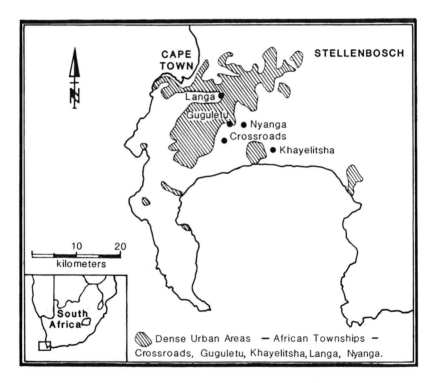

Research Area: Guguletu—Location of St. John's Apostolic Faith Mission

Under the Canopy

Introduction

I met Reverend and Mama Xaba on 16 June 1991 at an ecumenical worship service commemorating the death of several black children gunned down by South African police in Soweto in 1976. The service, which drew quite a large number of people from throughout Cape Town, was held at the Methodist Chapel in Guguletu. Earlier that day, Reverend Thabo Mkhize, the pastor of the church, picked me up so that I could attend the 11 A.M. worship service at his other church on NY 1, the main road in Guguletu. That service was quite lively and very familiar. Having pastored two Methodist churches in New York, I was well acquainted with the order of worship and the hymn tunes, even though the service was conducted in Xhosa.

Nosisa Mkhize, the pastor's wife, prepared a sumptuous dinner at their home, where I met several church leaders. Mama Nophelo Ngomana,[1] the lay leader, and I sat together in the small living room. Since I had been introduced at the service as Reverend Thomas from the Methodist Church in America, Mama Ngomana inquired about my reasons for being in South Africa in a manner that indicated that she assumed I would be conducting research in predominantly black South African Methodist churches. "Does your research require you to interview many people at our church?" she asked. I replied, "No, my research is on African indigenous churches, that are Zionist/Apostolic Churches of the Spirit." Suddenly, everyone in the room, having overheard my response, stopped talking and looked at me in disbelief; they did not understand why I was investigating Zionist/Apostolic churches rather than mainline Methodist churches. Moreover, their staring eyes and silence seemed to scream out, "How dare you?" During that year, I discovered that some adherents of mission churches disdain African indigenous churches (AICs) because AICs overtly use precolonial indigenous religious practices that are considered by many mainline church members to be incompatible with Christianity.

The ecumenical worship service commemorating the children killed in Soweto in 1976 began at 3 P.M. Reverend Mkhize and I arrived early so that he could see that everything was in order for the service. He invited me to process

1

into the service with clergy from other churches, who were gathering in a room next to the sanctuary. As I walked toward the robing room, I looked into the sanctuary and saw five women who were dressed beautifully in blue-and-white uniforms. Their heads were covered with white scarves, and they wore blue skirts and white blouses with a blue-and-white sash draped diagonally from their left shoulders to their waists. A blue cape flowed from their shoulders. While there were other people in the sanctuary, I could not take my eyes off of these women because they sat with regal stateliness. I went over to introduce myself and asked what church they attended. One of the women, Mama Xaba, leaned forward and responded with a warm smile, "St. John's Apostolic Faith Mission, which is located at the corner of NY 5 and NY 152 in Guguletu." Hesitating a bit, I told them that I was doing research on indigenous churches and asked if I could attend one of their services. All five nodded their heads at the same time. Wondering whether one of the women might be the pastor, I inquired about the name of that person. Mama Xaba answered, "He's over there," and pointed in the direction of the room where the clergy were gathering. I asked the women if I could take a photograph of them, and they consented. I promised to bring copies when I visited their church. Since June 1991 the image of these women, who were to become central to my life, has remained etched in my mind.

I entered the room where the ministers were robing and discovered that I was the only woman. My presence caused a stir because women did not normally enter the room where male clergy robed, but everyone settled down when they saw my clerical collar. The ministers were intrigued further by my American accent as I asked in a low voice, "Is Reverend Xaba here?" A hush fell upon the room as if E. F. Hutton had spoken. I was shocked and embarrassed by the silence. A tall, handsome man in his sixties wearing a white clerical collar and a blue velvet robe took a step toward me and said, "I am he." Once again the room became quiet, because everyone wanted to hear our conversation. I nervously explained who I was and that I had just spoken to several women wearing blue-and-white uniforms about coming to his church. "While the women told me to feel free to come to the church," I said, "I want to ask if it is all right with you." Reverend Xaba, a surprised expression on his face, smiled slightly and said, "It's all right. You can come to our church anytime." Behind me I could hear another minister whisper, "Why does she want to go to Xaba's church?" For a brief moment a little rivalry took place, with the ministers laughing and telling Reverend Xaba that I should attend their church instead of his. I knew that Reverend Xaba was being teased by his colleagues and enjoyed their spontaneous playfulness. By the end of the service,

I had more than twenty invitations to attend churches in black South African townships.

I decided to attend St. John's the following Sunday; a cold and rainy day. I was totally unprepared for such weather.[2] Since I did not have a car, I asked about public transportation. Thembile Moripa, a young man who worked at the front desk at Leo Marquard Residence Hall, my temporary quarters, told me that the walk to the taxi rank[3] was quite a distance, so I bundled up and headed out with my umbrella. As I walked down Main Road, the blowing rain turned my umbrella inside out several times. As I was alone on that dreary day, my senses were keenly attuned. Rain splashed and a southeasterly wind blew, causing cars to creep along. My overcoat was soaked, and although my suit jacket and shirt provided an extra layer of protective clothing, my body shivered like a leaf from the cold dampness. After what seemed like an eternity, I arrived at the holding area where minibus taxis usually gathered, only to discover that none were there. Sunday morning was not the time to get a taxi to the townships.

As I stood in the rain waiting, I heard a man's voice from a distance calling out "Wynberg, Kenilworth . . . Mannenburg." A white minivan with four young men drove by, and I wondered if this was the taxi I was to take to Guguletu. I did not hear the names of the black townships Guguletu or Langa called out, so I waited and was disappointed that no other minivans came along. I walked to a bus depot and asked if there was transport to Guguletu and was told that there was none. Suddenly, the white minivan with the same men came around again. I flagged them down and said, "I want to go to a church in Guguletu. Do you go there?" The driver, who had light coffee-colored skin said, "No," and pulled off. Fifteen more minutes passed and no other taxis arrived. The white minivan passed by again. I flagged it down a second time and asked the driver, "How much do I have to pay you to take me to Guguletu? I need to get to a church on the corner of NY 5 and NY 152." The three men who managed the taxi heard my accent and saw my clerical collar. I was glad that I had worn it, because it was a symbol that these men seemed to understand. The driver said, "It will cost fifty rand."[4] I said, "Okay," and climbed in, noting that I was the only passenger.

The driver looked at me through the rearview mirror and said, "We won't hurt you." I responded in a strong, clear voice, "I do not expect you to; otherwise I would not have boarded the van."[5] A mutual sense of trust seemed to emerge. The driver said, "There's a taxi war going on in Cape Town.[6] We are not supposed to go into Guguletu because it is not our territory, but we will take you there. We have to make some stops along the way to pick up people, but you will get to Guguletu." As I sat back and tried to relax, we entered a township called Mannenburg. I suddenly realized that these men were so-called Colored rather than black South African[7] and that I had encountered apartheid's race-stratification system where not only race but also the shade of skin color mattered. Apartheid's race-classification system placed Coloreds, who were the largest "racial" group in Cape Town, a notch above black South Africans. I now understood why the driver said that Guguletu was not part of his territory. Guguletu was a black South African township, and black South Africans and so-called Coloreds lived in separate areas in accordance with the Group Areas law (No. X of 1950).[8]

After the driver dropped off all the passengers, the journey to Guguletu began. Because the driver did not know his way around Guguletu, he stopped several times to ask people for directions to St. John's. Since most of the people on the street at that time of day were women, each time he asked for directions he began, "Hello, Mama. Can you help me to find St. John's at NY 5 and NY 152?" Each person he asked helped us piece together the route to the church. I told the driver that the members of St. John's wore blue-and-white uniforms. When he added that piece of information as he asked for directions, people seemed to know exactly where to direct us. As rain continued to pour down, we arrived at the church at the same time that Mama Ntiliti, one of the women I had met the previous Sunday, was walking into the driveway. I jumped out of the minivan and said, "Hello." She remembered me and with a smile said, "You've come out on such a rainy day?" I smiled and said, "Yes, I'm very happy that you came on a rainy day as well." I paid the driver fifty rand and asked if he would pick me up at 2:30 P.M. He agreed.

When Mama Ntiliti and I stepped out of the rain and into a small, dark room with a single white candle burning, I entered the cosmologically complex world of St. John's. Mama Ntiliti immediately got on her knees and uttered a prayer in a quiet voice. I respectfully bowed my head and quickly and curiously surveyed my surroundings, noting that the lone candle added warmth to the shadowy room as it glowed and flickered in a corner. Beyond the closed door, I heard muffled voices whose cadence reflected the sounds of a man chanting a prayer and female and male voices singing a response in unison. The text of the Lord's Prayer, a standard feature in most Christian worship, was being sung to a tune that was new to my ears.

Mama Ntiliti, who was in her mid-sixties, slowly rose from her knees. Taking off her coat, she told me in a hushed voice that we would enter the sanctuary when a song was sung. After a few moments a woman's voice started a fast-paced hymn that other voices joined. We entered the sanctuary as people rhythmically clapped their hands. I was invited to sit in the pulpit in front of a seat occupied by Mama Xaba. As I slid by, she nodded her head, offering a friendly greeting. Reverend Xaba, who sat on the right side of the pulpit directly across from Mama Xaba, likewise nodded his head to say hello. I looked out into a liturgical world in which people and ritual artifacts were surrounded by a sea of blue and white.

As ritual participants clapped their hands, their beautiful blue-and-white uniforms glistened against a background of blue-and-white walls and floor tiles. The Cross, a symbol central to Christian cosmology, had been designed into the floor with contrasting white and blue tile. A fluorescent light fixture in the shape of a cross hung from the ceiling, paralleling the cross on the floor. Blue and white are central colors in St. John's ritual life because the founder, Mother Mokotuli Christinah Nku,[9] is recorded to have had a vision about a church with twelve doors[10] whose members wore blue and white uniforms (August n.d.:1). These colors, which are laden with ritual meaning, are used in St. John's Apostolic Faith Mission churches throughout Southern Africa.

Specifically, the colors are a sign that unites ritual participants into a particular family of believers who have a common founder and rituals that offer therapeutic healing. The signs, symbols, and practices used in rituals build a bridge between African religion and western Protestant Christianity. While Christian symbols may seem more dominant, indigenous meaning systems are also present. Cultural signs and symbols of blended African cosmologies are evident in the ritual actions of St. John's members. Hence, the signs and symbols of the religion of the colonizers and rituals that demonstrate a blended African cosmological consciousness are synthesized to create St. John's religion. This synthesis of meaning systems joins precolonial and colonial pasts and creates a new religious consciousness. Many features of precolonial and colonial religion thrive in St. John's rituals and provide therapeutic healing for spheres of human struggle.

During services, men and women perform healing rituals created by, and passed down, from the church's founder, Mother Nku, who opened her two-room Prospect Township home as a house church and healing station for people in 1918.[11] During the early 1930s, she left the predominantly white Apostolic Faith Church and started St. John's Apostolic Faith Mission, a church focused on healing in a way that blended the signs, symbols, and practices of her own Sotho culture and those borrowed from Protestant Christianity. While Nku was a pioneer, one of a few women who initiated independent African churches, she also followed a stream of Africans who grew tired of being dominated by white Protestant Christianity and separated from mission churches to create new religious cosmologies that blended Christian symbols and practices into well-established precolonial religious systems.

5

St. John's healing rites have helped adherents to such an extent that the church is one of the largest denominations in southern Africa. The Guguletu congregation continued the healing methods of Mother Nku and adopted some begun by Archbishop Petrus Masango, who broke away from Nku's church and started his own in 1970. Although the church has fractured and branched off in different directions over the years, it continues to have a sub-stantial company of devotees who are committed to healing rites. The church attracts a disproportionately large number of ultrapoor people because fees are not charged for healing. Neither the church nor its ministers enjoy any monetary gain from healing work. People come to the Guguletu congregation from as far away as the eastern Cape[12] in order to get "treatments."

As an extension of the healing at the core of the religion of their African ancestors, healing is central to the religion of St. John's members. Religion at St. John's deals with any threat to one's wellness or health as it relates to an assortment of issues from violence, unemployment, and marital conflict to infertility, mental illness, and child abuse. In St. John's cosmology, sickness (*ukugula*) includes any one or all of these problems since they compromise the well-being of a person and the community to which he or she is attached. The cadre of healers at St. John's fuse the competencies of priest, medical doctor, psychiatrist, and welfare advocate.

Each May, the Guguletu congregation sponsors an *umgidi*, or festival, for the spiritual uplifting of members and the economic benefit of the congrega-tion. The diocesan bishop, visiting ministers, members, and friends gather for a four-day festival that includes a marching brass band, an all-night vigil, a service of Holy Communion, the baptism of initiates in the ocean, and the ini-tiation of women into the role of "mother" of the church. The umgidi also includes the ceremonial slaughtering of cows and lambs as well as the burning of their kidneys and intestines as a pleasing offering to God and the ancestors. Worship services in which members testify, sing, and clap hands to a critical transitional peak that causes some to be possessed by the Spirit (*umoya*) are themselves healing rituals. While services are held four times a day, it is toward the end of the worship service that adherents drink "prayed water," a com-munal healing rite performed by religious specialists set aside to pray for and lay hands upon those who walk under the canopy. This ritual assists the com-munity and individuals in their healing from ukugula. Discord is relieved and dissension remedied. At these services, the process of sharing significant life stories, drinking prayed water, and walking under the canopy strengthens important bonds in the group.

Because it incorporates the religious practices of the South African fore-bears into a Christian context, St. John's religion has a cosmological point of departure that is different from mainstream Protestantism. For example, the slaughtering of beasts, the initiation of members into age sets signifying movement from one life stage to another, and seating patterns that replicate the spatial arrangement used by clan groups reflect an integration of a precolonial past into a new religious movement. Moreover, while in St. John's cosmology the central faith claim of Christianity—the sacrifice of Jesus, the son of God, for the atonement of humanity's sins—is accepted, Jesus is also seen as an ancestor. Additionally, as the son of God, he is not equal to God as the Christian doctrine of the Trinity suggests, because St. John's cosmology, like that of many other African cultures, does not give children equal standing with their parents.

Another cultural category used to signify the centrality of human beings living in the context of community is *ubuntu,* which is assured through accountable relationships identified by the proper offering to the community of goods that are concrete (money, food, housing) and intangible (love, support, care).[13] When harmony exists, these goods move in an uninterrupted circular fashion that flows and crisscrosses with other circles among the living and between the living and the ancestors. Through the ritual of giving and receiving gifts, individuals participate in community life in a manner fitting to their place in the social universe arranged by role and duty. Responsible persons offer gifts in accordance with their status in the community.

It can be argued that the emergence of a European presence on the southern tip of Africa facilitated the economic strangulation of indigenous peoples. The religion of independent African churches such as St. John's persists because it responds effectively to the harmful impact of the oppressive system of apartheid that systematically produced a program of separate development that impoverished, undereducated, and kept landless the black South African majority. The legacy of underdevelopment has been a part of many black South Africans' lives for several generations. This is one reason churches like St. John's swell with people in search of hope and healing.

What lessons can we learn from members of St. John's as local communities throughout the world struggle to have a decent quality of life among governments and other macrosystem institutions that execute decisions ranging from benign neglect to compassionate care to detrimental assistance that is often given only after a crisis? Must grassroots peoples and others create rituals to provide meaning in a world that strangles those who are poor and so often are outside formal power systems? These are some of the broader issues about which this study can bring reasoned, compassionate, and intellectual insight.

As I participated in the community life of St. John's, I was given a place in the church's social universe. And I made offerings as a responsible daughter in the Xaba household. These gifts were both tangible and intangible. I sometimes bought groceries for the family or gave money to Tata[14] and Mama Xaba to attend an umgidi sponsored by another St. John's congregation outside Cape Town. The intangible gifts were the care and concern I gave Tata and Mama Xaba as they took on the role of loving parents to a daughter who came from far away. We deeply loved each other, and the affirmation that I received from their biological daughters, while usually harmonious, was sometimes strained, as sibling rivalry emerged toward this "outsider" daughter to whom the Xabas gave much devoted attention.

Tata and Mama Xaba had eight children, but only four were alive. The effects of apartheid shaped the size of their family; because of inadequate health care in the Transkei, three infants died of simple diseases like diarrhea.[15] Tata Xaba was so distressed by his family's poverty and the premature death of his children that he contemplated murdering his family and committing suicide. However, before he took any dire action, a member of St. John's told him about a woman priest who could heal his family's ukugula. Though reluctant to believe that a woman could assist him, he went to Cape Town to see Mama Shenxane, the minister of St. John's, and received treatments to allay ukugula. Tata Xaba's therapeutic healing precipitated his leaving the Methodist Church to become a member of St. John's and eventually to become a priest-healer in the church.

When Tata Xaba told me the story of the brutal death and decapitation of his son in Cape Town, I began to understand the impact of the cycle of violence on families in the church. It was difficult to hear this story and others in interviews and testimonies at services and remain a detached observer. Participating in the ritual life at St. John's, I drank the prayed water and walked under the canopy. I received the water and the laying on of hands as gifts. During my first months at St. John's, Reverend Xaba insisted that I lay hands on members since I was a Methodist minister. With some reluctance I did so; but in ensuing months and years I refrained from this practice because I simply wanted to walk under the canopy to receive the water and prayers as gifts of the community.

Since my research commenced before the end of apartheid, when I made inquiries about conducting research, Reverend Xaba and members of the church were suspicious of my motives. I was in a society that bred informants who worked for the apartheid state to identify people who fought against the system. I worked hard to be authentic and to show my eagerness to learn about the ways St. John's rituals helped people. I told Reverend Xaba and others that while I could never fully understand the whole of their lived reality, I wanted to experience what I could of it and write their story. In time, a bond

grew between members and myself, based in part on the mutual exchange of
our life stories and in part on the fact that our stories included pain from discrimination based on skin color. St. John's members were exceedingly aware of
the 1960s' Black Power and civil rights movements in the United States and
black Americans' struggle for freedom. As an African American, I was a black
person who had a good life and lived in a democratic society, a reality for which
members of St. John's hoped and yearned. Many times in the privacy of their
homes, members made statements connecting apartheid in South Africa with
racism in the United States. Nbilise, who had worked in the Johannesburg gold
mines, clearly articulated this connection when he said, "We know that your
ancestors are from here [Africa] and that you were stolen away from us. We
know that you fought for freedom in America and that you have now come
home to help us."

Such declarations, along with my commitment to work for justice for
black South Africans, prompted my intellect to yield at times to a reasoned
compassion as I remembered the pain of my experience of racism in the
United States. I united two ideas that are often disjoined, intellect and compassion, in order to seek justice. Anthropology's analytical tools helped me to
keep a balance.

My closeness to the St. John's community brought many learnings. I
received firsthand accounts of the meaning of ritual practices such as divination, the administration of a four-pronged healing method, spirit possession,
the role of the ancestors, the sacrifice of animals, and the relationship between
these practices and Christian biblical texts. While I initially understood rituals
of healing to include only the frame of the worship service in which people
drank prayed water, I came to understand how all segments of worship and
rites conducted outside of services were devoted to the healing process. St.
John's members lived in a perpetual state of material vulnerability that can be
documented by volumes of research on the black South African ultrapoor
over several generations.[16] Everyone I interviewed said they came to St. John's
because they or loved ones were sick and wanted to be healed. People came to
the church because of the hope it instilled in lives that were filled with suffering. I felt privileged to be admitted into the cosmologically complex and ritually thick world of St. John's. Because I risked feeling and caring about the
people with whom I established relationships, I gave and received many gifts.

In this ritual circle of giving and receiving, the world of healing opened to
me, and I, too, believed that in some way the blessed water and rituals healed
believers. I better understood St. John's religion because I opened my life to its
meaning and did not simply stand on the sidelines as a "rationally" minded
observer. There were many times when members said, "Linda, you really like

this church, don't you? We can see that you like this church. Will you take it to America?" An aura surrounded me as I intensely engaged in relationships with members of the church. It was easy to accept many practices of St. John's worldview because, as a member of the African diaspora, I wanted to learn about a subject that was not part of my primary, secondary, or liberal arts education in the United States—African cultures. I made a choice to learn, fully accepting that the worldview that I brought with me was being reshaped and restructured.

My personal involvement with the Xaba family and the members of St. John's had many risks, because I entered the field as an anthropologist whose life was steeped in a liberal and progressive Protestant worldview. Moreover, I had earned the credentials and had the experience of being a ritual specialist within the United Methodist Church. Therefore, I understood many of the symbols that St. John's cosmology selected from imported western Protestantism. I recognized how the signs and practices had been changed to fit the sensibilities of St. John's members. At the same time, I knew very little about, and had limited experience with, African religion other than the remnants of Africanisms that were transported to the New World on slave ships from West Africa and were present in the black churches I have attended all my life. While there was some potential positive gain from my having some symbols in common with St. John's members, there was also a potential risk in assuming that we shared synonymous meaning. Therefore, a large part of my interviews was spent asking questions about the meanings of symbols with which both I and the interviewee were familiar.[17]

I also knew that there was potential risk in not fully acknowledging a difference between St. John's religion interacting with the life of St. John's members and St. John's religion interacting with my very different life and worldview. In sum, my experiences of St. John's religion were similar to, and dissimilar from, those of St. John's adherents. My understanding of the rituals stood at a place between their experience and my own. I decided that it is important for the words and reflections of St. John's members to stand on their own as direct speech in this book, so that readers can experience the liminal space of meaning between themselves and St. John's adherents.

The layers of meaning in the words and actions of St. John's ritual participants were thick. Most adherents spoke English but felt most comfortable using their mother tongue, Xhosa. While my understanding of Xhosa was adequate, I hired an experienced research assistant who was fluent in Xhosa and English and also well versed in the terrain of the black South African townships. There were many times when I looked for maps of the townships only to discover how woefully inadequate were the few I found. Dirt roads and streets spontaneously sprang up overnight as poor blacks constructed shacks anywhere there was open land. These flimsy makeshift structures were built hurriedly because the promulgation of the 1986 influx control laws resulted in thousands of black South Africans moving to Cape Town and other urban centers. While Langa, Guguletu, Crossroads, and Nyanga had several decades of settlement history, Khayelitsha was a relatively new and sprawling township filled with new arrivals from the former Eastern Cape homelands. Because St. John's members lived in all the townships and because violence was so much a part of everyday life, I needed an assistant who not only had language skills but also people skills, "street sense," and knowledge about how to get around in the townships. I found all of these abilities in Barbara Manata, previously the field research assistant to anthropologist Mamphela Ramphele, who highly recommended Barbara to me.

Barbara lived in New Crossroads township, and people in her neighborhood knew her to be vivacious, talkative, opinionated, politically savvy, and a go-getter. She had worked as a community organizer and consequently had had several encounters with the South African police. During one confrontation she was so brutally beaten by the police that her left breast was severely mauled and scarred as a result. Nevertheless, Barbara was very zealous about the struggle for freedom and doggedly pursued people she believed had resources from which the community could benefit. She, too, was a member of an independent African church and was quite enthusiastic about a project in which the poor would have their stories shared.

During interviews, she encouraged people to speak freely and not be shy. She was an asset to my project, and yet there were some drawbacks. Barbara's outgoing nature was quite a contrast to the women who were members of St. John's. For instance, she spoke directly to men—a particularly sensitive point if she was speaking to ministers and bishops. Moreover, Mandlovu, the Xaba's oldest daughter, had worked previously with Barbara in a domestic setting and personally witnessed Barbara's activism on behalf of workers. Some church members saw Barbara's direct and straight-talking manner as too aggressive, and Mandlovu and others were at times uncomfortable with her style. With these two different communication styles, one aggressive and one meek, they maintained an unspoken truce to avoid open conflict. Mama Xaba intermittently complained about Barbara but on the whole supported her presence. What Mama Xaba felt, however, was that Barbara talked too much and was aggressive. In the words of Mama Xaba, "Barbara's too strong. She's like Winnie Mandela." Fortunately, Barbara assisted me primarily in interviews with members in their homes, which minimized her direct interaction with the Xaba family.

11

I used a tape recorder, camera, and video camera to record interviews and healing rituals because I wanted to foreground the stories and rituals using the spoken text of members. Moreover, I wanted a visual record of township life and the material circumstances in which members lived. Because this is a longitudinal project, my goal from the beginning has been to document events in order to trace change over an extended period of time. The videotapes not only recorded interviews, they also documented the environment in which people lived, their homes and neighborhoods, the shops in townships, and people's coming and going. These records chronicled both apartheid and postapartheid everyday and ritual life.

Because I was so often present at rituals with a video recorder and camera, people frequently asked me to videotape events such as funerals, initiation celebrations, and special church services. I responded positively to these requests and always made copies available.

Many casual conversations served as a source of much reflection in my field notes, which were written in a way that attempted to nuance what was said as well as the way it was said. In addition, I kept a journal of my own reflections on my fieldwork process that included comments on my feelings and reactions to what I experienced. Having committed a large part of myself to this investigation of St. John's religion, I put myself into the journal. My fond feelings about my relationship with the Xaba family are pondered in the notes. Reflecting on what was happening to me as well as recording data was a way to stay honest with myself, because I could note my guarded points and judgments when I later examined my notes. The process of recording data about informants' lives and consciously ruminating about my thoughts, feelings, and interactions with them is the essence of ethnography. In a nutshell, ethnography is the art of building and maintaining relationships. Through this experience, people are the living documents who are examined in a respectful and inquisitive manner. The dance of relationship building is sometimes unruly and yet beneficial. It is in part living with the unknown or living the questions while at the same time dealing with living with predictability. Building relationships for ethnography's sake means taking risks in order to experience the bond of intellectual engagement and a commitment to encounter the everyday affairs of people's lives.

This ethnography attempts to bring together intellectual engagement and passion for the lived experience of people whose voices are rarely heard. Their words and stories are "hidden transcripts" that represent resistance from total domination by oppressive circumstances and systems.[18] I am honored to present this rich material.

General Direction and Outline

This book endeavors to bring an understanding of the daily lives of members and of healing rituals in an indigenous church in South Africa. While apartheid laws were formally repealed in June 1991, the macrostructural relics of apartheid remain entrenched in South African society, particularly in its ideological/intellectual, political/economic, psycho/social, and secular/sacred constructions.[19] Thus, I argue that the repeal of the apartheid laws did not substantially change the deep structures that fortified apartheid in South Africa, leaving it still a country divided on the basis of race. My methodology reflects an attempt to integrate history, the speech of informants, their rituals of healing, and hermeneutics. My conclusion is an integrated reflection on the healing rituals used by poor, modern-day black South Africans who actively participate in an independent African church as a way to enhance meaning in their lives.

The book is divided into seven chapters, with chapter 1 outlining the purpose of the text and factors in the emergence of African indigenous churches in southern Africa. I feature St. John's as a present-day example of an AIC set in a larger historical context. An overview of the setting in which the book is based is the core of chapter 2. I introduce readers to the history of Guguletu and other African townships in the Cape peninsula.

Chapter 3 presents an ethnographic profile of members of St. John's Apostolic Faith Mission–Guguletu focusing on life narratives. Chapter 4 explicates the theology and rituals of St. John's–Guguletu and examines the belief system of the church. This chapter also analyzes sermons and considers the issue of syncretism in the particular context of South Africa. Chapter 5 examines the ritual use of symbols of healing at St. John's, highlighting particular symbols that members viewed as significant.

Chapter 6 formulates theoretical approaches to the cultural construction of illness. The chapter includes discourse from St. John's members illustrating their understanding of illness. I delineate a detailed exploration of health, factors compromising wellness, and steps taken by St. John's members to preserve well-being. Chapter 7 offers concluding remarks about the healing rituals considered in this book. Appendix 1 provides a summary of the specific anthropological methodology used while conducting field research in South Africa. Appendix 2 provides demographic information about St. John's-Guguletu members, while appendix 3 presents the schedule of questions asked during interviews.

This book will not specifically address the broad political, economic, and sociological ramifications of apartheid. Rather, I seek to provide a detailed examination of one central aspect of the life of an African indigenous church, its healing rituals, and the ways in which these rituals enhance life for a particular group of black South Africans. My operative assumption is that healing takes place in a variety of secular and sacred institutions and that there are important inferences that can be made about healing in the context of an African indigenous church. By choosing one particular theological and ecclesial tradition—St. John's—I will be able to illustrate concretely how the legacy of apartheid adversely affects poor black South Africans and how and why healing rituals provide one way to respond to systems that oppress people.

Since St. John's is part of Protestant Christianity, I will not deal at all in this study with other religious traditions, such as Roman Catholicism, Islam, or Judaism. However, my methodology should provide a means for other researchers to approach the dynamics and dimensions of healing in other religions.

It is important to acknowledge that I am an ordained minister of the United Methodist Church who visited South Africa in 1985 with a United Methodist delegation hosted by the Methodist Church of South Africa. I am thus an active participant in Protestant Christianity and a religious specialist of sorts, in that I not only know personally, but have been formally trained in, theology and ritual practices that are similar to, and different from, those described in this book.

My interest in South Africa spans a number of years. I wrote my first statement about South Africa in 1978, when I responded as a scholarship applicant to an essay question asking me to discuss a critical global issue that would concern the international community in the 1980s. My essay dealt with apartheid in South Africa, and writing it helped me to crystallize my profound interest in the politics of racism in that country. I continued to follow events in South Africa via scholarly journals and the media and became involved in the antiapartheid movement in the United States. In time, I realized that my personal experience with racial discrimination, as an African American woman born and reared in the United States, piqued my commitment to understand the dynamics of legalized racism in South Africa as structured in apartheid. More particularly, I wanted to understand the mythology of racial superiority in South Africa, hoping that such a cross-cultural study would give me insights about my experience in America. My personal experience of racial discrimination in America and my decision to locate this study of healing rituals in South Africa may or may not be a limitation for this study. Readers will have to decide for themselves.

CHAPTER 1

An Inquiry into an African Indigenous Church

Religion must be understood for "its function as a social field and social medium of communication and struggle."
—Otto Maduro, *Religion and Social Conflict*

Under the Canopy examines the relationship between the everyday life of poor[1] black South Africans who are members of St. John's Apostolic Faith Mission Church, located in Guguletu, an African[2] township in the Western Cape[3] of the Republic of South Africa, and the healing rituals they perform in order to survive in a hostile social environment at the close of the apartheid era. St. John's, an African indigenous church (AIC),[4] brings together a community of people whose cosmology arises from the synthesis of precolonial African religion and Protestant Christianity.[5] While participating in church services, being a part of the daily activities of several families, and conducting in-depth interviews, I sought to understand the ways that members singularly and collectively designed adaptive support systems to oppose degrading social conditions that were the result of race discrimination and an economic scheme that created conditions of perpetual poverty for the majority of black South Africans (Evans et al. 1992; Chidester 1992; Wilson and Ramphele 1989; Kiernan 1994). St. John's members conducted healing rites four times daily. These medicinal ceremonies played a central role in creating a ritual process in which individual members who experienced *ukugula* (sickness) participated in dramatic presentations ameliorating their afflictions. These ritual actions positively affected participants' minds, bodies, and spirits so that they shared a mutual sense of accountability for one another's well-being. Individual members, consequently, were less likely to be overwhelmed by social difficulties. An entry from my 1991 field note journal describes the significance and power of healing rituals practiced at St. John's–Guguletu:

I remember meeting a young man who was interested in becoming a member of St. John's. He was unemployed, unable to support his family, and quite depressed. During worship, he sat with the other St. John's men. His rumpled and wrinkled shirt and pants were quite a contrast to their sparkling and neatly pressed white coats and blue belts. His quiet demeanor revealed an emotional affect of discouragement with life. As the congregation sang songs and the movement of the Spirit (*umoya*) possessed some of the evangelists, he sat unaffected. This young man came to St. John's several consecutive Sundays and had many conversations with Reverend Xaba.[6] In time, he partook of the blessed water and participated in the rituals. Over a period of three weeks, I noticed that his countenance changed. The most significant change occurred when he was baptized and was given a white coat and blue belt to wear. It was as if a new person had arrived in the same body. Now as he stood with the St. John's men wearing his sparkling white coat and blue belt, his face shone. He emoted a happiness that I had not experienced from him before. He began to testify about what St. John's meant to him as his life took on new meaning. Over a period of time, this man took a key role in facilitating worship services. When he testified other members listened intently. His new role at St. John's stood in stark contrast to who he was when he first came to the church. Previously, he was forlorn and dejected, now he had vitality and hope. His unkempt appearance and sense of insecurity were exchanged for a neat, ordered, and hope-filled life. He began to work and support his family. His status indeed had been elevated.

As a cultural system, St. John's cosmology and rituals play a significant role in supporting affirmatively the lives of its members.[7] Symbols, words, and dramatic activity integrate the way ritual participants make sense of their lives, and accountable relationships make it possible for them to endure in a local context where they struggle against apartheid's insidious legacies that harshly affect human life.

Social Context for the Rise of African Indigenous Churches

The origin of independent African churches is related to the complex history of race relations in South Africa and the negative effects that segregation policies administered by local authorities had upon the lives of Africans. Before and after the inception of the Union of South Africa in 1910, laws existed that rigorously discriminated against Africans.[8] For instance, as early as 1910, there were approximately three hundred reserves, similar to Native American reservations in the United States, set aside exclusively for Africans, dispersed throughout the country.[9] Africans could not purchase land, vote, or live in white areas. Any amenities granted by the state or municipalities to Africans were second rate. Africans did not have the freedom to move about without a pass; moreover, curfews restricted the time of day that they could be on the street, with or without a pass (Ngubane 1963:55).[10] Thus, segregation legislated a race-based political inequality that, according to Saul Dubow, was established on two presuppositions. First, Africans' right to own land was contingent upon the renunciation of their citizenship. That is, Africans could own land in segregated areas only, but if they did so, they were not permitted to be citizens of the country. This was because the goal of segregation and apartheid was to create political inequality for Africans as fully as possible. Second, Africans were to be cared for by white custodians and therefore would be forced to have separate and unequal development (Dubow 1989:1).[11] Commenting on race relations in South Africa and the American South, John W. Cell argues that segregation "must be recognized as one of the most successful political ideologies of the past century. It was, indeed, the highest stage of white supremacy" (Cell 1982:18). In sum, African independent churches were a vehicle for a dignified and resilient people to fight against white racism and ecclesiastical control.

Missionary Control and African Indigenous Churches

The late-nineteenth-century European missionary movement was a vigorous effort by Christians to convert African peoples conquered by European countries.[12] As benevolent caregivers and soul-savers, missionary societies played a pivotal role in executing evangelistic strategies that were both helpful and harmful to indigenous African peoples (Kiernan 1990; Comaroff and Comaroff 1991:5–11; 1992:235–63; Majeke 1953). Using Jesus' final instruction to his disciples to "[t]herefore go and make disciples of all nations, baptizing them in the name of the Father and of the Son and of the Holy Spirit" (Matthew 28:19),[13] the advocates of Christianity justified their actions, which often further subordinated indigenous people, as evangelization. Furthermore, many missionaries perpetuated the attitudes and behaviors advanced by settlers who practiced racial separation in the social spheres they controlled. In so doing, the Christian emissaries supported the implementation of macrolevel secular racism into the microlevel institutionalization of congregations.[14] Hence, the signs and symbols of missionary religion augmented racial discrimination in imported Christianity and created foundational structures that assisted in the eventual establishment of apartheid.

The advocacy of cultural superiority on the part of many missionaries was also evidenced in their attempts to eradicate precolonial African religious rit-

17

uals (Pauw 1975:21; Wilson 1969:265). These same Christian emissaries did not consider Africans to be equal to whites; moreover, they regarded as unimportant African spiritual needs existing prior to colonial religion.

Recognizing the oppressiveness of white rule, many Africans responded with acts of resistance. Some refused to accept Christianity in any form, while others separated from mission churches to renounce their inferior position and to challenge European evangelistic efforts. Many Africans, feeling muzzled and frustrated, left the mission churches because they were not willing to submit to white Christian cultural indoctrination and attitudes of cultural superiority (Saunders 1970:555; Vilakazi 1986:17; Kiernan 1995). Others turned to their own resources in order to restore their human dignity. As Absolom Vilakazi observed, "If the opportunity for the maintenance of that dignity is denied to the Africans by the white man, then the Africans will create and inhabit their own world and its own values" (Vilakazi 1986:17).[15]

Seeing the negative impact that missionary culture had on their cosmology and culture, a few Africans created independent churches to restore honor and purpose and to oppose white Christian control (Verryn 1972:17–30; Barrett 1968:83–158; Makhubu 1988:5; Sundkler 1961a:29–32; 295–97; Kiernan 1995). Like Vilakazi, Harold Turner identified the ways in which many Africans adapted the message of the mission church to their own heritage, noting that African indigenous churches were institutions "founded by Africans who usually have some kind of Christian background and who have developed forms of Christianity expressed in African cultural ways to meet the needs of African peoples as they themselves determine" (Turner 1977:105).[16]

In 1882, African activists living in the Transkei founded the first African political organization in the Eastern Cape.[17] Two years later, in the same region, Nehemiah Tile, tired of racial discrimination in the Methodist Church in the Transkei,[18] initiated the first independent African church, called the Thembu National Church. Tile, one of the few ordained African ministers at that time, was directly influenced by African nationalism and identified strongly as a Thembu.[19] While he had previously worked with missionaries in the Wesleyan Church, their cultural bias against African cultural practices forced him to leave. His influential spirit, along with his commitment to Thembu culture and its incorporation into the life of the church, generated a positive response from Africans but criticism from European missionaries. Hence, the Thembu National Church started with the assistance of the Thembu paramount chief and began as a reaction against discrimination against Africans and missionaries' support of colonial politics.

In 1892, as a response to injustices experienced by blacks in mission churches, an African member of the clergy started another independent church. Reverend Mangena Moses Mokone resigned from the Wesleyan Church in Pretoria to form the Ibandla LaseTiyopiya, or the Ethiopian Church. This first nationwide indigenous church was named after the first black nation on the African continent to be free of colonial control. That Ethiopia was mentioned in the biblical text Psalm 68:31 also gave hope to blacks oppressed in mission churches and in a segregated society. Furthermore, the Ethiopian Church movement was a part of an emerging African nationalism facilitated by black urban workers educated in mission schools. Educated black Christians launched, directed, and promoted African nationalism (Wilson and Thompson 1971:433); they also assisted in the formation of the South African Native Congress, which was the forerunner of the African National Congress.[20]

Government authorities had grave concern about the political nature of independent African churches, which were experiencing phenomenal membership growth in South Africa (Kritzinger 1993:248; Pretorius and Jafta 1997:211) and throughout the continent (Barrett 1968:41, 65–66). A dynamic interplay between politics and religion in AICs was apparent in church leaders' questions to authorities about voting and land rights as well as wage and labor prerogatives. John De Gruchy argues that there is "little doubt that the independent churches were concerned about more than just religious freedom. They wanted the liberation of their people from all unjust bondages" (De Gruchy 1986:44–45). Indeed, independent African churches constituted forums for black people to institutionalize social solidarity in a religious sphere laden with political overtones because many members were influenced by African nationalism.

State authorities were not the only ones concerned about the pride and power of AICs. Commenting on the rapid increase of these churches in South Africa[21] and the disquiet this caused members of white mission churches, G. C. Oosthuizen and Irving Hexham note: "There was a time when these churches were treated with great suspicion from the White population and with contempt by educated Blacks. Missionaries considered them theologically dangerous while Christian Blacks [who were part of the mission churches] considered them out of step with true Christianity which, of course, was defined by the missionaries" (Oosthuizen and Hexham 1992:1).

They continue: "These churches are on the front-line of the indigenization process of Christianity in Africa, particularly South Africa" (Oosthuizen and Hexham 1992:1). Although often repudiated by both whites and black South Africans in the mission churches (Pauw 1995), independent African churches developed their own rituals, drawing on African religion and culture.

The independent churches thus have a much closer relationship to black South Africa than does the white mission church.[22]

St. John's Apostolic Faith Mission Church:
An African Indigenous Church

Founded by Mother Christinah Mokotuli Nku in 1938,[23] St. John's Apostolic Faith Mission of Guguletu is one congregation within the historic politico-ecclesiastical movement of independent African churches in South Africa. Acting upon a vision she believed came from God, Mother Nku launched her own church, which drew upon precolonial African religious practices and imported Christianity. Her church grew so rapidly that new congregations developed and spread throughout Southern Africa. Its present total membership exceeds two million. Most St. John's congregations have no more than twenty-five to sixty members, who come together to perform rituals in "bands" (Kiernan 1976a). These rituals, which are a summation of St. John's cosmology, have as their goal the transformation of members' lives and the social situation in which members find themselves on both the micro- and the macrolevel. The congregations have a strong sense of community, focus on mutual aid, and use the majority of their income assisting members who are in need.[24]

The lives of members of the Guguletu congregation, who live in Cape Town's black South African townships, reflect the effects of apartheid, as all are minimally educated, have limited employment skills, and earn very little money.[25] Their economic deprivation means that their homes are small and crowded, their daily food intake unpredictable, and medical insurance unaffordable. The majority of members came initially to St. John's–Guguletu because they were sick and were referred by others who had been healed at a church considered by many to be a hospital.

Context of the Study and Research Questions

The field research upon which this book is based was conducted during the period immediately following Nelson Mandela's release from prison on 11 February 1990. Mandela, the prominent leader of the black independence movement in South Africa, had been incarcerated by the South African apartheid government for twenty-seven years. The interlude between his release from prison and his election to the presidency was a time of rapid transition in the country, with macrolevel politics and grassroots activism intermingling to produce a season of contradictory societal incidents. For instance, in Cape Town's black townships, children could not attend school because of random violence; migrant workers living great distances from their families in the Eastern Cape were unable to send money or return home to relatives because of poor pay; and a turbulent taxi war erupted, making it difficult and dangerous for Africans to commute from black townships to their work in white areas.[26]

Other contradictions were more global. For example, in 1991, the apartheid laws were repealed and the all-party Convention for a Democratic South Africa began talks in December. Meanwhile, a "third force"[27] of unknown persons operated to destabilize the possibility of black rule, despite the all-white affirmative referendum vote in March 1992.[28] During all of these transforming national events, the quality of life at the local level did not shift in any dramatic way for poor black South Africans.

The research questions that I posed during this time of rapid transition and social contradiction in South Africa probed the relationship between the daily lives of poor black South Africans who are members of St. John's and the rituals they performed at the church. The questions were: What role do healing rituals, as exhibited in St. John's Apostolic Faith Mission Church–Guguletu, play in the lives of members during this period of liminality in the political life of South Africa? Does the incorporation of indigenous African religious practices within a Christian context, as expressed in healing rituals, represent a health care system that successfully functions outside the conventional realm of hospitals and doctors' offices? Are healing rituals symbolic forms that assuage some of the contradictions in the lives of poor black South Africans?

These contradictions indicate an "in-between time," or a period of liminality (Turner 1969:93). Liminality, as reflected in South Africa, was a period between balance and chaos, between self-determination and authoritarian rule, between equality of rights, opportunity, and fair treatment and inequality, barriers, and injustice. It was a period of extreme ambiguity, uncertainty, and suffering for disenfranchised persons.

In light of these historical circumstances and within the context of these contradictions, I argue that religion and ritual life functioned on symbolic levels to assist St. John's members to integrate their everyday lives so that they could live tenaciously in micro- and macrosystems that discriminated against them racially and economically.

CHAPTER 2

The SETTING

A sequence is clear. Each time Cape Town grew out and enveloped their
previously distanced "locations," the Black Africans were moved.
—John Western, *Outcast Cape Town*

Guguletu, located in the Western Cape of the Republic of South Africa, is one
of six African townships inhabited by Xhosa-speaking Nguni peoples whose
predecessors migrated from the eastern Cape Province from 1840 onwards to
take jobs as road laborers and dockworkers.[1] From the time that Africans
began to return to the Cape Peninsula, controversy among the ruling class of
Afrikaners and English raged about the types of jobs they would occupy and
the regions of the peninsula in which they would live. These volatile and contested issues put Africans in a vulnerable position from a political, economic,
ideological, and psychosocial perspective.

This chapter gives an overview of the social history of African life in the
Western Cape from the 1880s to the 1980s. It is necessarily the saga of the
forced removal of Africans from one location to another, as well as a chroni-
cle of the promulgation of laws that on the one hand restricted the movement
of Africans and on the other controlled their employment opportunities.
Finally, this chapter considers the repeal of laws that effectively opened an era
that granted Africans uninhibited influx and free movement as well as residential rights. These changes, however, did not significantly modify residential or employment patterns for a majority of Africans, who continued to be
economically disadvantaged. As a consequence, while the 1991 repeal of the
Group Areas Act of 1950 made it legal for blacks to live in mixed neighborhoods,[2] many could not afford to do so; and while employment opportunities
were opened to all persons, only a minimum number of Africans had the skills
necessary to take higher-paying jobs.

Africans Come to Cape Town

By 1879, there were 3,778 blacks in Cape Town. As their numbers multiplied, regulations to restrict their presence and movement were enacted by the local municipality (Wilson and Mafeje 1973). The City of Cape Town Mayoral Minutes records that whites living in Cape Town's fifth and sixth districts petitioned the Corporation of the City of Cape Town to take precautionary action to deter the intrusion of Africans into these areas lest "respectable working classes" find it unsatisfactory to move into these vicinities (Mayoral Minutes 1898:48). Many whites believed that large numbers of Africans dwelling close to their homes made their neighborhoods undesirable as well as vulnerable to contagious disease. In 1899, the Cape Town medical officer of health, Dr. Barnard Fuller, argued that: "an undesirable feature of the present distribution of Kaffir[3] dwellings is that they are often in immediate contact on either side with European Artisan dwellings" (Makosana 1988:7). Fuller recommended that Africans be relocated to areas a great distance from the center of Cape Town. Thus, beginning in 1901, Africans were, over a period of years, forcibly moved to outlying areas, which later became townships known as Ndabeni, Langa, Nyanga, Guguletu, Crossroads, New Crossroads, and Khayelitsha.

While city officials intended for Africans to live solely in townships, this was never fully accomplished because the population of blacks grew so rapidly that townships could not contain their large numbers. For example, although Uitvlugt, the first residential area set aside for blacks in 1901, had a thousand small dwellings with two rooms and a kitchen, up to 6,000 Africans continued to dwell in central Cape Town (Wilson and Mafeje 1973). Those Africans who lived in proximity to "civilised [sic] [white] communities" were considered a chronic and aggravating problem to local and central governments (Makosana 1988:8). Various white citizen groups petitioned the city to find accommodation for homeless Africans who wandered around prominent areas such as the slopes of Table Mountain, Lion's Head, and Signal Hill. The city council, while initially reluctant to assume the cost of establishing homes, finally in 1923 agreed to build a new African township, Langa, that accommodated 7,600 people. Nevertheless, in twenty years, approximately 50,000 Africans lived in the Western Cape (Kinkead-Weekes 1983).

When it became apparent that the Cape Town municipality would not implement a housing program to accommodate the rapidly increasing population of Africans, legislative measures—such as the 1923 Natives (Urban Areas) Act, section 17, which ordered the removal of "idle, dissolute, or disorderly natives"— were promulgated. The city council provided the opportunity for the South African government to apply the 1923 Urban Areas Act to Cape Town in 1924, but the African squatter area continued to grow, and attempts to control the influx of Africans failed. Large numbers of Africans migrated from the eastern Cape because the economic conditions of the Ciskei and Transkei were disastrous. The Great Depression of 1929 devastated the subsistence economy of these rural areas, forcing Africans to come to town for employment, only to discover that jobs and housing were inadequate.

In 1943, approximately 40,000 unemployed Africans lived in the Western Cape.[4] Yet, with Langa only accommodating 7,600 people, most Africans were illegally in the area, making the squatting situation extremely difficult. In an attempt to stop migration, the city council refused to give "seek-work permits"[5] to Africans and, moreover, declared the Western Cape a Colored Labor Preference Area. Notwithstanding, these measures failed to prevent Africans from coming to Cape Town.

The Cape Colored Preference Policy and African Unemployment

Though the South African government officially announced the Cape Colored Labor Preference Policy in 1954, already by 1946, influx of Africans was even more meticulously regulated in the Western Cape than in other parts of the country through enforcement of the Black Urban Areas Consolidation Act, No. 25 of 1945 (House of Assembly Debates [H.A.D.] vol. 10, 1986, col. 7660). The Cape Town City council, the South African government, and various Western Cape employers acted together to ensure labor preference for Colored people (Goldin 1984:160–161; 1987:71). In 1946 more than nine thousand Africans were expelled from the region, and regulations were rigorously applied to keep others from entering the area (Bodow 1976:41–42).

The victory of the National Party in 1948 meant a radical shift in the quality of life for both Coloreds and Africans in the Western Cape. Yet, this change must, on the one hand, be understood relative to the degree of subjugation each group experienced and must, on the other, be perceived in light of the way each was controlled by the government. Some Nationalists believed that the future strength of their party and its philosophy could be made palatable to Cape Coloreds (J. Albertyn quoted in Goldin 1987:86). In contrast, "Natives," or Africans, were considered a threat and associated with the demise of the party and its command of the country. Thus, though Coloreds and Africans were both disenfranchised and subjected to the Group Areas Act of 1950, through the Reservation of Separate Amenities Act of 1953 and other apartheid legislation the National Party executed a damage-control plan for Cape Coloreds in order to cultivate a group consciousness or identity[6] that was both appreciative of the National Party and radically separate and unequivocally different from that of African people, who were even more rudimentarily and callously oppressed than Coloreds.

Many divide-and-rule tactics on the part of the government created a chasm between Africans and Coloreds. Coloreds, for instance, were not required to carry passes, nor were they subjected to influx control (Goldin 1984:179; 1987:86). Though the 1954 announcement by the South African government that Colored laborers in the Western Cape would be given preference was a statement of a reality already in effect, it also signaled a more overt and aggressive action against Africans, especially African women. An assault was immediately launched, and in mid-1954, African women in the Western Cape were the first people in the country forced to carry passbooks (Horrell 1978:185; West 1983:17).[7] By the end of 1954, twenty thousand African women had been cataloged and were required to have a permit for their jobs and tenancy (Horrell 1957:71; Goldin 1984:182; 1987:87).

To add clarity to the Nationalists' intention to appease Cape Coloreds in light of a growing Colored resistance movement,[8] and on being advised by several governmental agencies to enact a Cape Colored Labor Preference policy to elevate the status and conditions of Coloreds in the Western Cape (Goldin 1984:181;1987:78; Kinkead-Weekes 1992:564),[9] in January 1955, Secretary of Native Affairs, Dr. W. M. M. Eiselen, reported the establishment of a "Colored Labor Preference Area" to oust all Africans from the region (Eiselen 1955). Eiselen explained that such an area was being created because Coloreds had an honorable prerogative to seek job protection or work preference over Africans. Furthermore, he argued that the Western Cape was the "natural *lebensraum*" of Coloreds and that relations between Coloreds and Africans needed to be curtailed because it was destructive to both groups (Eiselen 1955:18; see also Eiselen 1955 as cited in West 1983:16). To reinforce Eiselen's announcement, Dr. H. F. Verwoerd, the minister of Native Affairs, also in 1955 stated in a House of Assembly speech: "the Western Province [is] the area where, due to a whole series of circumstances, the policy of apartheid in regard to the Bantu can be applied with the greatest ease and where it is most essential to take certain steps" (H.A.D. vol. 87, 1955, col. 200).[10]

Through a series of governmental notices and acts, Eiselen and Verwoerd swiftly and vigorously implemented previously approved apartheid legislation in the Western Cape. By order of Government Notice 1032, for instance, there was immediate enforcement of laws forbidding Africans seeking work to be in the Western Cape more than fourteen days annually (Goldin 1984:182; 1987:87). Moreover, the Native Law Amendment Act of 1952, that controlled where Africans could live in urban areas and limited the movement of

Africans out of rural areas, was rigorously enforced. These laws, being more stringently applied in the Western Cape, meant that not only was the movement of blacks regulated, but also that blacks were effectively barred from employment and housing in the region. The aim of the Group Areas Act, the Reservation of Separate Amenities Act (which repressed both Coloreds and Africans), and the Cape Colored Labor Preference policy (which elevated Coloreds over Africans) was to appease and assimilate many in the oppressed Colored community through a positive "affirmative action program" for Coloreds and a negative and fierce assault policy for Africans. Goldin comments on the situation between Colored and Africans in the Western Cape during this period: "From 1948, however, the position of Coloreds deteriorated sharply as they fell victim to legislation designed to institute residential segregation, disenfranchisement and job reservation. At the same time, their position was improved relative to Africans: this was achieved through an unprecedented attack on the African population of the Western Cape" (Goldin 1987:87; see Golden 1984:179–80 for a slightly extended rendering of this quote).

Although unauthorized, many Africans moved into the area and lived with family or constructed shacks in open areas.[11] Influx control measures also changed the way migrant labor was utilized (West 1984:17).

Pass Raids and the Breakup of African Families

Police officers frequently conducted pass raids to ascertain whether Africans were in residence illegally in Cape Town. In addition, all African men were determined by the government to be bachelors, that is, unmarried, in order to prohibit African women and children from living with their husbands and fathers in Cape Town. According to Solomon Makosana, this measure effectively destabilized African families, curtailed increasing numbers of Africans in the Western Cape, and supported the government's plan to establish a second black township in Nyanga West, later called Guguletu, about nine miles from central Cape Town (Makosana 1988:13).

Squatter Camps and the Demolition of Pondokkies

Over the next several decades, the government attempted to enforce rigorously the influx control of Africans. Horrell's 1953–54 *Survey of Race Relations* reported, "influx control is operated even more strictly in the Western Cape than elsewhere in the Union" (Horrell 1954:41). However, Africans continued their illegal migration, and squatter camps were established in Windermere, Blouvlei, and in other areas known by government officials as "black spots."[12] By 1957, the population of Africans in Cape Town had risen to 105,000. Consequently, the government initiated an even more active program of forced removals. In order to increase control of Africans, the government set up an emergency camp to determine Africans' eligibility for housing in either Langa or Nyanga West. Up to 15,000 "unqualified" Africans were expelled from the Western Cape in 1957, and more than 23,000 Africans were removed from the area between January 1959 and March 1962 (H.A.D. vol. 108, 1992, col. 1542).

The *Cape Times* carried a quote by a Mr. Madlebe, who described the heartless manner in which city council officials and the police appeared at 4 A.M.[13] to destroy the *pondokkies*[14] of Windermere residents: "On January 10, the City Council officials, accompanied by police, arrested a large number of people in the early hours of the morning. Mothers with babies on their backs and expectant mothers were among those taken from their beds and locked up in police cells."[15] Protesters denounced this action, and groups of Windermere women, the African National Conference (ANC) women's league, as well as a social worker, Mrs. Sheila Truswell, who witnessed the event, sent letters to the mayor (Makosana 1988:19). With such actions continuing, eighteen months later the government declared a victory in its removal program, and the headline in the *Cape Times* read "Unlawful Entry of Africans Almost Stopped."[16]

Those Africans who remained in the Cape Peninsula were restricted to living at the emergency camp. In December 1958 the local government, having made a deliberate decision not to use brick to construct homes for Africans because it would encourage their permanent presence in Cape Town, assembled five hundred two-room corrugated structures (Makosana 1988:20). Three categories of people were accommodated in these dwellings: (1) those whose legal status and eligibility to live in the Western Cape were still to be determined by the government; (2) those who, while not qualifying to live in a shack erected by the government, were permitted to build their own homes; and (3) those who were displaced and did not qualify to live in Cape Town and, moreover, had neither families nor homes to which to return in Ciskei or Transkei. Despite challenging circumstances, all these people lived together and formed a sense of cohesiveness. They established organizations, such as the Masakhane Thrift Club. They also shared times of celebration (e.g., weddings) and bereavement (e.g., funerals). In addition, communal activities, such as initiation rites, clan meetings, and worship services, were opportunities for them to have meaningful exchanges with one another (Makosana 1988:21). At the same time, public services, such as post offices, hospitals, libraries, sports fields, and recreation centers were not available, nor were basic necessities like water or electricity provided.

The Establishment of Guguletu

Not until 1961 did the city council make earnest efforts to fund a more permanent infrastructure for Nyanga West. As plans evolved for this township to
have a new face through the construction of four independent residential sections, it was renamed Guguletu, meaning "Our Pride" (Makosana 1988:25).
Plans called for section 1 to have 1,244 permanent houses, which were built by
1967. Sections 2 and 3 contained transitional homes without sewage lines.
These homes did not have an infrastructure because the government only
wanted those Africans who provided necessary labor to reside in Cape Town.
Thus there was a systematic plan to build underdeveloped and rudimentary
facilities for Africans.

As people began to live in these new homes, a stratification system evolved
that differentiated Africans on the basis of criteria related to the Urban Areas
Consolidation Act of 1945 and its amendment in 1952. These acts designated
the four categories of persons eligible to live in Cape Town: (1) those who were
born in Cape Town qualified under section 10 (1) (a) of the act; (2) those who
worked in the area for ten consecutive years with the same employer qualified
under section 10 (1) (b); (3) migrant workers employed prior to the Bantu
Labor Regulations of 1968 and who applied to remain permanently qualified
under section 10 (1) (b); and (4) migrant workers in the area after 1968 who
could be employed under the Tribal Labor Bureau for a maximum of one year
qualified under section 10 (1) (b). Those who qualified under section 10 (a)
were eligible to live in a house in Guguletu. Those qualifying under Section 10
(1) (b) were required to live in bachelor quarters or hostels.

By these stratification criteria, permanent and legal residents had high
status, whereas migrant and illegal workers had low status. Hence, there was
considerable social distance between permanent residents and migrant workers (amagoduka). Legal residents were highly regarded, while illegal residents
were considered to be riffraff who did not make a positive contribution to
Cape Town. Wilson and Mafeje note that Langa township also had a class
stratification system, which consisted of migrant workers, males considered to
be bright boys, elderly males (amatopi), and elderly women (amatopikazi)
(Wilson and Mafeje 1973:21). Social distinction was also evidenced as those
residents who lived in pondokkies were rebuffed. Occupants who had four-
room houses had higher status than those who lived in two-room dwellings.

Effects of Overcrowding

In time, overcrowding became a major problem. Since government policy dictated that Africans were not to have a permanent place in Cape Town

and that Colored people were to have job preference, as of 1972 only 3,868 houses had been constructed in Guguletu. Even with government policies that controlled African migration and employment, the population of Guguletu in 1970 was 65,068; by 1980, it had increased to 73,480 (Granelli and Levitan 1977:14). By 1982, however, the housing stock in Guguletu had increased only to 7,392 units. Even if we assume that in 1982 Guguletu's population was the same as in 1980, this would mean that 9.9 persons lived in dwellings with no more than four little rooms.

M. Lipschitz reports a positive correlation between overcrowded homes (more than six people per housing unit) and the high incidence of respiratory infections among Africans (Lipschitz 1984:6). Tuberculosis was associated particularly with populations living in overcrowded quarters (Lipschitz 1984:12).

Migrant Worker Accommodations and Liquor Outlets

Migrant worker accommodations in Guguletu, known as hostels, housed sixteen men in six rooms, each measuring 4 by 3 meters. Each hostel had common cooking and eating areas and cement bunks without mattresses. Privacy did not exist, as cold-water showers and toilets were constructed without walls. Moreover, since there were no separate areas for entertainment, the potential for conflict was great. When additional hostel dwellings were erected by the city council, electric plugs and rubber floor tiles were added.

In 1961, the government enacted the Liquor Amendment Act, which made it legal for Africans to purchase alcohol. The Cape Town city council established five liquor outlets in Langa and Guguletu. Profit from the sale of liquor was funneled into accounts set aside to administer townships. A report issued by the city council's auditor-general in 1975–1976 revealed that a higher level of revenue was generated from the sale of liquor than from the collection of rent (Makosana 1988:45–46). Dwellers refused to pay rent because government officials took little responsibility for maintaining rental houses. As African communities were devitalized through liquor consumption, township services were improved by the city council (Kraak 1984:18).

National Party's Continued Support for Cape Coloreds

In 1978, P. W. Botha, wanting to improve relations with Coloreds further, promised to make the laws more secure, thus guaranteeing Coloreds political and economic advantage over Africans. This is demonstrated by the large number of Africans who were arrested between 1978 and 1981. Over 13,694

Africans were arrested for violating influx laws in the Western Cape, a number 10 percent higher than the de facto number of Africans in the Western Cape (West 1983:21; Goldin 1984:359).[17] With the average fine being R70 per person,[18] which represented at a minimum two weeks' wages, the total of the fines exceeded R283,500 (Goldin 1984:349).

At the conclusion of the 1982 Cape National Congress, the government vigorously renewed their policy of influx control. Three weeks after the congress, three thousand blacks in the Western Cape were detained. The majority of them were unable to provide defense for themselves; hence, the South African government collected more than R60,000 in penalties (Goldin 1984:359). With the exception of the Western Cape, influx control arrests decreased in urban areas (West 1983:20). Moreover, during the late 1970s and early 1980s, African women were arrested more often than African men in the Cape Peninsula (West 1983:21; Goldin 1984:360).[19] The *Cape Times* reported that a "war" had been declared on Africans in the Western Cape (*Cape Times*, 28 October 1982).

In 1984, in what was heralded as a capitulation on the part of the Nationalists, the Cape National Party withdrew the Cape Colored Preference Policy. This was not, however, an authentic capitulation, because amendments to the Black Labor Act of 1964 effectively continued the policy. Nonetheless, one benefit of the repeal of the policy was that permanent African residents were permitted to purchase ninety-nine-year leaseholds in Khayelitsha (Goldin 1984:377;422). Otherwise, there was very little change in influx control in 1984.

The Abolition of Influx Control

Africans in the Western Cape continued to be harshly affected by influx control until the 1986 Abolition of Influx Control Act was passed. The effect of the bill was not only the initial dismantling of apartheid but also the removal from urbanization programs of discrimination based on race or color. Moreover, the bill aimed to prevent chaotic squatting and adverse conditions that might lead to health risks in cities and rural regions (H.A.D. vol. 10, 1986, col. 7662). During the debate on the bill, Professor Nicolaas J. J. Olivier, a member of the Progressive Federal Party who had moved from being a supporter of apartheid to being its critic,[20] made a significant speech about the consequences of influx control legislation and the importance of its repeal:

> I do not think there is any other legislation in South Africa that has caused so much resentment, so much bitterness and so much alienation as the legislation

which is about to be repealed by this Bill. I do not think there are any measures which have caused greater alienation between Black people as a whole, and the central authorities, the police and officialdom—all of whom were burdened with this legislation—than these very measures. The aftermath of these measures . . . will remain with us for a very long time, because the removal of these measures will not be able to wipe out in an instant the resentment and the bitterness which these measures caused.

Over the years, . . . literally millions of Blacks were arrested and sent to jail. In terms of the night permit system alone, according to calculations since 1945, no fewer than 4 million Blacks have been sent to jail—and this figure is the lowest of all!

None of us will ever be able to overestimate the effect which these measures have had on the quality of life of the Blacks, on their human existence as a whole. (H.A.D. vol. 10, 1986, col. 7668)

In the Western Cape, where influx control and apartheid legislation were initially applied, [21] the quality of life for blacks was particularly adversely affected.

Summary

This chapter has chronicled several key challenges faced by thousands of Xhosa-speaking Africans who left rural areas of the eastern Cape and migrated to Cape Town in the late nineteenth century. Fleeing their homes in the Transkei and Ciskei because economic blight irreversibly impaired their quality of life, they ventured to the Cape Peninsula searching for a productive life and gainful employment. Instead of positive opportunities, they confronted acute discrimination from white residents and government officials. Panic among whites created a reactive environment in which the laws were passed making it illegal for blacks to live in and move about Cape Town freely. Since white employers needed the labor power of Africans, occupational niches considered undesirable to Colored laborers opened to blacks at low wages.

White citizens did not want the families of black workers to live in Cape Town. Thus, African laborers' wives and children resided in rural areas separated from their husbands and fathers and hoped to receive a portion of the income earned by their loved ones. While black workers earned paltry wages in the city, their families continued to live in economically depressed conditions in rural areas. Although Cape Town government officials did allow family members of essential laborers to move to Cape Town, they were not the majority of unprotected workers, who suffered miserably because they lacked political rights.

The social history of Africans in Cape Town between the 1880 and 1980 is replete with aggressive actions by government officials forcibly removing Africans from white areas to locations designated exclusively for blacks. Temporary emergency camps and townships housed Africans in places away from the center of town and out of the sight of whites at an insignificant cost. The Cape Town government was reluctant to provide adequate housing for black employees because Africans' permanent residence was the rural areas. Thus, laws enacting limited employment opportunities and minimum wages dictated the quality of African life in Cape Town. Moreover, the government elevated Cape Coloreds, another disenfranchised group, one notch above black Africans with the establishment of the Cape Colored Labor Preference Act, thereby granting affirmative action to Coloreds as an attempt to drive a wedge between two communities that shared race discrimination in South Africa. In addition, this policy was an effort on the part of Afrikaners to seduce Coloreds to support the National Party.

In 1986, influx control of Africans was lifted and the African population in Cape Town soared. Free access to the Cape Peninsula caused overcrowding in black areas. Crime burgeoned because black unemployment was extremely high and wages very low. Africans erected shantytowns of shacks in any open space, and new townships (e.g., Khayelitsha) emerged.

As African townships such as Langa and sections of Guguletu stabilized, class divisions increased. Nonetheless, the majority of black Africans at a subsistence level lived below the poverty line. Large numbers of destitute black people were attracted to African indigenous churches because their cosmology integrated African culture and ritual life. Moreover, indigenous churches affirmed the humanity of black people disregarded by the larger society.

A priest at St. John's baptizes two initiates in the ocean.

Xolisa does a holy dance during the worship service.

An usher washes a priest's hands in preparation for blessing those who walk under the canopy.

A member walks under the canopy as Mama Xaba lays hands on in blessing.

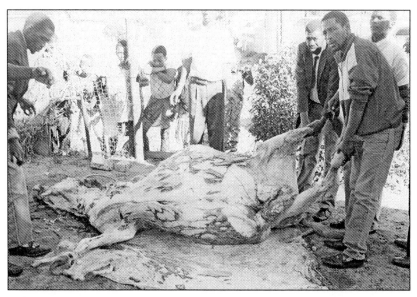

Men remove a cow's skin as a preliminary action to extracting its entrails.

The bishop and his assistant bless the entrails of a cow and sheep prior to burning them in a special ritual.

The bishop and his assistant burn entrails to honor the ancestors.

Members receive communion.

CHAPTER 3

Ethnographic Profile of St. John's Apostolic Faith Mission Church–Guguletu

> What the ethnographer studies is how people create meaning or significance in their lives, how they interpret objects and events. . . . A corollary of this position is that the people who are being studied should be allowed to speak for themselves whenever possible, for they are the only true experts on themselves.
> —Karen Brown, *Mama Lola: A Vodou Princess in Brooklyn*

My interviews with members of St. John's–Guguletu began in 1991, shortly after Nelson Mandela's release from prison, and the repeal of the final pillars of apartheid. Even though apartheid was no longer legal, it still had a firm grip on the nation, particularly its intellectual, psychosocial, political, and economic life. With apartheid's legal, political, and economic infrastructure having solidified over a period of eighty years, it was impossible to dismantle in a short time. Extracting apartheid's underpinnings from all macro- and microstructures will take several generations.

In the early 1990s, apartheid was firmly entrenched throughout various structures and systems of the nation. For instance, the notorious African "homelands" were still in existence, and unemployment among Africans was extremely high, creating a labor surplus that kept wages low. Additionally, violence was the order of the day all over the country. Indeed, it was a liminal time, as the African National Congress (ANC) set up a new government administered by newly elected comrades who had little or no government and management experience because they had either recently returned from exile or had just been released from prison. Moreover, the ANC, the Afrikaner National Party, and other political entities were debating and negotiating a

33

new constitution. At the same time, preparations for the first democratic election in the history of the nation, scheduled for April 1994, moved briskly. Social distress was great, as a nation in transition experienced extremely high rates of crime and uncertainty about future business with international companies. In spite of this uncertainty, many lived with hope because Nelson Mandela was heir apparent to the presidency. Many believed that the first black president of the nation would usher in a new South Africa because apartheid was at last unraveling. Hope and struggle were the watchwords.

National events had consequences for the lives of grassroots communities like St. John's. Members of the church represented a segment of the black South African population that was desperately poor and lacked basic amenities. Most adherents were women who worked as domestics in the homes of white families, while men held jobs as unskilled laborers, if they were employed at all.

Social unrest was endemic to members' lives, as was a cycle of unemployment and violence in the aftermath of apartheid. The transition from a white supremacist to a democratic government created economic uncertainty and unemployment in addition to racial and criminal violence. Apartheid's legacy exacerbated the problems marginalized people experienced. Simply because they had black skin, and lived with the ramifications of the accumulated effects of poverty, they were devalued by white culture and discriminated against by South African society—especially if they were female. St. John's members were the victims of the social havoc wreaked by the interlocking dynamic of race, gender, and political economy. Adherents called this accumulated stress, consternation, and complexity *ukugula,* meaning sickness or ill health.

I entered the world of St. John's members within the larger context of the demise of apartheid. Having received permission to conduct research, I interviewed members in order to examine their everyday lives and to learn about the ways their religious cosmology was woven into the fabric of their identity. My questions explored the reasons they were devoted to the St. John's community, the dimensions of their family life, and their experience of black township life during a time of discord and rapid social change.

The members of St. John's–Guguletu were like a family who gathered in varying configurations to grapple with, struggle against, and confront the ever changing circumstances of life under apartheid. For instance, three women living together in a one-room shack located on the church's property shared food from their limited incomes, looked after one another's children, and supported one another's struggle for fair treatment and dignity at their workplace. Members living in individual homes scattered throughout Guguletu and adjacent townships[1] gathered at the church on Wednesday and Saturday mornings to assist ailing people who came for healing treatments. On Sunday mornings, most adherents gathered as a larger group to worship together and support those who experienced difficulties during the week. Throughout the week, various members assisted sick people who lived on the church premises. Whether the cluster of people gathered was a fluid informal group or a formally structured subgroup, there was cohesiveness and a dedication to the cosmology and healing works of the church.

This chapter integrates interviews with eighteen members in the form of personal narrative. What these members tell us about their reasons for joining St. John's and the nature of their everyday life reveals both the challenges faced by economically disadvantaged black South Africans and the ritual world they produced to fashion a constructive, creative way of being in the world.

In this chapter, I respond, by way of application, to queries and challenges posed by postmodern anthropological methodology (Marcus and Fischer 1987; Rosaldo 1989)—how few ethnographic texts take seriously the need to hear the voices of black South Africans, particularly the poor; the importance of being intentional in permitting the point of view of poor black South Africans, who are members of an African indigenous church (AIC), to speak for itself; the need to encourage readers to draw their own conclusions about what St. John's members say about their experiences rather than overlay their insights with heavy authorial interpretation; and the importance of taking seriously what leaders of AICs have called for in their own volume, *Speaking for Ourselves*. In this text, grassroots people implore outsiders to allow the voices of AICs to emerge on their own merit at different points in whatever books are written about them.

The information on apartheid, violence, the taxi war, employment, personal challenges, reasons for coming to St. John's, and the healing process, which is outlined below, is from men and women who articulated clearly their life experiences under apartheid and the spirituality of St. John's. The following paragraphs serve as introductions to those interviewed in 1991.

1. Tshawe

Tshawe was the daughter of Jezile, a minister of a St. John's congregation in Paarl, two hours from Cape Town. Tshawe came to the St. John's–Guguletu congregation on the first Sunday in September 1991 because she wanted to go to the ocean with Reverend Xaba for the monthly purification ritual in which members were expected to participate. Tshawe talked with me about worship services, ancestors, customs, and initiation rites for girls and boys. She was a part of St. John's because her parents were both ministers of the denomination.

35

2. Thole

For less than one year, Thole lived in a shack on the church's premises with four other men. He was thirty-eight years old, divorced, and the father of three children. Two of his three children lived with their mothers; one died of unknown causes. Thole came to the church through the assistance of a maternal aunt who knew about Reverend Xaba. Thole's aunt was extremely worried about him because he tried to commit suicide. Reverend Xaba invited him into the church community after discerning that he wanted to be healed.

3. Nyawuza

Nyawuza, Reverend Xaba's nephew, lived with Thole and three other men in a one-room shack. He was twenty-three years old and had been at St. John's–Guguletu for six weeks. Before coming to the church, he lived with his mother in Willowvale, a province in the Transkei. His mother was very concerned about the voices he heard in his head and pains he had in his neck and back. While he had been examined by a medical doctor and received a prescription, his condition had not improved after a few weeks. His mother thought it best that they journey to Cape Town to be with her brother, Reverend Xaba, who she believed would know how to heal her son.

4. Mama Ntiliti

Mama Ntiliti's home of origin was Bophuthatswana, in the Northern Province. She was Tswana[2] and moved to Cape Town in 1942. A very dedicated member of St. John's and an enthusiastic church evangelist, Mama Ntiliti lived in a small three-room house situated a few blocks from the church.

5. Myira

Fifty-six years old, Myira was born in the Lady Frye province of the Transkei. She was divorced and lived in a four-room house in Guguletu with twelve other family members.

6. Banzi

Banzi, a thirty-one-year-old man, had been at St. John's for nine months and was very devoted to the church. He credited St. John's members with helping him to develop a positive relationship with God and to heal from scars upon his life inflicted by political and social violence. As a young man he had worked in the mines; so he understood life in South Africa from the perspective of a migrant worker. Banzi willingly answered most questions during our conversation but declined to disclose his monthly income.

7. Mama Joxo

Mama Joxo affiliated with St. John's because she believed that Mother Shenxane, the minister who preceded Tata Xaba, could help her son's mental illness. The congregation provided support as she and her family experienced many difficulties.

8. Thobeka

Thobeka joined St. John's because ukugula was manifested in two ways in her life. First, her child was sick, and second, she believed that she was called to be a diviner and wanted to resist this summons from the ancestors. She talked about her struggle with *amafufunyana,* a sickness typically acquired by those called to be diviners.[3]

9 and 10. Ndsilibe and Yoliswa Beliqoco

Ndsilibe and Yoliswa, residents of Nyanga, an African township adjacent to Guguletu, inhabited a two-room shack without plumbing, located across the street from a male hostel in a crime-ridden neighborhood. Ndsilibe traveled to St. John's seeking relief from an illness that had plagued him since childhood. Yoliswa worked as a domestic in the home of a white family. Her oldest child lived with her family in the Ciskei, and her youngest, an infant, lived with her and Ndsilibe. She participated actively in the housing reform program in her community.

11. Mama Mazibula

Mama Mazibula, born in Ngqamakwe, Transkei, was sixty-two years old. During her marriage, she gave birth to ten children; four died in infancy. She also had two miscarriages. She had six years of formal schooling and attended a Methodist church before becoming a member of St. John's. Mama Mazibula resided in Guguletu in a three-room house with her husband, two of their children, and two grandchildren.

12 and 13. Reverend and Mama Mjoli

Reverend and Mama Mjoli were both born in the Transkei, in the Mount Frere and Qumbu districts, respectively. They had been married over forty years and had two adult children. Unemployed at the time of our interview, Mama Mjoli had previously worked for several years as a domestic. She had completed six years of schooling. Reverend Mjoli had been unemployed since 1988. He had formerly worked in township administration in Langa, an adjacent township, and had completed eight years of schooling. The Mjolis received R295 (U.S.$74) each month from pension funds. They usually received no income assistance from their children, who lacked jobs. Their daughter and her little boy lived with them, intensifying the financial strains. Occasionally, however, their son sold beer and sometimes gave them money.

14. Nozipo

Born in the Transkei, Nozipo gave birth to five children, but only two survived. Her little girl, Thembisa, and her son, Mthetheleli, lived with her at St. John's. She had not seen her husband for several years. Since the violence in Old Crossroads[4] made it unsafe for her to remain in her own home, she chose to stay at St. John's.

15. Thozama

Thozama had been a member of St. John's for two years. She lived with several other women in a one-room shack behind the church and was employed as a domestic. Her only child died while they lived in the Transkei.

16 and 17. Manqwati and Xolisa

Manqwati and Xolisa resided with Thozama and several other women and children on the church's premises. Both were employed as domestics.

18. Nonceba

Residing a short distance from the church, Nonceba initially went to St. John's because she was sick. She became an evangelist after being a member for five years.

Demographic information on the eighteen interviewees appears in appendix 2.

Apartheid and Violence

After giving an overview about my research, I asked each member to reflect on ukugula and other apartheid-related challenges they experienced in their day-to-day life. Banzi explained his understanding of the interconnections between apartheid and violence. He focused on the ways apartheid placed undue pressure on black people, causing, in his opinion, the erosion of relationships. This was very troubling to him because Banzi personally and various South African indigenous cultures highly valued interconnections between friends, neighbors, and clan members, paramount paradigms of a communal lifestyle. "The violence here in South Africa happens because we are under pressure.[5] The pressure is like this: black people don't get what they want. Apartheid divides black people. People are living in a terrible way. For example, the Group Areas Act divided us in our place."

Mama Mazibula's view of the chronic violence in South Africa was succinct. "The situation in South Africa is terrible. It is a very bad time because of the violence. It's so terrible. Terrible." While Banzi and Mama Mazibula gave gripping descriptions of their experiences and impressions about violence in daily life, they also shared stories related to apartheid. Banzi not only linked violence and apartheid; he also explained the ways prayer assisted him in everyday life.

Apartheid affected me very much because some members of my family are in jail. Some members of my family died, so it is something that affects my life. It has been very bad for me. For example, when I went to Johannesburg looking for work, there was a time when we were in the train and the soldiers and policemen came and hit and shot us. I used to pray very hard because every day when I went to work I didn't know if I was coming back. So I prayed and God helped me a lot because I'm still alive.[6]

I can say that my church plays a big role in my prayers. I pray for myself because there is so much violence. I was one of the people on the train and didn't know that the soldiers were hitting people and killing people who were on board. When I got off, I found out that there was a problem on the train. You see, God helps me a lot. I prayed there. I also thanked my church because there was a problem and God helped me. God helps me a lot. But I also play a big role because I pray for myself. Yes, I was safe. There was also a time that I didn't have a ticket in my hand, but I just looked down and I found a ticket. I gave it to them because otherwise they would hit me. Others had nothing to give them. We had to push to get off the train. I can say, I praise my God because he helped me with that problem. Even the ticket I picked up from the floor, I know that God helped me to get this ticket because I just found it and gave it to the soldier. Then I was safe.

He recalled an experience from 1985, a particularly volatile time in South Africa, when he and other migrant workers conducted a labor strike at a gold mine in Johannesburg. For Banzi, the heinous work conditions and low wages were linked to apartheid. "In 1985 I had a problem while in Johannesburg. There was not so much violence by a black toward a black. The Inkatha[7] business was not involved. We were all on one side, so I was safe. Among the hostel dwellers there was a strike. We were fighting against our oppressors. We demanded the wages because our oppressors were the white people."

Mama Mazibula likewise talked about the way apartheid functioned.

> I don't know how to explain apartheid, because most of the time I am working in the house, but I can say this. Sometimes you go and get on a bus. Then they say, you can't get in this carriage because it's for whites only. You can't go to this place because it's for whites only. You can't go on the bus, and even in the train, you can't get in first class unless it's first class that is for blacks only. There is a special first class for whites only on the trains. If you are late, you have to go to your own class on the train. They make a special third class for blacks. These are some of the things I see with my own two eyes.

When I asked members whether they believed apartheid was over because Nelson Mandela had been released from prison and segregation laws repealed, they asserted clearly that nothing had changed in their lives to make them believe in the truth of such a notion. Banzi recounted how he did not support the De Klerk[8] government and how the situation in South Africa was deteriorating. "I don't support De Klerk, so I won't say anything about him. I don't see any results from the removing of the rules of apartheid. Not one. What I see is that instead of making things better, he's making things worse. Maybe, though, there's a very good future for the new South Africa since I see there are people who stand up and go and fight for us."

Mama Mazibula conveyed a similar thought: "I don't see that apartheid has ended as De Klerk says. I haven't seen any action to end it. I just see that things are as they were before. I might see a white person sitting next to me, but with other things there is no movement. It is still the same."

For Nozipo, apartheid did not encourage blacks; though headed for a sure demise, apartheid's structural and personal effects maintained their grip: "It is still very difficult to talk about apartheid, because there's so many things that don't encourage us; that don't give us hope. Apartheid is slowly, slowly going away. But still you can see it's difficult to die. It doesn't die. It still exists.

"As for me, what I can explain is that I don't see any changes at the moment. There are places where they don't allow us to enter, even our wages are not the same with Colored people. I don't want to say anything about it."

Amid the instability and volatility in townships of the Western Cape, poor blacks experienced violence on at least two distinct levels. One level is related to a general malaise and deterioration in the social web of relationships and the physical atmosphere of township life. A segment of the black population living in townships was not only dissatisfied but angry about blatant inequities that were the result of unequal development and segregation policies. The second level, while related to the first, is somewhat different. A taxi war between two competing companies had a devastating impact on people who risked their lives to get to work and other places on the most reliable form of transportation available in townships.[9] Banzi articulated the reasons for the taxi war: "The taxi war is caused by two companies that do not have the same views. There are the two organizations called Laguna and Webta. They won't work together. The drivers disagree. Some say, 'We are to do one thing,' and then others say, 'No, we can't work.' So there are differences between the taxi drivers and the taxi owners."

Mama Joxo attested that her son, a taxi driver, often risked danger because of the disagreement between Laguna and Webta. Instead of picking passengers up at taxi ranks in the townships, he opted to pick people up at hotels and drop them off at less volatile stops in townships.

> The violence has affected my family directly. My son in Khayelitsha was affected by the violence because he had a taxi there. He was working for his boss by going to collect people who were staying at a hotel with this taxi one afternoon. About three o'clock, they wanted to kill him. They wanted to shoot him. There were guns around him. Then they took him out and they ran away with his taxi. This happened about three months ago. It's still new.
>
> My son is still working. He still drives a taxi. My son always comes to my house, especially on the weekends. The violence in Khayelitsha is so terrible for him. Sometimes he doesn't work in the taxi rank but instead collects people at the hotels at night. Then, sometimes the people there in Khayelitsha stop his taxi, so he sleeps here to avoid the problems. I don't know what the cause of the taxi war is because we haven't got a person who's got a taxi nearby.

Children suffered extreme peril because of the multiple layers of violence, particularly when they tried to attend school. Even in 1991, education for black children remained substandard as black schools were not funded at the level of white schools nor were black teachers as well trained as white teachers. Nevertheless, parents wanted their children to have an education. Nozipo depicted the traumatic impact of violence upon her life, and why she hastily departed from Old Crossroads[10] squatter camp to a shack on the church's premises. "It's like this. My little house in Crossroads was burnt down. I had to flee from Crossroads. I took my two kids and came to stay here. I was waiting for the trouble to finish; to come to an end. It doesn't come to an end. That's why, now, I say I don't see the future of the country." She also detailed how various incendiary conditions negatively affected the children in her life, particularly her daughter, niece, and nephew, and spoke of her own fear of sending her daughter to school in Old Crossroads.

My little girl can't go to her school in Old Crossroads. We used to live in Old Crossroads. I had to move out of the house where I lived because of the fighting in the neighborhood. So, I can't take my child to the school. My sister came here last Sunday. She said she was going to take her back, because they had a meeting to make peace. But after the talks, they started shooting again. So, my sister did not come. That's why Mama Xaba didn't take her to school. The last time I was at Old Crossroads, I went to see my sister. There was another meeting, but we hadn't heard about it. The other children from Crossroads are now going to school, but my little one is here. I don't want to take her to my sister, because she lives close to the shooting and where they throw stones.

Nozipo's sister's children also had to stay away from their school. This was especially disappointing because both were almost ready to graduate, which meant that they could have sought employment to help with the household economy. Her sister expressly expected and desperately needed her son to work to help support the family.

My sister's got two daughters and two sons. The big daughter is doing the matric[11] for the second time. She's in a school now, in Langa. One of her boys is doing Standard 9. His sister, the little sister, is also doing Standard 9. They have to stay away from school for a couple of months. I don't know even now if they go to school, because of the violence and the fighting that's going on. They are so clever. I mean, this son is so clever at school; he's wonderful. But, he can't go to school because the fighting is going on. Somebody's just running behind him to shoot him. There's nowhere to stay because somebody's waiting for him—to kill him. So there is more pain—more pain, because we were just thinking that in a few years' time, he will be finished with school. And he will have to help his father and mother, who have nothing. They are just struggling to educate their children.

Ever mindful of the danger of living and traveling to work or to school, Nozipo concluded by sharing a story about a bus driver's murder. She declared that violence needed to stop immediately and linked it directly to inadequate wages. "Even today, they killed a bus driver and hit the people in the bus. The people must stop fighting one another and let the children go to school. The violence is because of dissatisfaction with the government. I think the fighting is carried on because the people are not satisfied about money."

The circumstances of her life led Nozipo to make a final comment about the reason she lived in a one-room shack with other women and children. "We are here together now in this small room because we want to pray together. If one of us is not back from our job, we become so frightened for that one, because we don't know how we would get help. It's Khayelitsha and Nyanga townships that are the problem. That's why we thank God, because sometimes we get in a place and then they tell us that somebody was shot, but we always come home after that thing has happened. Now we feel that we can stay here where we can pray every time."

Banzi was exceedingly aware of the negative impact that violence had in the Western Cape townships. He linked his faith in the church with the cessation of violence and explained the reasons he believed that the church could play a role in peacemaking.

> I think the church can play a big role in working against the violence. For instance, all the churches can come together and pray to God. The church can pray for God to give light to the people so that they can understand each other. So if there is fighting between people, through the light of God, there won't be blood. People will understand each other.
>
> The church can call both taxi organizations and then ask them to make peace. It's not necessary to know about deep beliefs as long as they try to make peace between those two organizations. Then after they pray together with these two organizations, maybe God will do something.
>
> While I don't know too much about Archbishop Tutu, I do know that he always goes where there is violence and tries to make peace. He goes and tries to make peace and to ask the people to come together.

The Release of Nelson Mandela

Nelson Mandela's elders groomed him from birth to be a chief in Thembuland. However, as he grew older, he had an ardent drive to prepare himself to make a difference in the struggle for democracy in South Africa. Trained as an attorney, in 1952 he held the title of national volunteer-in-chief in the Defiance Campaign of Unjust Laws, which the ANC initiated to produce a mass civil disobedience movement involving grassroots people. The apartheid government arrested him for this work and for his battle against worker exploitation, pass laws, embryonic Bantustan policy, and the segrega-

42

tion of open universities. Because of his activism in the 1950s, the government restrained the growing movement to fight apartheid by making him a "banned" person and imprisoning him. In the mid-1950s he was accused and tried for treason, and in the 1960s he was charged with sabotage in the Rivonia trial and sentenced to life imprisonment. When Mandela was released on 11 February 1990, the entire world rejoiced, especially broad-minded South Africans who recognized that a wind of freedom was blowing. Mandela continued his life's work: the fight for freedom and democracy in South Africa; the goals he and others had outlined almost forty years earlier.

Mama Joxo, connecting many of her life's struggles with apartheid, expressed how disturbing it was when Mandela was in prison and how heartened she and others were when he was freed. "It was a terrible thing when Mandela was in prison. I don't know the things of politics. I was happy when he was released because he was a long time in jail." Likewise, Banzi communicated the grief he felt that Mandela was jailed and his confidence in Mandela's leadership. "Mr. Mandela has done the best. It means a lot to me that he is free. Since he's been out of jail, the exiles are coming back home, and political prisoners are to be released. We cried for Mr. Mandela for many years because we needed him outside, so that he can do what he's trying to do now. He is sitting down with Mr. De Klerk to talk with him. We knew that if he could come out, he would do that."

Employment Issues

Employment and unemployment issues loomed large for black South Africans, particularly during the peak of the resistance movement from 1985 through 1991. Unemployment was at a record high, and a corresponding level of violence ensued as a result. Those who were employed were exposed to at least two risks. First, employers subjected them to exploitation, because the labor surplus meant that wages were very low. Second, their safety was jeopardized because violence often occurred en route to work or at the workplace. Banzi, a laborer in the Johannesburg mines, recalled the harsh treatment and the small amount of money he received for his work. Banzi reported that this was a deplorable existence.

> I understand what's going on in South Africa because I worked in the factories. I worked in the mines, so I tasted some of the bad things. I saw who the oppressor was. I noticed many things. That's why I understand what is going on in South Africa, because I'm a worker.
>
> To work in the mines is a very troubling thing. It's really bad. You exist between dying and being alive. It's very hard, because while you are working,

you are not working in a happy way. You work just because you have problems. There's a lot of things to say about it. While the white people are kicking us, while we are busy digging, we don't get money. There we work very hard and we don't get money. While we are busy working, they are kicking us. They do everything that they want to do under the ground.

I am thirty-one years old and when I had a problem I went here and there. Maybe I worked in Transvaal from January to June.[13] Then I changed jobs because there was a white person who wanted to hit me while I was working. I ran away from there and went to Vrystaat to take a job.[14] I got there and had the same problem I had the first time. So this is how we move from work to work.

Mama Joxo, a long-term domestic, likewise talked about the underpayment she and other black South Africans received for their toil. She asserted that the elite, whether in industry or in private homes, did not pay Africans the wages necessary for a decent standard of living.

When I worked, I was a domestic in the houses of white people. I worked in the kitchen. I cooked and looked after their children.

Even the work here, there's no work for blacks and no money for blacks. If you work in the factory, they don't want to pay blacks. I see that some blacks are working, but there's no money for blacks.

What I can say is that there's no money in South Africa. I was working in the kitchen. I never get anything. There is money for white people, and they share amongst themselves.

Banzi and Mama Joxo represent an array of members of St. John's as well as unskilled laborers in general. They lived on a subsistence wage and had limited alternatives to enhance skills necessary for higher-paying jobs. Indeed, apartheid restricted black people's earning power and promoted minimum subsistence levels. This acute survival mode, underscored by the remnants of apartheid's separate development policies, had a debilitating effect on black workers and their families.

Furthermore, the dialectics of black womanhood in South Africa meant that grassroots women were usually domestics in the homes of white families or were self-employed street vendors, seamstresses, or shebeen queens in their homes.[15] While most of the women at St. John's were domestics, at least one, Mama Mazibula, sewed at home. The daily activities of women show that they were diligent workers who sacrificed their esteem and their bodies and, in spite of these losses, managed limited incomes creatively. For instance, some women shared living accommodations. Nozipo, who worked as a "tea girl," stayed in a shack with nine other women and their children. A mutual-care network existed among these women, who shared their wisdom and meager resources. During an interview, Nozipo explained her daily life and work responsibilities.

> I get up at five o'clock when the St. John's bells ring for the first prayers in the mornings. I go for prayer, which lasts for half an hour. At half past five, I come back to the room, put the paraffin stove on, warm up some water, wash myself, get dressed, and at half past six I walk to the Heideveld station, where I catch a train at about seven o'clock to Bonteheuvel and then change for the Belleville train. At Belleville, I take a taxi that costs R1.20 to R1.50 a journey. I'm supposed to get to my job at eight o'clock and start work. My work is to clean. I start cleaning in the poolroom, which is like a bar. After I finish at twelve noon, they open up for their customers. Later, I do the banking and make some tea. When I come in the morning, I make tea for the secretaries, the staff, and all the bosses. I also do banking for them. I go to the banks for statements and sometimes I go to bank some checks for them, like a messenger.

Nozipo, with a zealous spirit, imparted that she remained dissatisfied with an income of R120 a week ($50), because such a low wage did not compensate for the amount of work she performed. Although she was unhappy with her income, she worked hard and used her paltry earnings wisely as a single mother with two children.

Mama Mazibula contributed an account of the activities of her daily life, which included sewing, washing, and taking care of her husband and family. "During the week I wake up, and by 7:30 A.M. I am dressed. I am always busy with my housework. I do sewing. I do washing. I clean my house and cook for my husband. I also look after my grandchildren. I go to bed at 8:00 P.M. after watching television. I have never had a holiday." While not employed outside of the home, Mama Mazibula nonetheless endured a very full work life.

A retired domestic laborer receiving a pension from the government, Mama Joxo chronicled her daily life and described an injury she received working as a domestic. "I get a pension, so I don't work outside my home during the day. I clean my house, and when I can, I relax. I had a knee operation some time ago. It was necessary because of the work I did in the kitchen where I worked, and going up and down stairs."

These three women worked under arduous circumstances to support their indigent families. Because her husband was employed as an unskilled laborer, Mama Mazibula remained at home and took in sewing. Nozipo and Mama Joxo, however, did not have the support of spouses during their working years.

These three contrasting portraits of African women proletarians point to the resolve of folks whom apartheid designed not to rise above a certain level of economic existence; and yet, despite the tension of living in an almost unbearable economic climate, these women survived with resilient spirits.

Personal Challenges

Adverse macrostructures frequently yielded negative consequences that, added to the precarious nature of members' lives, particularly with respect to their employment, income, and encounter with ascending levels of violence. In addition, they weathered challenges caused by their own human fragility. Nozipo's and Mama Joxo's life stories offer examples of the repercussions precipitated by macrostructures as well as difficulties related to human fragility. Nozipo, like many black South African women at St. John's, grew up in a rural area but later migrated to the Western Cape. Her experience also replicated the strength of St. John's women who gave birth to several children but buried one or more during infancy. She gave birth to five children, but three died during the first six months of their lives because of the paucity of medical facilities in rural South African villages. Infant mortality was a perpetual problem, particularly in rural areas. Nozipo explained the similar deaths of three of her children: "My second, third, and fourth children died. I think they died because I had to leave them at an early age. The second one was a little girl. I was still living with my mother in the Transkei when my daughter died. She was a very pretty girl, and she just started turning the eyes upward. Her eyes couldn't come back. I didn't know what she had. She had terrible pain that lasted a day. On the second day she died. My third child died at five months. I had come to Cape Town and left him with my mother. The same thing that happened to my daughter happened to him. It was diarrhea."

While Nozipo did not comment on the death of her fourth child, she did describe her feelings of utter grief and disclosed that the fathers of her children had not provided money for child support or burial expenses. The apartheid state bears much responsibility for the death of Nozipo's children, because medical clinics, clean water sources, and other basic necessities were not provided to black South Africans, especially in rural areas, because of separate development policies.

The personal challenge of Mama Joxo related to family dysfunction and to the macrolevel structure's systematic disregard for black people. Mama Joxo's mentally ill son received no assistance from the state; so friends and St. John's members provided all of her support for daily living. In addition to being responsible for the care of her son, Mama Joxo cared for her grand-daughter when her daughter (the child's mother) worked. One day Mama

Joxo had to be out of her house for a period of time, leaving her son and granddaughter at home alone, leading to disastrous consequences. Mama Joxo detailed the trauma of her devastating experience.

It is a terrible story. One day I left my son at home alone with my granddaughter. He was a man and my granddaughter, a little one. On that day, he raped the little one. When I returned home, I thought that she was frightened, because she was carrying on. He raped her, and after that the child never told anyone. I could see that the child was sick and that she did not seem better for a long time. I took her to the Red Cross Hospital, and then they found that the child was raped. The hospital took action against the rape. They made a case. We tried our best to get my son admitted to Valkenberg or Lentegeur Hospital. The social workers asked the police to go and fetch my son because a place was being prepared at one of the hospitals. Instead, the policemen put him in jail. When I went to the jail to see my son, I couldn't find him.

She told me about her diligent search for her son. "I went all over the jail, but I never found my son. I went to the Pollsmoor jail to find him. I was told that he was there and that he was all right." The apartheid court system tried Mama Joxo's son, found him guilty, and sentenced him to prison. He was to be held at Pollsmoor jail for another month and then transferred to prison, but while at Pollsmoor, he died. When Mama Joxo told me what happened to her son, her tone suggested that the police were disingenuous about the cause of his death. "His case came up, but he did not win. He was given a three-year prison sentence. He stayed in the Pollsmoor jail for one more month, which was in February. In March my son was dead. They said that he died of kidney failure. The police told me that I could take his body to bury at home, so that is what I did. I don't know what to believe about my son's death. I was told that they took him to Groote Schuur Hospital. I heard from a friend that she did see my son in the hospital."

Although the rape of her granddaughter, the death of her son, and the malicious neglect of the macrosystem left Mama Joxo with little hope, the St. John's community supported and affirmed her existence.

Reasons for Coming to St. John's

All the members whom I interviewed said that they came to St. John's because they or someone to whom they were intimately connected had ukugula. The social and cultural construction of ukugula makes it a flexible category whose meaning ranges from disease of the body (physical) to distress to a body (family, community, or nation). Ukugula assumes diverse manifestations, as described in the following scenarios.

47

Malaise to the Physical Body and the Mind

Ukugula as mental depression and personal despair is evidenced by Thole, whose testimony discloses his suicide attempt.

> I came to St. John's nine months ago. My life was a wretch, and I did too much drinking. The real reason for my coming was because I had too many enemies. I was very depressed—so depressed that I took a knife and cut my neck. I wanted to be dead. I was found by friends who took me to the hospital. My friends told my Aunt Bongiwe what happened, and she came to see me. My mother's sister looked at me and said, "My sister's son, what causes you to do this?" I could not look at her, for I was so ashamed. She said to me, "I am going to take you to the people at St. John's. I have heard about their healing. I know Mama Xaba, who is at that church. You must go there to be healed." I had never heard of St. John's before, but I had nowhere else to go. So on the day I was released from the hospital, my Aunt Bongiwe came for me. We went by taxi to the church in Guguletu. I met Tata Xaba.

The intervention of friends and a maternal aunt provided Thole enough support to declare his desire to be healed. Assurance also came from Reverend Xaba, mediator of the divine, whose power initiated a transformative healing process in Thole's life.

Mama Ntiliti traveled to St. John's because the ukugula manifested in her body was not relieved by biomedical treatment. She attended St. John's because she believed she could be healed. "I came to St. John's because I was sick [ukugula] and I could not get well. Medicine didn't help. I heard that I could get help from the St. John's people because they prayed. So I went there to the church. Well, I got well and I decided to stay." Grassroots African Christians throughout southern Africa knew St. John's excellent reputation as a healing community, and Mama Ntiliti was one of many who sought relief from various illnesses. Her results were positive, and she transferred her membership from the Methodist Church to St. John's.

Likewise, Mama Mazibula entered a hospital because ukugula plagued her body. While recuperating at home, she had a vision of St. John's and decided to investigate its healing ministry. "One day after coming from church, I got sick at home. My family took me to the hospital. I came home from the hospital because I was not serious like before. I was just a little bit better, and then I had a vision. I saw St. John's Church in my vision. It didn't take long for me to heal after I went to St. John's."

Mama Joxo moved initially to St. John's because her son displayed ukugula as a little boy. Having sought help from many sources to no avail, she immersed herself in St. John's ceremonial activities with hopes of improving his life: "I began to go to St. John's because my firstborn child, the one born before I was married, was sick. He was a little boy and had Xhosa sickness [*izifo sesiXhosa*]. The people used to say that he had "white sickness," which is connected to the diviners. We went all over the place trying to find people who could help him. No one could help him. Then, he began to get sick mentally. This made the problem even more difficult." Although Mama Joxo hoped the rituals would help her son, his mental illness continued. The rituals performed in the context of community provided a balm for Mama Joxo and her son, as a circle of support generated love and affirmation during positive and arduous times.

Affirmative changes in a their physical and emotional selves motivated people to seek out St. John's and undergo baptism into membership. A chain reaction ensued, as men and women who believed themselves to be healed proclaimed the power of St. John's ritual to restore health. Hence, seeking the recipe for healing, others arrived at the church.

Ukugula Manifested as Misfortune

Mama Ntiliti told me that people flocked to St. John's burdened and distressed by unemployment or misfortune: "St. John's is a church where people mostly thank God for helping them to get through their problems. You know, like on Sunday, a lady said that she was unlucky. She was looking for a job and she couldn't get a proper job. She heard about this church and came to us. Tata Xaba prayed for her. They did everything that is usually done for everybody. We prayed for her and she went home. She went and looked for a job and found one. Now she is never without a job. You see, it's that kind of church!"

She also attested that people prayed for their sick or troubled children.

People thank God for their children. Sometimes people come and pray for their children. The children do all sorts of naughty things. The parents come to church to pray for their children, and their children will get better and some will come to church. I remember a story that Archbishop Masango told about a mother whose son was in jail. She came to St. John's to pray for her son. One day it happened that her child came out of jail. He started coming to St. John's. Archbishop Masango said, "When I was sitting in my office, I heard the voice of a child. He was asking for prayer and remembering how his mother prayed for him when he was in jail." When the child left jail, he came back home a different person. He decided to go to church.

49

Moreover, Mama Ntiliti professed that many joined St. John's when ukugula manifested as a domestic problem or infertility: "You can even go to St. John's when you have problems at your house. One lady at church said that her husband loves to quarrel for no reason at all. Ever since she came to St. John's church and asked for prayer for her husband, he has stopped everything. They live like a perfect family. So, some people at St. John's are sick, some are not sick. Some come to church because they are unable to have children. They ask for prayer. They say, 'We don't have children,' and the minister or bishop prays for them. Afterwards, God gives them children."

The Healing Process

The healing process at St. John's had several dimensions. Sick people usually had initial contact with Reverend Xaba, the healer with divine authority and power. For example, Thole, taken to St. John's by his aunt because of a suicide attempt, met Reverend Xaba immediately upon arrival at the church. After Thole's aunt explained their presence, Reverend Xaba asked him immediately, "Do you want to be healed?" Thole found this question startling: "My aunt explained what happened; how I tried to kill myself. Tata Xaba looked at me and said, 'Do you want to be healed?' I was frightened that this man who I did not know should ask me such a question. In a hesitating way, I said, 'Yes.' He pointed to the shack and said, 'You can live there. Put your things inside. You will live with the other men who are sick, and we will show you the way of St. John's.' My aunt was very gracious to Tata Xaba. She took his hand to express her thanks, looked at me, and then left."

Because Thole's arrival at St. John's depended upon his aunt's initiative rather than his own, Reverend Xaba's question was significant because it was linked to Thole's motivation. Being a discerning healer, Reverend Xaba, through his question, provided the means by which Thole could take responsibility for initiating his healing process. In essence, by consenting to live at St. John's, Thole chose to reframe his life and thus demonstrated a desire to be a well-adjusted person with agency.

Once homeless, Thole now lived with four other men participating in St. John's healing process. Reverend Xaba taught Thole about St. John's, propheted him,[16] and prepared a ritual bath for cleansing. Thole described his first days at St. John's to me: "I lived in a shack with four other men who were sick. One had come all the way from the Transkei to be healed. The three others had been healed but still lived in the shack. Over the next days, Tata Xaba instructed me in the ways of St. John's. He propheted me by looking in the Bible and telling me everything about my life. He told me that I must go to

50

church four times a day and that I must take a bath in the blessed water in order to be healed." There were others in the St. John's community who had the authority to heal and still others who assisted with the various stages of the healing process. Thole had the full array of St. John's ritual works, which included a bath (with special healing agents added to the water), an enema, and self-induced vomiting.[17]

Thole said: "Other members came to the church on Wednesdays to help Tata Xaba with the sick. The women prepared a bath for me to wash myself. During my first month I took a bath, I had an enema, and vomited bad things out of me with the water."

With the attention and care Thole received, he began to recover. "I began to feel better and I could see how the God of Mother Christinah Nku and Tata Masango was working in my life.[18] I began to read my Bible and stand in front of the congregation and testify and ask God for help. So now my life is better." His participation in the community and witness to the works of healing testified to the transformation occurring in his life.

St. John's ritual works and their capacity to engender reassurance surfaced in a story Mama Ntiliti related to me about her daughter's unexpected illness. St. John's ceremonial process greatly favored the ritual expressions of prayer and liturgies. The latter, performed by the priest-healer, Reverend Xaba, required a person seeking restoration to offer six white candles, a box of matches, and a bag of salt to the church. Mama Ntiliti, who sought special prayers for her ailing daughter, believed fervently that St. John's rituals made a difference in her life. She boldly claimed: "The prayer works wonders. Every time I have problems, I run to the church and ask the minister to pray for me or for my children. You know, my daughter phoned me, the youngest one in Mmbatho. She told me, 'Mother, my sister is to go to Kimberley to a hospital. It is possible that from Kimberley, she will go to Cape Town to have an operation.' The moment I put down the phone, I ran to the store and bought candles, matches, medicines, and everything. I took all these things, candles, matches, salt, and R2 to Tata Xaba. I told him my problems about my daughter."

St. John's ministry featured special quarterly festivals (imigidi) in which members received uncommon spiritual power. When Mama Ntiliti discovered that her daughter suffered from a grave illness, the St. John's clergy had already scheduled an umgidi a week later. Members from St. John's congregations throughout the country would gather at Newcastle,[19] the district headquarters, to celebrate church liturgies in which the energy of members generated a healing force that protected and empowered people. Mama Ntiliti believed that if she attended the festival, she would receive the power necessary to support her daughter. Consequently, she consulted with Tata Xaba. "I asked

Tata Xaba if I should go to the festival where they do healing in Newcastle. I was doubting about whether I should go, but the moment I heard my daughter was sick, I decided to go. Tata Xaba said to me, 'Yes, go.' I went to Newcastle."

St. John's members had a profound faith in the power of ritual to make a qualitative difference in their lives. Mama Ntiliti left the Newcastle festival certain that her daughter would receive the benefits of the liturgies performed on her behalf. She articulated her confidence to me claiming:

> When the festival in Newcastle was finished, I went to my sister in Johannesburg. When I got there with my sister, I was afraid to phone my daughter in Mmbatho to find out how her sister was and whether she was in Kimberley or Cape Town. I hoped that she had not yet gone to Cape Town since I had not yet returned home. I left for Cape Town on August 21, and she also left Kimberley on the same day to go to the hospital in Cape Town. You know, that was very wonderful to me because all that was done through prayer. You see, I went to Newcastle and prayed there. I asked everyone there to pray for my daughter, and things went smoothly. She had an operation and there was no problem. She is in the hospital now. She is waiting to get better.

The words that follow reflect her certainty that St. John's rituals altered life-and-death circumstances and that other churches could not possibly have the same efficacy. In addition, she testifies to her personal use of the ceremonies. "I don't like other churches. They don't do what St. John's does. When I don't feel well, I ask for the water. I drank the water and brought it back up again. I had an enema and I had a bath and food. That's what I like about St. John's."

Mama Ntiliti continued by professing that children received successful treatment with the ritual works, just as adults benefited. She went on to share a story about a woman whose children manifested ukugula in an unusual manner. One of the healers at church recognized the sickness and worked to bring about healing. Mama Ntiliti related this story: "One woman once said to me, 'My children were sick. One was more sick than the other. But both were so sick. I took them to St. John's and whenever I sat down, my feet would rise from the ground. A mother in the church took my son and put him in the place where my feet kept rising. She looked at me and said, "Why don't you give God what's God's? Why don't you get on your feet like God wants you to and stop stamping your feet?" The woman said to me, 'I wasn't sick but I had sickness in me. It was in me, but hidden. It made my children sick.'" St. John's cosmology allowed for the transference of ukugula from one person to another. In this case, the healer sensed that the mother had not responded to her obligations to God and reprimanded her for not doing so. Then members set her on the path of healing for herself and her children.

Finally, Mama Ntiliti explained why she sent her grandson to Reverend Xaba because her grandson complained about his legs and his inability to walk normally. She believed wholeheartedly that St. John's rituals would bring relief to her grandson.

> My own grandson was healed at St. John's. He was sick from the waist down and couldn't walk straight. He kept saying to me, "I can't walk properly." His knees started knocking. One Saturday morning, I told him to go to the church. I gave him soap and said, "Go to the church and they will do everything for you." He went to the church and saw Tata Xaba. Tata Xaba could see that he wasn't walking properly and began to talk with him. When they sat down together, my grandson started crying, and Tata Xaba asked him, "What's wrong?" My grandson said, "I can't walk properly." Tata Xaba told him, "Go and tell the one working with the water to do everything for you." The water was made and he was given an enema and a bath. Tata Xaba prayed for him and my grandson was well.

As a final refrain, Mama Ntiliti proclaimed St. John's success in mediating transformation in people's lives. Even though members of her family knew about the healing rituals, not all attended the church. She talked to me about her family's "knowing." "I mean, the church knows about the healing. My grandson knows about it and my children know, although they don't go there. But they know."

When Mama Joxo, whose story was presented above, attempted to get help for her son when he was a little boy, several older women, referred to as "mothers," visited her at home, including one who lived in the Transkei. After an initial treatment session, Mama Joxo began to work with Mother Shenxane, the priest-healer at St. John's–Guguletu prior to Reverend Xaba. Because St. John's ritual works had a long history in Mama Joxo's life, she talked about them from a historical perspective.

> Some mothers from St. John's came to my house. One of them was from the Transkei. She told me about my child's sickness. She couldn't stay to help him, because it was the time of the pass laws.[20] After she left for the Transkei, I began to go to St. John's in Guguletu. I took my son with me and told the priest about him. The priest was a woman named Mother Shenxane. She gave him water to vomit. She also bathed him and gave him an enema. Unfortunately, this mother did not stay at St. John's–Guguletu a long time. When she left, my son did not want to go to church. He refused to go, though I tried to force him. I decided to go and joined St. John's. I asked the new priest, Tata Xaba, to come to my house to hold my son. Tata Xaba used to bring the rituals to my house.

Mama Joxo received support from the priest-healers and members over an extended period of time; and to express her gratitude, she contributed salt, a ceremonial medium, to the church. She expressed her fondness for the services and explained how specific rituals such as vomiting and bathing functioned.

> I like everything in St. John's because when the people preach, you can feel it in your blood. You can feel it in your blood when they sing. You can feel the spirit.
>
> As for rituals, I buy salt and take it to the church.
>
> There is a special place outside the church, where we put our things. We call it the lake (*ichibi*). We take all the things like salt and water. We take them every Sunday. The minister prays for the salt and water and then I take it home. With the water, I spray my house all over, including outside, so that I can stay away from the evil spirits. The children also drink the water.
>
> In our church there are healing rituals. When people come, members pray for them. Then the person vomits and takes a bath. These are all important rituals that are done in our church. And then, the sick must attend the services in the church.

Many of those who participated in rituals attested that they had dreams with messages from their ancestors. Dreams have a significant role in African religion, and those who received messages from ancestors were required to prepare Xhosa beer, a ritual drink honoring the ancestors. Mama Joxo narrated to me the interaction through dreams between living persons and their deceased relatives and the responsibilities the living had regarding their obligation to these ancestors: "Following these rituals, many people dream clearly, and see everything. A person may get messages through their dreams. If the messages are not followed, then it's bad luck for you. Sometimes you dream about your ancestors and they tell you what you must do. Then sometimes you dream of something that happened in the church. Sometimes your ancestors, your grandfather, your mother, or the ones who have passed away a long time ago appear. You dream of them talking to you and they say, 'I'm thirsty.' Then you have to make Xhosa beer so that everybody can come and drink it."

When a person received such instructions from an ancestor, he or she prepared Xhosa beer and relatives and friends gathered to honor the ancestor with a feast. An elaborate communal meal connected living relatives with kin from their past, and in so doing the present generation was reminded of the moral agency and tradition of persons important in their lives. Such gatherings usually pleased and appeased the ancestors, allowing both the individual who had the dream and the community to which he or she was connected to be comforted and restored to an assured relationship with their ancestors.

On Thursday afternoons at 4 P.M. women members gathered to enact another type of ritual. Throughout the entire country, Thursday afternoon was understood to be the time that African women united to pray, sing, and share words of strength. Mama Mazibula enjoyed the services and looked forward to the time she met with the "mothers" of the church. "I like to come to the church on Thursdays, because it is mothers' day. The service starts at 4:00 P.M., and all the mothers are there. If we have problems, then we share them and we pray. The scriptures that are important for our church are Nehemiah 10 and Leviticus 5."

She also gave an overview of some of the other rituals dramatized at St. John's. "We do many rituals at our church. We have Communion, but only at night time. We do washing of the feet. On Sunday, we ask of God the things we need. We pray for the world and sing. Then we have the healing service where everyone stands in the queue to drink the water. We call it going to the lake [ichibi]." She continued by interpreting rituals she performed in her home: "I do some rituals at home. All the little children who are sick come to me. I give water and enemas when a parent brings a child to me. I use salt and water to spray my house. That is how I pray for my house." Finally, she instructed me about the healing services conducted at every Sunday morning worship service. She painted a picture of the congregation being at a lake, represented by a long blue-and-white cloth, designated by one of the archbishops of the church, Tata Masango, to be used in healing services. As the cloth was lifted, a canopy formed under which members walked and received blessings after they drank holy water. "When we have our healing service during worship, we call it going to the lake [ichibi]. We put up the blue-and-white cloth that the reverends stand under as they pray for us after we drink the water and walk under the cloth. Tata Masango propheted about the blue-and-white cloth. That is why we walk under it after drinking the water."

This series of ritual works supported St. John's cosmology and provided the means by which people used signs and symbols to reinforce a sense of security, protection, care, and transformation. All of these assurances enhanced the lives of grassroots people and helped them to function in a chaotic world whose structure aimed to destroy self-esteem, inner spirit, and physical bodies. In this sense, poor people combated the affects of ukugula.

Healing rituals and works of transformation were only two of the sources of renewal for St. John's members. The realm of the ancestors, mentioned previously, was an additional source. The role of the ancestors will be more fully discussed in chapter 4; in this chapter we must consider the ways interviewees understood their deceased, yet "living," relatives.

The ancestors, a firm source of support, could be called upon during times of distress. They were a link to the persons of worth and wisdom who had died but to whom the living could turn for solace, sustenance, and power. The ancestors helped clarify challenging situations and often presented solutions to problems in the dreams or visions of the living. The ancestors were vital to the continuation of culture, life, tradition, and meaning. Mamas Joxo and Mazibula told me about the valuable connections the ancestors have with the living. Mama Joxo described how the ancestors provided safety and security. Mama Mazibula recalled a conversation she had with her deceased father, who instructed her to have a special dinner with Xhosa beer and also gave her a stick symbolizing the way to her healing. Mama Joxo presented the following account:

> The only thing that I know is that the ancestors help you. They always keep you safe. The ancestors are related to the living because we come from them. Sometimes I slip into trouble and feel an evil spirit, but at the same time I feel that there is something safe that surrounds me. I can feel that there is a heavy thing that is around me. Then I become safe because the ancestors are living. They help me. God is also there. I make Xhosa beer and even slaughter something for my ancestors to show my respect and thankfulness for their protection. The Bible tells about the ancestors. Sometimes you see your ancestors, and sometimes they come straight to you. They say, "Don't go that way." Then if you force yourself to go that way, you have problems. I believe that we are together with the ancestors.

Mama Mazibula verified that ancestors are an important part of the cosmology of St. John's members by talking about her encounter with her deceased father.

> I believe in my ancestors. When I was sick, my father gave me a stick in my dream. He gave it to me straight in my hand. When I received the stick from my father, I saw my whole family, not the ones who are alive, but all my people who are dead. In the dream, I went to my brother and told him that I was going to make a dinner for my family. In the dream I thought to myself, I will call my mother's family to come and sing to her. Then I cooked. I didn't have something like a sheep that we slaughter now. I cooked white beans and poured on a little bit of fish oil. Then I made kaffir beer—that is our cultural beer.[21] While my family was eating, some of them sang. My ancestors gave me a St. John's uniform. They gave me a blue-and-white uniform, with a white cape and head covering.

Explaining further, Mama Mazibula said that she did not disclose to others everything she received in a vision or dream, because it could cause consternation and worry. If a vision had an unfavorable outcome for a person, it was best not to share the vision. She narrated the reasons for her decision. "I don't always tell my dreams and visions because sometimes you see something where you or another is hurt. If you tell this kind of vision at church, the members won't be nice to you. That is not good, so I would rather keep my visions to myself unless it is such that I can't do otherwise; then I have to tell."

While the ancestors served as a spiritual resource for members, community organizations operated in the civic realm to render support in day-to-day life. Mama Mazibula said that community organizations assisted during times of bereavement, marriage, or neighbors' disagreements. Moreover, the community association fought against unjust government policies.

> There are community organizations that help our neighborhood. When someone on our street dies, we give money to the people. We help by working hand-in-hand through the burial association. We also give money when someone has a marriage party. We give money to a mother once a month to uplift her. I also belong to the civic association which helps if I'm fighting with my neighbor. The association sorts out all the fighting between me and my neighbor. If maybe my child is naughty, I take him to the men of the association executive committee. If the child needs a hiding,[22] they give it to make the child straight. If there is someone who wants to fight, who wants to take my house, then the association helps me. They help with the things we need in the community. If the government is fighting against the community, then the civic association fights against the government for the rights and needs of the people in the community.

In addition to neighborhood associations, members' memories about their family life and its structure during the years they lived in rural areas gave them the fortitude to face the daily struggles they endured. Mama Mazibula recalled her childhood in Cofimvaba, Transkei, and her schoolteachers, who taught her the benefits of consistent church attendance and the importance of completing household chores.

> I will tell you about my childhood. We grew up in Cofimvaba, Transkei, in a nice way. We were three girls and two boys on our farm. Our teachers expected us to go to church on Sundays. On Monday, you had to tell your teacher if you went to church. So, we were supposed to go to church even if we did not like it. As children, we always listened to our parents. Every day, including Saturday, we had to wake up and keep the house clean and cook. On Saturday,

we prepared everything for Sunday. On Sunday, we went to church. Once we came home from church, we gave dinner to our parents and then we went with other girls. Sunday afternoon was when we met our boyfriends. We went to youth meetings together. At six o'clock we had to go back home and put on the light. We had to do everything so that it looked like we hadn't gone out.[23] We had to make everything look nice and clean to satisfy our parents.

Mama Joxo remembered her childhood and the difficulty her mother had after the death of her father because her maternal grandparents arranged a second marriage in order for her mother to have financial support. While this arrangement was not the best, it illustrates the role families played in caring for young widowed women with children. "I completed standard six[24] at school, but could not go further because my father passed away. Financially, everything was quite tight, because my mother was alone. She struggled to educate me. Furthermore, my mother was a stepmother to my father's children. My mother and the stepchildren were always fighting. I grew up in a terrible way. My mother's parents forced her to marry another man, and it was very bad for her. She was forced to get married because when my father died, he left nothing. My mother had to work. She did the washing of students who went to St. Matthew's College." She continued by informing me about the customs and rituals enacted by her community when a child was born and when boys completed initiation rites. "The customs that we had at home included *imbeleko,* which is done when a child is born. We slaughtered a goat and had a dinner. We also slaughtered a goat when boys came back from the forest from circumcision school."

Mama Ntiliti's story weaves her early life with her present circumstances:

I was born March 23, 1923, on a farm where my father worked in the northern Cape. We are Tswana and our clan name is Batlharo. I came to Cape Town in 1942 in search of a job. You see, I couldn't get a job in Kimberley, where I actually grew up. I had to establish a firm address here in order to get a job because of the laws.[25] They don't do that any more—that is, the pass laws. We don't have to have special documents in order to work here now. I was a domestic servant and I had to stay where I worked but my home was actually in Kuruman. I still want to go and live there because I'm old now and I'm not working any more. It is poverty that keeps me from going. I live only on my pension which is R222 (U.S.$55) every other month. Every now and then one of my children will send me R50 (U.S.$20), but that is not reliable. I have no other source of income, and I have three boys to care for. Two of my grandsons live with me, and a grandson of my friend. We all live here together. Two boys live in a shanty in the backyard and one sleeps inside with me.

The healing process at St. John's embodied a tapestry of converging signs, symbols, speech, and actions that called on the sick to build upon the faith, belief, and life-changing experiences of members who believed themselves to have been restored, in order that the ailing might be healed. The mysterious power of community charisma flowed through a priest-healer, whose culture and history secured a lively past, including a cult of the ancestors who influenced the present. The power of the priest-healer, the gathered community, and the ancestors together manifested a holy alliance of African and Christian symbology. The signs and symbols and faith and action of St. John's adherents brought into existence a liberating pattern of healing and transformation. People whose path could have easily led to destitution circumvented the effects of an undesirable macrosystem through creative management of their microsystem. Whether it was talking about the negative impact of violence (thereby building a safety net by sharing with others concerned for one's welfare) or having safe space to reflect about life's challenges (as they related to a spouse and children) or simply recalling past customs (remembering those who reared you and made unexplainable events plain), healing rituals were a way to make meaning, to create solace, and to take liberating action on micro- and macrofronts.

Reflections on the Future

In 1991, it became clear to all the world that South Africa had entered a period of transition. Poor blacks who had lived with the consequences of apartheid and the history of antagonistic relations with government were hopeful and ambivalent at the same time. They would require strong character and communal support systems to move into the future free of bitterness and fear. As St. John's members contemplated the future, their remarks and questions indicated an understanding that present problems would not disappear suddenly. Their words exhibited a profound sense of the extraordinary change necessary on all levels of their society. Banzi and Nozipo enunciated frankly their thoughts of what the future held for them and other black South Africans. Banzi believed those elected to lead the country would make a considerable difference in what happens in the future. Moreover, he hoped that a black president would be elected, because black Africans suffered so much during the apartheid years. "I won't tell you how it is going to be, but the only thing I can tell you is this: I pray to God for my future because I want to see who's going to be the leader in the next years and how he's going to rule. I want to see how he's going to treat my people, who have been suffering for a long time. That's the only thing I pray to God for. Please God keep me and I want to live a little bit longer, so that I can see my future and who is going to be the leader. I wish a black man would lead our country because all of Africa is for black men. We have been suffering for a long time. I wish the leader of our future could be a black man."

He further articulated the imperative for South Africans in exile as well as black people in the diaspora to aid South Africa's redevelopment program because both groups of people had experiences from which a new black South African government could profit.

> I wish those people from South Africa who were in exile could help with lead-ing. I think they learned a lot when they were away and they are educated. They understand how to rule people. These South Africans were in America and England. These people who were overseas know everything and they have been educated. Each family has got somebody overseas. Yes, they are the Africans. Yes, I will make an example. I think these people are our families. They were Africans, and some of them can't even speak our language. They speak English like you. I know that you are black and you came from this world, from South Africa. I'm definitely sure that your parents were from South Africa and of Africa. But maybe your parents were running away from the oppressors or maybe they go there for other reasons. But, I know that you are from Africa. I'm talking about those people who can help us.

Nozipo's analysis presented the problematic prospects for the future. The haunting reality of violence and the ongoing loss of life were of immense impor-tance to her. Indeed, her concerns had immense substance, because the crime rate in South Africa soared during the period of transition. Faith and God sus-tained her as they manifested in St. John's community of care; they helped her and others to persevere despite apprehension about a complicated future.

> Our own future is a problem. It's a problem, because you go out and you wait for death. You go into the train and you wait for death. You go into the bus and you wait for death. You go to sleep and you're afraid somebody will shoot you. Somebody will burn your house. Somebody will just shoot you. So you just pray for the day that God will come.
>
> That's why now there's no hope for us. Now the only thing we can do is pray while we are in our houses. As you go out of your house, you get a bullet. You don't know where to go to be safe. So, the only way to be safe is to come to God, and pray and wait for your day to die. We only keep on working, try-ing to earn a little money to get what we need. The little things that we can get. If you get the chance to put away R2, you put it away, but you never know what's going to happen tomorrow.

We keep on going because, we get the spirit from God because we know ourselves to be under God. We have to pray. Even on our way, everywhere we go we have to pray. While we're on the train we have to pray. Even when we leave the children behind we just say, "God, you're going to look after our children." And then, sometimes when we're at work, we hear the people say that in the location,[26] the houses are burning.

We need a future for our children, but we want to know how can we go through all these problems and get a future for our children? How can we have a good future for our children? That's why we pray every time because we also think that the only thing that can help us is to pray to God. We haven't got the power. We haven't got the tools to fight against the white people. We haven't got the things to fight against them. If we can't fight against them then we can pray about us. So instead of fighting, we'd rather pray.

The apartheid era created an atmosphere in which people of African heritage took control of their lives on a microlevel by combining spiritual, physical, emotional, and financial resources. Black South Africans knew extraordinary effort was essential for them to survive the war declared against them by the South African apartheid government. The brutal effects of apartheid coerced poor people into particularly vulnerable positions. Mandela's release from prison sparked renewed vigor and hope; yet the lingering economic devastation caused by decades of apartheid was sobering. Therefore, hope coexisted with a somber sense that it would take time and endurance to create a new life. During this period (1991–1994), people at St. John's proclaimed God's ability to heal a broken body in order to renew human spirits. Those who attended services, participated in congregational events, sang the hymns, drank the holy water, and walked under the canopy claimed restoration on various levels. Despite an oppressing macrosystem, St. John's members experienced renewal exhibited in their agency. St. John's cosmology enabled liberating acts and is therefore a tribute to the ingenuity of those called to bring back to life the dispossessed hovering on the threshold of death.

CHAPTER 4

The Ritual and Theology of
St. John's

The anthropological study of religion is therefore a two stage operation:
first, an analysis of the system of meanings embodied in the symbols which
make up the religion proper, and second, the relating of these systems to
social-structural and psychological processes.
    —Clifford Geertz, *The Interpretation of Cultures*

This means therefore that authentic theological speech arises only from an
oppressed community which realizes that its humanity is inseparable from
its liberation from earthly bondage. All other speech is at best irrelevant
and at worst blasphemous.
    —James Cone, "Black Theology and Black Liberation"

Ritual and theology are the cornerstones of St. John's Apostolic Faith
Mission–Guguletu's faith and practice. Together they constitute the center
and foundation of the church's cosmology. Ritual cannot exist without theology and vice versa. This chapter explores their synthesis in the life of St. John's
Church and its members.

Ritual is culturally defined communication rendered by a community's
goals. In addition to expressing a group's collective values, ritual secures results
beyond the original expressive intention of participants. Moreover, it serves
adaptive purposes, including techniques of reversal wherein acts not condoned
in nonritual space are performed. Ritual, like all ceremonial rites, is both action
and assertion. When ritual and religion are joined, human drama unfolds,
building a relationship between people and their beliefs about the supernatural.

Ritual expression at St. John's–Guguletu was usually associated with moral
problems, social conflict, and healing of *ukugula* (sickness).[1] Furthermore, ritual performances by hardworking and resilient church members reconstituted

these believers, who were undermined intellectually, psychologically, spiritually, and even physically maimed by apartheid culture. These dramatizations merged St. John's disciples with symbols from various streams of African religion and Protestant Christianity or African indigenized Christianity. Moreover, these ritual dramatizations were the means by which transformation occurred in members' bodies and social relations—all demonstrating the existence of a powerful source creating order out of chaos.[2]

In a mysterious way, communicative mechanisms of ritual curtailed disorder and perplexing complexities, thereby permitting participants to have an adaptive response. As such, ritual created an orderly world where members believed themselves to have some semblance of control. In the apartheid cosmos in which members of St. John's dwelled, ceremonial rites provided steadiness during crisis, coherence during transition, and balance during tragedy. Ritual furnished peace of mind in a threatening, demonic world. Thus, performance and imagination resolved conflict and also expanded and enriched the social dimension of followers' lives (Kluckhohn 1942; de Coppet 1992:9; Parkin 1992:11–12).

St. John's participants' perceptions of the activity of supernatural forces coincided with their liturgical actions (V. Turner 1968; 1969; 1982:84–85). The way members knew things, how they felt, and what they did were all linked intimately to ritual activity. The cognitive, affective, and volitional characteristics of the forces, while essential for these endeavors, were rarely manifested in their absolute form. Rather, these attributes were understood in the context of members' lives (V. Turner 1967; 1982:84–85). Adherents' liturgical behavior in relationship to their belief in God took seriously cultural context, personal experience, and symbolic roles and patterns of human transactions. These factors were decisive and of critical importance to ritual healing and theology at St. John's.

The Religious Belief System of
St. John's Apostolic Faith Mission–Guguletu

Belief in God

In Xhosa religion, the Supreme Being is an exalted person or absolute being identified with the sky (Pauw 1975:76; Hodgson 1982:101). The Xhosas believe that qualities of the Supreme Being, who created all in existence, were revealed in the conception of the natural world and the genesis of the universe. Likewise, they believe that good is inherent in mortals and that evil, caused by human beings, exists. One's well-being, inclusive of health and fertility, is considered part of the normal cycle of life, and any aberration is attributed to the influence of pernicious persons (Peires 1981:67). The unseen world, as created by the Supreme Being, is understandable, and human beings can influence it. Religion pervades all aspects of life, and thus there is no religious/secular dichotomy. Practitioners, such as diviners, understand and interact with the unseen world in order to help people enjoy success and happiness in life (Soga 1932:149–51; Peires 1981:67; Hodgson 1982:107).

Xhosa cosmology responded in various ways to missionaries and the threat of Christianity. Some Xhosas readily sanctioned specific aspects of Christianity and disregarded those parts with which they were uncomfortable; others reacted differently. For instance, many Xhosas acceded to Christianity's notion of God, while others, believing missionaries' connection to colonial government restricted Xhosas' lives, found it impossible to trust or embrace a foreign God. These latter Xhosas reconfirmed their commitment to the Xhosa God, Mdalidiphu,[3] creator of the deep, while the former continued their allegiance to Thixo, the God of Christian emissaries, as well as Thixo's son, Jesus, and submitted to the peace and protection associated with these deities. Indeed, both responses were ways that Xhosas constructed a new worldview to come to terms with the presence of Christians (Peires 1981:73; Kiernan 1990).

At St. John's in Guguletu, those persons interviewed referred to God exclusively as Thixo and Jehovah. When I asked the origin of these names, interviewees, the majority of whom had Bibles written in Xhosa, responded uniformly, "This is the name the Bible gives to God."

Inasmuch as God was the ultimate power of the universe, members spoke directly to God about their concerns. Commenting on township violence, one woman repeated unrelentingly, "We must pray to God," adding, "We must talk to God about this violence. If we pray to God, everything can be changed." For most adherents, God was a perpetually accessible caretaker addressing their needs in a loving and protective manner. One informant summarized these attributes while discussing violence in her community, saying, "The only way to safety is to come to God." God, the protector, gave this woman a sense of security in a violent environment.

Another woman, characterizing God as "a spirit," expressed her certainty of God's dependability, uttering, "God is our shepherd. He helps us all the time." She continued, "He is father to us. He is the man to the widow."

Devotees of St. John's regarded God as an all-knowing Creator. One follower described God as "the man who created the people, us." While contemplating God's ability to know the best in all situations, a participant distressed about township violence remarked, "Only God knows and only God will allow this violence and will stop this violence." An associate, linking her limited income and struggle to pay her bills with apartheid, said, "We don't know how to pay accounts; that's why I can say we believe in God. God helps us in so many ways, even apartheid. God helps us sometimes to pay accounts."

Finally, disciples accepted God as a healer who was concerned about suffering individuals and travailing humanity globally. One informant commented, "God is King. No one has the power that God does. God is the one who heals us in this world." Another member asserted, "I think that God does anything for you. He heals. God helps you to do everything."

Revelation and "Propheting"

Revelation played an important role at St. John's because members believed in personal transactions between God, who revealed, and human beings to whom disclosures were made (Oosthuizen 1992). More often than not, Reverend Xaba was the medium through whom revelation emerged because he had the ability to divine or to "prophet."[4] Church constituents flocked to him and other designated prophets to discover why a particular event occurred, the reason a sickness developed, or the explanation for the death of a loved one. Most of Reverend Xaba's oracles, as well as those of other church prophets, communicated personal messages, helping people understand the origin of misfortune and the surest means to restore harmony to life.

St. John's cosmology attributed fragility to individuals who lived alone or who did not have regular contact with kin. For such individuals to fulfill their destiny, they needed the support of their ancestors.[5] Adherents were aware of these spiritual beings' constant presence and their importance in the cosmos and, thus, in people's everyday lives. It is about such matters that Reverend Xaba propheted or divined. Informing me of Reverend Xaba's ability to divine, Mama Ntiliti remarked, "He propheted me," meaning Tata Xaba, acting as diviner, notified her about important things in her present and future life. Thole corroborated Mama Ntiliti's testimony about Reverend Xaba's propheting ability, declaring, "He propheted me by looking in the Bible and telling me everything about my life."

Use of the Bible and the ability to tell a person about his or her past and future life were key elements of prophetic revelation in this Christian context. At Tata Xaba's funeral,[6] a woman confided in me, saying, "I am not sure what I am going to do. Tata Xaba was not only my spiritual father, he always told me what to expect through his prophecy." Clearly, patrons of St. John's viewed Reverend Xaba as a prophet. For instance, Nyawuza linked his prophetic abilities with his power to restore health, proclaiming, "He is a healer and prophet."

Other members of St. John's also mediated divine oracles. Informants talked about them in a general way without naming specific persons. For instance, Mama Joxo, responding to a question about the role women played in the church, remarked, "Sometimes they [women] prophet people who have been away, and those people come straight in the congregation." Her answer suggests that women prophets reconnected inactive adherents and redirected their lives after an absence for sundry reasons.

Tata Mjoli articulated unreservedly his appreciation for St. John's prophecy, asserting, "What I like most about St. John's is when the people prophet. The prophets can see the illnesses of the sick people." Like others, Tata Mjoli saw prophecy as including the ability to tell people about their lives and their ailments. As ritual process, prophecy was essential to healing and foundational to the prophet-patient relationship because a diviner's revelations uncover his or her power. Likewise, a patient's affirmation of the prophet's interpretation of his or her life elevated the prophet's confidence in his or her competence.

Spirits and Ancestors

St. John's members accepted continuation of the spirit after death, and adherents were faithful to their ancestors. They handled any contradictions between imported Christianity and African religion by incorporating respect for, and remembrance of, the ancestors into their Christian faith and practices. Followers of St. John's respected their forebears out of commitment to familial descent and heritage. They also viewed their progenitors as the guardians and conservators of ethical behavior based on moral values associated with ideal conduct. Kinship ties, through the clan, bound people to each other. The living dead embodied the sacred nature of the family and reinforced goodwill among people through unending unity between the deceased and the living. Commitment to the ancestors honored them as trustees of standards of the family group or community; hence, a person was expected to exhibit conscientious behavior by devotion to, and respect for, the ancestors.

St. John's followers' lives intertwined with spiritual beings rather than with objects because they truly depended upon their forebears. Members approached the ancestors as often as they called upon God. On some occasions believers asked the ancestors to be intermediaries to God (Oosthuizen 1991:21).

Since God created the universe and all matter, the ancestors are considered to be the framers and supporters of the world in which their descendants live. Furthermore, the living dead were perpetually in the company of their relatives and acted as forerunners who maintained contact with the community of their descendants (Shorter 1974a:60).

To illustrate St. John's members' relationship with ancestors in a Christian context, I refer to a worship service held on Sunday, 20 October

1991. While giving a testimony on Deuteronomy 16, Mr. Mantolo incorporated a faith claim about a "great grand ancestor": "We have all heard the words . . . God has taken the Israelites out of Egypt. . . . He is now sitting with them; making a deal with them; telling them about what should happen in order that he and they can travel the road of life harmoniously. . . . The book says, let every male three times a year, on the place chosen for the celebration of the feast of the Passover, not come to the temple without anything in his hand. I will ask that you support me in prayers that God may allow the very great grand ancestor to be there as I hold a customary occasion at my home."

A "customary occasion" was a feast typically held in the home of black South Africans when a family member dreamed of a deceased relative. This affair, to which friends and neighbors were invited, occurred within a month of the dream. The living honored the deceased relative by offering roasted meat from a freshly slaughtered animal to the ancestor and guests. Descendants hoped the dinner pleased and appeased their ancestor so as to reestablish balance and harmony in the lives of the dreamer and the family.

The Moral Order and Evil Spirits

At St. John's, the integrity of the community involved honest and responsible living as reflected in a person's trusting relationship with God. God's moral order was represented in the deep structures of society. A breach of God's command interrupted the balance of life and engendered discord, which indicated that a transgression had occurred.

Members believed spirit forces often caused bodily sickness because of imbalance in community. On 20 October 1991, Mr. Mantolo spoke on Deuteronomy 16, speaking about sickness caused by "spirits": "This Scripture says: Now that you are here these people were bitten by mosquitos, beforehand in this world. . . . We too when we came here were suffering; some of us were inhabited by *amafufunyane*. These spirits instruct the person they inhabit to perform different things. Some are so overt that they are audible as they talk. God is reminding us of what we are in the world." Amafufunyane was a unique demonic illness generated by spirits inhabiting human bodies (Pauw 1975:272; Ngubane 1977). Mr. Mantolo implied that some members, prior to affiliating with St. John's, were directed by spirits. Accordingly, he believed that God, in Deuteronomy 16, instructs people not to forget their previous struggles with demonic forces. Rather they ought to make a proper sacrifice and remember what their lives were like "in the world" before they came to St. John's.

Jesus as Cosufferer, Liberator, and Healer

The members of St. John's understood Jesus to be God in the flesh who suffered death for the sins of humanity, brought healing to those spiritually and physically broken, and offered liberation to the oppressed and the oppressor. As such, Jesus was the savior of all humankind—the one who died, was resurrected, and remained victorious over death and death-dealing situations.

Jesus' suffering during his earthly existence is symbolic of the misery many St. John's believers and their family members experienced under apartheid. The Truth and Reconciliation Commission of South Africa, appointed by the ANC (African National Congress) government and chaired by Archbishop Desmond Tutu, has recorded the atrocities that many South Africans endured during the apartheid era.[7] These death-dealing circumstances are part of the grotesque history that South Africa is attempting to resolve. As so many St. John's believers and members of other African indigenous churches (AIC) suffered under separate development polices, Jesus is cosufferer with those who lived under apartheid's tyranny. He qualified as cosufferer because he announced that God's kingdom had final authority and thus ultimate power over the Roman Empire and its officials. Church members believed that, in a parallel fashion, Jesus became their highest authority, even above the apartheid government.

Furthermore, Jesus announced that in God's time the poor and disenfranchised would have a place of respect and value on earth and in a new dispensation. This proclamation elevated the oppressed to a condition and position equal to those of their oppressors. In the cosmology of St. John's believers, this alternative worldview posited by Jesus caused him to be persecuted and eventually murdered by the Roman Empire. All four biblical Gospels record the story of Jesus having a final supper with his disciples and as suffering servant praying to God in the Garden of Gethsemane on the night before he was crucified.[8]

Persecution, death, loss of hope about the future, and prayer are themes reflected in stories about Jesus' life on earth and are also familiar in the lives of St. John's members. Following the model of Jesus on the night of his death when he prays to God for renewal, Nozipo discussed the bleak future of black children and the importance of prayer: "I don't see nicely the future of our children because there's a lot of war and there's a lot of fighting between black to black. Even for children who are only fifteen years old, there's no future. We can just see there's no future for them. If the things that are happening now go on, the future of our children is bad. That's why we pray every time because we also think that the only thing that can help us is to pray to God.

We haven't got the power. We haven't got the tools to fight against the white people. We haven't got the things to fight against them. If we can't fight against them then we can pray about us. So instead of fighting, we'd rather pray." Prayer was the medium through which to ask God for a better future when life conditions are overwhelming. Not having power themselves to overturn a lethal system, St. John's members saw prayer to a holy and sacred source as one way to rebuild hope.

Jesus was also a symbol of liberator because he broke the power of death in his resurrection and appearances to his twelve disciples. His victory over the forces of death, which were associated with evil, meant that Jesus symbolized life beyond death, and therefore power and liberation over the profane world. The gospel story's central message is humanity's salvation through the death and resurrection of Jesus. Resurrection as liberation[9] is a view found in *Speaking for Ourselves,* which Dr. Lydia August, the daughter of St. John's Church's founder, Mother Christinah Mokotuli Nku, wrote with other AIC members. The book is a response to many outsiders who have studied AICs. In the chapter "An Outline of Our Theology," the writers assert their dedication to Christian doctrine and biblical theology.

In their discussion about Jesus Christ, the authors relate that AICs' greatest expression of unity occurs at Easter, when many congregations gather at denominational headquarters to commemorate the death and resurrection of Jesus Christ. Their own words best reveal the meaning of Jesus Christ exhibited in their Easter celebrations: "This is the most important activity of our church-life. Here we remember that Jesus, who is God made flesh, suffered as we also suffer. We remember that through his suffering he saved us from sin. We remember that he conquered sin and suffering and rose again from the dead. And finally we remember that it is through him that we have the gift of the Holy Spirit today. It is a happy occasion for us, a great festival—much more than Christmas" (African Independent Churches 1985:30). This statement evinces church members' acceptance of Christianity's core beliefs. In this sense, St. John's members remain within the mainstream of orthodox Christianity. At the same time, they connect this surface appearance of a conservative theology to the empowerment of the Holy Spirit in the transformation of life today. Therefore, it is important to note how the suffering, death, and resurrection of Jesus are linked to their understanding of the Holy Spirit or the spiritual power to alter social relations.

This transformative spirit was central to the work and hope that adherents had for liberation from their status as disempowered victims of apartheid to citizens of a free South Africa with all attendant rights and privileges.

Admittedly, the convictions of St. John's and other indigenous church members that the resurrection is a symbol of victory over the forces of death do not appear to be particularly at variance with the view of missionary churches. Perhaps the point of distinction was the social situation in which St. John's members found themselves as poor black people living with violence in an apartheid and postapartheid South Africa.

Possibly the best illustration of how the members of St. John's applied the symbolism of Jesus' victory over death to their own lives is seen in their healing rituals. These ritualized medicinal dramatizations represented grassroots believers tapping into a spiritual world of holy power and then, as transformed beings, returning to a world and a system intent on destroying their sense of self and being in the world. Evidence of this system's destructiveness was its denial of adequate health care to black people. Rites providing alternative healing methods were a sign of liberation. Thus, Jesus the liberator was crucial to the theology and work of the church.

During worship on Sunday, 8 December 1991, Mr. Ntili preached on the New Testament Scripture John 9, in which Jesus healed a man born blind. Mr. Ntili connected the role of Jesus healing the blind man to Jesus' liberating power to revitalize and open the eyes of "blind" South Africans who perpetuated the oppression of black people. Below is his exhortation:

> Mothers and Fathers . . . I greet you all in the name of our Lord, Jesus Christ. We have heard today the . . . reading [of] John 9, . . . a story of the opening of a blind person's eyes. A powerful story, especially if we can delve deeper and find out what God is saying to us. Some meanings have already been exposed by others who witnessed here. We come across a blind person in a world where there was a belief that when a person is born blind; when a person is born a cripple or dumb, the mistake is with the sin of the parents, so he should be ostracized. . . . [I]n such a world a blind man . . . suffers. A blind person had a problem of not being accepted by his world. In some cases, such people had a problem of being ostracized and squashed out to live outside residential areas or in the deserted areas because they were branded sinners. So, we find Christ defying the norms, beliefs, and expectations of the day, renouncing such beliefs. . . . So Jesus said, when a person is born blind, it is not the mistake of the parents. This was done so that God could reveal himself among people. When we see things happening in the world, it is not necessarily that people are wrong. . . . God is at work to help us know him. When things seem to be out of the way; when they seem not to be in God's control; it is not that God is out of control. He is in control, but God is trying to create a situation that will enable us to understand his words. In other words, God is urging us to part

with our anxieties. We must trust that God can solve our problems. Let us do so then, even when battles, wars, and all violence takes place. We should not throw away our hope, knowing that the time always comes when blind people's eyes are opened. When we see the oppression that takes place in this world, we should not throw our hope away, because we know that the time of the opening of the eyes of the blind always comes. When we see the exploitation in places of workers, we should remember that the time of the lifting of people's burdens will come. When we see the world in a state of unrest, when we see crime, when we see women raped, one of the most common crimes today, . . . we should remember that this time comes. This time always comes. The time of the opening of the eyes of the blind. Even where you live, being unloved, uncared for, the world talking things about you, the world accusing you,—you must know that there is a time when the blind are liberated. Let me stop here. Let us pray.

In this passage, Mr. Ntili drew a direct correlation between the biblical passage and the social circumstances in South Africa. His resounding message urged members to remain hopeful even during aggressive oppression. Just as Jesus opened the eyes of the blind man, so too would the eyes of black South Africans be opened. Black people recognized their exploitation and knew that apartheid caused violent crimes such as the rape of women. Mr. Ntili's reference to the time when the eyes of the blind would be opened thus had a twofold meaning. Black people, blinded by oppression, would fight for freedom and power. White people, locked in a debilitating pattern of perpetuating violence upon black people, could choose to free themselves from their evil activities. Thus Jesus identified with the suffering "blind" conditions in society, offered healing by way of fresh sight, and as liberator provided the possibility (and for Mr. Ntili the inevitability) of a new humanity for both the victims and the victimizers of the apartheid system.

The Holy Spirit

Healing works at St. John's were executed through *umoya* (the Holy Spirit),[10] which empowered the church and all aspects of its life.

The Holy Spirit as a spiritual power usually took possession of persons during worship services in a spontaneous and unpredictable manner. It is difficult to describe because people responded in several ways. During a particular morning worship, for example, Ndsilibe was suddenly possessed by the Holy Spirit and began to jump up and down rhythmically as the congregation was singing a hymn. While in this possessed state, he moved throughout the church. His eyes were closed, and his arms moved in a fashion that gave him balance. Occasionally he cried out an ecstatic utterance. When the hymn came to a close, the pace of his jumping slowed, and he walked around calming himself. When he was ready, he returned, quite exhausted, to a pew.

Possession by umoya expressed itself in other outward signs. Some possessed persons made jerky movements with their arms and legs. Others bent over and became completely limp. Still others became stiff. All usually showed great emotion not easily contained quietly or serenely. One woman commented on possession, saying, "No matter what your problem may be, if you have been possessed by the Holy Spirit, you are always safe." When asked whether she had been possessed, she responded, "I don't know, but I am always safe."

During structured interviews, St. John's members were asked about the Holy Spirit and whether they had been possessed. Mama Mazibula responded: "I know that there is a Holy Spirit [umoya]. Everything we do, we do through the Holy Spirit. When we are possessed by the Holy Spirit, . . . we dance. You can't dance if you don't feel the Holy Spirit on you. We also do some other things. For instance, people tell you, you did something, but you didn't know. It's there where we see everything, while we're in the Holy Spirit."

In an interview with Reverend and Mama Mjoli, I asked about rituals performed in the church, and they replied by talking about umoya. "If a person is just listening to a song and the song satisfies that person—sometimes you will see that person jumping but the person doesn't know this. You might think that person is mad. And, that is the Spirit [umoya] in that person. He's working through a person."

A final comment on the Holy Spirit came in Reverend Xaba's words of welcome to me during a worship service on 30 June 1991. Since this was only the second time I had worshiped at St. John's, he prepared me for seeing members possessed by the Holy Spirit by saying: "We thank our visitor for coming to this place. We thank her a lot. The Bible tells us that receiving visitors is receiving the angels of heaven. We welcome you wholeheartedly. We want to apologize that you did not understand what is happening here. When the Spirit comes upon us, we jump. You should not be amazed." These comments from Reverend Xaba and members of St. John's document the Holy Spirit's significance in the life of the church. Because many people did not recall that they had been possessed by the Holy Spirit, those who witnessed possession shared what transpired with others. Some people experienced a "lightness" in their bodies. Mama Mjoli said that "once I have been possessed by the Holy Spirit; I feel myself very, very light. The way you see me when I'm dancing—you won't believe I'm an old lady."

The possession of a person by the Holy Spirit usually took place in the context of the worshiping community. The "holy dance" typically accompanying possession most often occurred during congregational singing.[11] When people danced, many clapped their hands, and the entire assembly experienced a shift in energy as song and movement created an ecstatic state that penetrated the moment. Members often described the feelings evoked during these moments as "a lightness" or said, "I did not know what I was doing." Sometimes the possession of one person set off a chain reaction in which others were also possessed. Spirit possession saturated members with an experience that could not be ignored. While not everyone present was necessarily possessed, everyone was aware of a shift in the modality of the ritual moment. Indeed, what occurred could be called a liminal state in which emotions, sensations, and time were suspended.

In addition to the holy dance, umoya made it possible for people to speak in tongues, have visions, prophesy, and heal. Umoya "inspires, reveals, and fills with power and spiritual gifts" (Ndiokwere 1981:90). Kiernan suggests that umoya is associated with the movement of air and breath (Kiernan 1972:200). It is often invoked to cool the overheated body of a sick person (Dube 1991:10). Vilakazi suggests that umoya's power (*amandla*) is central to life and is a part of one's being. He writes: "The spirit, breath or air . . . *umoya*, is the vital force of the body. . . . This spirit . . . also gives strength. A tired person halts in his exertion to 'take air' . . . *athathe umoya*, which is the same as 'to take strength'" (Vilakazi 1962:87). The strength umoya gives is multiplied when people gather communally.

The feeling accompanying the presence of umoya kept St. John's members bonded together against the difficulties of life. Indeed, the awareness evoked in people by an encounter with umoya was one of the factors that kept them involved in the church. As Nonceba commented: "Once I joined St. John's, it is the Holy Spirit that makes me to know the word of God and to understand what's going on in the church. I think that this church provides the only way to live."

When the Holy Spirit possessed one person during a worship service, the experience affected the entire worshiping community. The shared moments of being in the presence of one who was possessed drew the community together, and further bonding occurred among members as they cared for those who had been possessed during the service. At the conclusion of the service, when others told the person who had been possessed what had occurred, he or she faced the reality of having participated in a drama in which a powerful force had created an altered state of consciousness. Both for the individual and for the worshiping community, the experience validated the power of umoya and strengthened belief in the Spirit. Thobeka commented on the ultimate result after people were possessed, saying, "If you have been possessed by the Holy Spirit, you help other people."

Service of Healing

The climax of every Sunday morning worship service at St. John's was a healing ritual. After the sermon, Reverend Xaba announced, "It is time to prepare to go to the lake (*ichibi*)." To "go to the lake" was symbolic language signifying the commencement of the ritual drama of healing. The drama unfolded in the following way. First, a member, usually a woman, began singing the hymn "*Seteng Seliba Samadi*" (There is a Lake of Blood). The words follow:

Seteng Seliba samadi	There is a lake of blood
Aletareng ya tefelo	in the altar of atonement.
'liba se eleng setlhare	The lake which is a medicine
Maatla a sona	the power of which is life.
ke bophelo.	
Esale ke I tlhatswa teng	I have been washing myself there,
Kentse ke bina topollo	Singing the song of salvation
ke be ke kene Moreneng	until I enter to the Lord
Madulong a dinyakallo.	in the places of joy.
Motlhang o retla kopana	One day we shall meet
khanyeng le bohle baa	in the light; glory with all
hlotseng.	those who conquered.
Babinang pel'a konyana	Those who sing in front of the lamb,
rato le ba lopollotseng.	About the love that redeemed them.
Bare Amen Haleluhah	They say, Amen Hallelujah
Hoboraro boo teroneng	To the Three in the throne
Ntate le Mona le Maya	Father, Son, and Holy Spirit
	Let this song be sung eternally.

The words of the hymn, rich in symbolic meaning, say that the lake of blood is an altar of atonement signifying Jesus' sacrificial death. It is also a counteragent giving power to life. Thus, Jesus' blood is metaphorically a healing medicine, signified by the blessed water members drank.

While singing this hymn, members transformed the sanctuary into a lake representing the healing pool where Jesus cured a man who had been an invalid for many years. The lake, called Bethesda in John 5, offered hope to people who wanted to be healed. Everyone had the opportunity to drink blessed water and receive prayer during the service.[12] A large, spotlessly clean white cloth with blue borders, six feet in length and three feet in width, was raised above the center aisle. In the floor of the aisle was a cross outlined in white tiles against a solid blue background. The tiles had been scrubbed until they shone. Over the aisle was a fluorescent light bulb, also shaped like a cross. Thus, the symbol of the cross completely surrounded the blue and white canopy. Two members brought water in a large container to the front of the sanctuary. After the water was blessed by Reverend Xaba,[13] it was poured into little plastic cups and handed to those who stood in line. After Reverend Xaba's death in 1992, Mama Xaba, as the head of the church, blessed the water. Upon obtaining the water, people walked under the blue-and-white cloth to receive a blessing from the ministers and their spouses, who laid hands upon them.[14]

After the ministers gave water and blessings to everyone, Reverend Xaba walked throughout the church and sprinkled it with healing water for a final cleansing and benediction. Members believed blessed water and healing rituals changed their lives because the Holy Spirit, which came from a powerful God and Jesus Christ, was present.

An example of the power of water blessed by the Spirit came from Reverend Xaba during Sunday worship on 27 October 1991. As the service was about to end, he declared: "God's people, time is against us. Time is up. We have people who must live having drunk the water. We live by the water and the laying on of hands. Some people don't understand this. We live by the water anywhere and the laying on of hands. . . . May God develop a new well of water. . . . May those people who are ill be healed." Like several of his members, Reverend Xaba lived many of the same challenges and expected healing and the maintenance of health by drinking the water. Congregants drank the water at least once a week and believed its healing properties kept them spiritually and physically well.

The blessed water was used not only for drinking but was also for bathing, vomiting, and enemas. The water was a purifying agent cleansing bodies internally and externally. Dirt entering a person's body from foreign sources was removed ritually through enemas and vomiting. During structured interviews, members discussed candidly the various uses of blessed water. Thole remarked, "I had an enema and vomited bad things out of me with water . . . I began to feel better." Mama Ntiliti said, "I drank the water and brought it back up again. I had an enema and I had a bath." A bath accompanied the ritual acts of vomiting and enemas.[15] When unclean elements touched a person's skin, a ritual cleansing was performed. After the funeral of Reverend Xaba on

8 August 1992, I wrote this description, which illustrates the importance of removing unclean spirit elements from the skin.

Saturday was the day that black South Africans buried their dead. It was the day that most people did not work, and the community always honored the dead and their families by attending funerals. Services were usually held in the open air. It was difficult to accommodate large crowds in the small structures in which people lived or worshiped. There was, however, another compelling reason that funerals were held outdoors. Most Africans believed that the body of a deceased person was unclean. Those who handled the body, those who attended funerals, and those who entered the cemetery entered an unclean state of being. The resolution of being in a polluted state was to wash one's body with water as quickly as possible so that others would not be exposed to the uncleanliness carried by the person who had been exposed. After the burial of Reverend Xaba many people returned to his home. At the outside gate there were large basins of water for people to wash themselves. By washing in this way, each person was cleansed and could enter the home of widow Xaba.

Thus, blessed water had power and was used as a primary cleansing element to remove unclean spirits. One informant, Thobeka, said that she sprayed her house with the water, particularly when her children cried during the night. Adherents believed that children were vulnerable to harm from evil spirits. Water was the means of removing the spirits or preventing them from entering a home. Reverend Mjoli explicitly stated the connection between evil spirits, children, and blessed water, declaring, "We spray with prayed water in our home. We do this when the children don't sleep in a good way. This is how we must fight the evil spirits."

Water, then, was a source of healing, an element employed to cleanse impurity, and the means through which St. John's members fought evil spirits. It was a source members used continually in many areas of their lives. Thozama provided valuable information when she discussed the ways St. John's members taught her to apply blessed water and how she was healed: "Then they told me to drink water so that I could vomit and take in water for an enema. They also gave me a bath. They told me that I must also have a bottle of water to take home. They said to pour some of the water in the bath. They stressed that I must always use this water while I bathed. It did not take long for me to get well and find a job. I found a job quickly. At the present time I work as a domestic in the home of a white family. I started the job in December 1990."

The use of "prayed water" transformed the lives of people who endured ambiguity caused by micro- and macrostructures working against them.

Sermons

St. John's members' acceptance of, and rigorous engagement with, the Bible was directly tied to the symbiotic linkage between particular texts and their life conditions. From reading passages about a God who healed the sick, protected people in hostile environments, and sheltered those in need, members received the benefit of feeling increased security. The following exhortations from St. John's adherents during worship on 10 November 1991 illustrate the power that the struggles of biblical characters had for indigenous-church participants.

Mr. Molo, reflecting on David in Psalm 23, confessed:

> I also on this day wish to give thanks in the house of prayer. I give thanks to the finger that pointed me to lead worship. I give thanks to the angels of the prophets who always support me under the readings that fell upon us today. In the Book of Psalms we hear David giving thanks for God's deeds and asking for prayers. He says that the Lord is his shepherd, he shall not want. God makes him to lie down in green pastures. He says that God leads him in the pathways of righteousness. David is saying this because he saw God's work. He says that even though I walk in the shadow of the valley of death, I shall not fear. He says that even if anything may happen or if all enemies can come from anywhere, I shall not fear because of the word of God.
>
> I am also under this great reading of the psalm. I ask that God may be with me. May he give me to know that I won't go far, but I will ask those who are with me in the plan to be with me. Pray with me.

Identifying with the biblical character David and taking David's metaphor of God as shepherd for his own life, Mr. Molo believed that if God provided for David's needs, then God would do the same for him.

Shortly after Mr. Molo's speech, a second Scripture was read, Revelation 3:1–29. Reverend Xaba gave the following sermon:

> Today we have been given a great book that threatens the nations. We have been given the Book of Revelation 3:1–29. It says that each person must choose where she/he wants to go. God says, "I know your name. You say that you are living only to find that you are dead." This Scripture reading scares me. I am scared of standing here and talking about such a great book. It says that you may sit here and think that you are alive but, in fact, you are dead. A book which needs a person who can diagnose you as you sit here because as for me it has exposed me. A book which says that I think I am alive but I am dead. I do not do God's work. The book says that you may sit and worship only to find

that there is nothing that you are doing. You talk about God's name but you do not do God's work. Down at the bottom it says that if you conquer, I will not leave you out of God's books. I feel afraid of this book. I wish to be assisted in asking today. That I may ask God to give me power to serve where I am. . . . I am asking to be written in God's book. I ask to be assisted as I pray.

The congregation prayed with Reverend Xaba, and he continued:

The book is Revelation 3 from the beginning to the end. But there is a place I like most. . . . the fifth verse says that the one who conquers will wear white garments. You cannot wear white garments if you have not gone through battles. There is a big battle that a human being engages in this world. When you go to the right, the devil on the left is pulling you. This is why this book of revelations says he/she who wins shall be dressed in white garments. His/Her name is written in the book of life. There is a destiny. This battle that we are involved in here shall come to an end. God will call you to him. But there is something challenging, and that is when this battle is over, what will you be holding as God calls you. He/She who conquers shall wear white garments. This word is a reminder . . . if you call yourself a Christian. Be patient and endure in your Christianity, because you are not going to go along in goodness. When you make a choice to be Christian, the devil wants you. Trust in God who created you and put you in this world. When God sends you down to earth, he wants you to do his work. He sends a person down to earth in order to praise him. On the last day God rewards you because you have been a good child. He then will give you eternal life. If you can see people killing one another here, you will be surprised as to where they say God is. What makes them to kill themselves this way here outside? Are they not afraid of God? Are they not afraid of what will be of them up in Heaven? May God give me a new Spirit. I am asking for repentance under this book of John. This book has been turned open for people who are like you and me; a person who is in a battle. The battle . . . makes it necessary for you to ask for the Holy Spirit.

Reverend Xaba's sermon was tied intimately to the lives of St. John's members. He began by claiming that Revelation 3:1–29 was a threat to the nations (a metaphor for African indigenous churches), and the congregations of St. John's in particular. The Book of Revelation threatened the church because it spoke boldly and exposed the truth. Even Reverend Xaba confessed his fear to the congregation, "I am afraid of such a great book . . . it has exposed me." His apprehension about being unmasked was related to whether or not people followed God's laws, which entailed living a holy and righteous life, including obedience to the commandments and other biblical codes. Reverend Xaba and the congregation believed people who lived a godly life would be "written into God's book."

Reverend Xaba specifically addressed the fifth verse of Revelation 3, which referenced white garments, a sign of goodness and purity. According to Reverend Xaba, if a person was given the privilege of wearing a white garment, it meant the person, having turned to God, was victorious in battles with evil forces.

Reverend Xaba concluded his comments by relating the Scripture to the violence occurring in townships where members resided. He asked, "What makes them to kill themselves this way here outside? Are they not afraid of God?" Drawing a distinction between St. John's members and "them" who were killing "themselves" outside, Reverend Xaba asked the ultimate question, "Are they not afraid of God?" who had the power to decide whether a person was written into the book of life. Reverend Xaba drew sharp contrasts between the elevation of God's power and the demotion of human beings, who took away life given by God. Church members would do well to remain separate from those who kill and do violent acts. There were battles in life requiring people to ask for help from the Holy Spirit. Obviously, for Reverend Xaba, this was what people who were not members of St. John's or other churches needed in their lives.

These exhortations related biblical narratives to the challenges in the daily lives of church members. Thus, they confirmed the thesis that indigenous churches do not separate religion from the circumstances of daily life. This is one of the reasons that these churches are so popular with poor people. In South Africa destitute people struggle for life in ways alien to others, black or white, who have greater financial security. These churches form a liberating source of renewal for their members and respond to the challenges of their lives by offering hope.[16] It is important to ask, what is the concrete meaning of liberation? Does liberation motivate people to live with their religion as an opiate, or does it radically transform the lives of those it touches?

The authors of the previously cited text *Speaking for Ourselves* respond to this question. Dr. Lydia August's participation in writing this volume ties St. John's members directly to the views it articulates. Indigenous-church members write:

> Our communities are sometimes accused of being too inward-looking and people ask us what we think about politics. It is difficult for us to know how to answer this question. The members of our Churches are the poorest of the poor, the people with the lowest paying jobs or with no jobs at all.
>
> Our people, therefore, know what it means to be oppressed, exploited and crushed. Those who came from the 'White Churches' will tell you how even in the

church they felt humiliated and discriminated against and dominated just as they are at work and in the rest of society. But we also know that God does not approve of this evil and that racial discrimination and oppression is rejected by the Bible.

And so what do our people do about it? They join political organizations or trade unions and take part in the struggle for our liberation. But it is a matter of individual choice. Members of the same Church will join different political organizations or trade unions and some will choose not to join anything. . . . The 'Churches of the People' and the political organizations or trade unions of the people have different roles to play. It is often that the same people belong to both. (African Independent Churches 1985:30–31)

Drawing upon the comments made by these writers and applying them to St. John's–Guguletu, one can conclude that the church's cultural system provided members relief from daily psychic, social, and political hardships.[17] Oosthuizen argues that indigenous churches like St. John's play a healing and transformative role in people's lives and offer restoration to their members because they are "churches in the true sense of the word, they are hospitals and they are social welfare institutions. The liturgical approach, the healing procedures, the strong sense of community in these tremendously dynamic independent church movements in Southern Africa owes much to the approaches in the traditional religious context in spite of their rejection of many aspects of the traditional belief system" (Oosthuizen 1991:33–34).

The genesis and raison d'être of St. John's were its healing rituals. According to Adrian Hastings, indigenous churches across the continent of Africa have a similar focus: "All across Africa independent churches, while divided on whether or not to reject all use of western medicine, have adopted services of prayer healing dependent upon the throwing out of spirits, the ecstatic utterance of strange tongues, but also the acceptance of long hours of intense prayer of a fairly conventional kind, all based upon a deep sense of the relationship of physical health to spiritual health and the will of God" (Hastings 1976:70). St. John's, like independent churches throughout Africa, attracted people because healing was a central religious activity.

Selective Conservatism

While the cultural system of a particular congregation is represented in the healing rituals at St. John's and in the cognitive reflections that support them, the literature and comparative field data indicate that similar rituals of healing are found in other African indigenous churches (Daneel 1970; 1983a; Jean Comaroff 1985; Kruss 1985:150–202; West 1975:91–124; Kiernan 1976b; Schoffeleers 1991).

Many scholars of religion suggest that indigenous churches' influence on the lives of black South Africans, within the particularity of apartheid, generated a religious movement in which African peoples selected religious beliefs and practices from past generations, and integrated them with components of a received Christianity to meet their specific needs (Mosala 1985:109–11; Pato 1990:27–35). Anthropologist Monica Wilson proposed the category "selective conservatism" to argue that indigenous people in South Africa chose integral parts of their own "traditional cultures" and integrated them with those of an intruding culture in order to fortify their own cultural authority, expresses precisely this phenomenon (Wilson 1936:548).[18]

The concept of selective conservatism can be used to examine religious experience in light of problems specific to South African society. This analytical idea is inseparable from South African cultural history, a record that shaped and reshaped a bundle of social relations through an interactive field constitutive of the white and black world. Thus, selective conservatism provides a framework for interpreting the emergence of an innovation in the religion of a growing number of South African Christians. While African indigenous churches exist elsewhere in Africa, they proliferated most rapidly in South Africa, where poor and oppressed black people struggled to live in a society that systemically discriminated against them.

The social context in which St. John's members find themselves is changing rapidly. Flux and transformation were particularly pronounced as South Africa moved away from structural apartheid toward a democratic political process. However, from the historical perspective of African indigenous churches like St. John's, transformation began when the first black South Africans separated themselves from mission churches. Thus, St. John's–Guguletu is a result of founder Mother Christinah Mokotuli Nku's separation from the Apostolic Faith Mission, a white denomination that originated in the United States. The racial dominance in the social and cultural patterns of the mission churches led black South Africans to refuse to relinquish, or in some cases to reclaim, rituals and practices predating the arrival of Europeans.

German scholar H. J. Becken writes about AICs' use of selective conservatism: "[The African indigenous churches] express their faith in forms which are understandable by their members and by their environment: the symbolism of their clerical and congregational gowns in many colors with their specific meaning, the rich ritual connected with every service, the unreflected acceptance of the explanation and understanding of richness from their environment, all these are not syncretic remnants, but genuine results of the incarnation of the Christian message in Africa, which is more closely related to the understanding of healing in the New Testament" (Becken 1971:16).

Perhaps the most prudent way to assess the symbols and actions of the African indigenous churches, and of St. John's Church in particular, is to employ the approach of David Chidester, who suggests that rituals demonstrate "how western Christian power symbols have been mobilized to make strategic claims on traditional symbols of power" (Chidester 1989:25). Chidester amplifies this point by adding that "'Christian' beliefs, practices, and forms of association have been appropriated by Africans primarily as vehicles of power in a world of increasingly disempowering power relations. AICs may not be an acculturation, or an Africanization of Christianity, but rather an ongoing, complex mobilization of certain symbolic forms as alternative instruments of power in Africa" (Chidester 1988:85). Selective conservatism serves in the way Chidester suggests and also explains how poor black South Africans, such as the members of St. John's, have transformed received religion in light of a historic struggle for liberation from the oppression of apartheid.

Selective conservatism also implicitly acknowledges the issues of hegemony, which are extremely important in South Africa. I argue that this category points to syncretism's failure to explain adequately the historically unique power dynamics in the interactions of the Afrikaners, the British, and black Africans in South Africa. Indeed, although "syncretism" is not an inherently pejorative term, in the context of apartheid South Africa, its meaning is not neutral (Daneel 1983a; 1984; Stewart and Shaw 1994). While elites may attempt to control cultural meanings to explain the fusion of religious ideas and practices from several sources, people from disadvantaged positions have successfully contested old meanings and created new ones. Those without access to formal structural power do have agency to make cultural choices. St. John's members' use of their power demonstrated that subjugated African peoples claimed their past and altered received Christianity to form a very specific belief and symbol system contesting the oppressive systems. The power of the indigenous churches is their resistance to received religion. Despite the domination of imported Christianity, indigenous people held onto ancient materials from African religion and intertwined them creatively with received Christianity (Jean Comaroff 1985).

Syncretism

In the South African context there are plausible reasons to argue against the "syncretism motif" (West 1975; Pato 1990:25–27; Goba 1988:52) to explain the synthesis of old and new religious belief systems (Lévi-Strauss 1966:16–30; Hannerz 1987; Herskovits 1967:423–29; 1990:17, 249–51). In some instances, interpretation by theologically trained scholars of religion has misrepresented Christianity in Africa, particularly as it is displayed in African indigenous churches (Goba 1988:52).[19] Furthermore, according to many indigenous scholars of religion in South Africa, the notion of syncretism has been misapplied. While on the one hand many anthropologists construe syncretism as value free, on the other, as constructed by some scholars of religion, it implies that African religion has contaminated Christianity. While Christianity itself is syncretist, many scholars of religion have refused to view it as such.[20]

Since the construction of meaning in South Africa has disadvantaged black South Africans, it is necessary to have a radical shift in epistemology with respect to syncretism, which for several reasons is an inappropriate category as it relates to indigenous churches. First, the syncretism motif is an etic explanation postulated by outsiders examining a "foreign" or "culturally different" phenomenon. Second, as an etic category, syncretism carries an overtone insisting that Christianity is the benchmark against which other religious expressions can and should be measured. This elevates Christianity to the status of a pure form that is not itself a product of syncretism. Third, syncretism is a pejorative paradigm when used to explain the emergence of the African indigenous churches, a phenomenon best described as selective conservatism (Pato 1990:25–27; Goba 1988:52).

A more readily acceptable explanation is that independent African churches emerged from the growth of a "new self-awareness which is the result of a lengthy sociocultural and political onslaught on the Africans" (Pato 1990:24). The African indigenous church thus became a symbol of autonomy for many poor people, because it originated in a context of social struggle as black people separated themselves from the dominating ecclesiastical structures that were introduced by white Christian emissaries, structures that reflected domination in the larger society. Colonization pushed African converts into a new society that forced them to submerge their own religious symbols. The hegemony of the missionaries' religion denied indigenous people the power of their own symbols (Pato 1990:26). When syncretism is used to explain the evolution of African indigenous churches, it gives no consideration to Christianity's status as an imposed ruling-class religion that disallowed Africans' use of their own symbols. If those symbols had not been forced underground, other religious forms might have emerged. Moreover, the symbols that Christian couriers introduced might not have been used at all. Pato argues that the African indigenous church "represents a continuity of the struggle which began when the African indigenous cultures were first confronted by colonized power and the world view of European Christendom" (Pato 1990:27). Thus, syncretism is an unacceptable way to explain the

African indigenous church because it assumes an "illegitimate mingling" of religious traditions (Pato 1990:25). Because the blending of the religious elements was forced instead of voluntary, syncretism does not explain adequately the dynamism with which African indigenous churches sprang forth. Since these churches arose from an active battle against the religious values of the oppressor (Mosala 1985:110; Pato 1990:25), it is valid to call this etic category into question. It is not a neutral term, but it carries a bias that assumes power equity between the cultures from which the religions derive.

Martin West, a South African anthropologist of independent African churches, has similar objections to the use of syncretism. Because his concern about the value ladenness of syncretism in the South African context was so great, he chose not to use the term in his writings, explaining that "'sect,' 'cult' [and] 'movement' . . . are generally used by people who do not belong to the groups they describe, and often give the impression that independent churches are not proper churches, and are in some way inferior; 'separatist' and 'syncretist' also have negative connotations when applied to these churches, and are consequently not used" (West 1975:3).[21] As a student of Monica Wilson, West understood the unique political situation in South Africa and its impact on problematizing particular anthropological terms.

In sum, syncretism is not a neutral category in the context of South Africa. The challenges to its use are compelling because of the concrete reality of apartheid for black people. Furthermore, objection by indigenous scholars to its use signals an abnormality in the power dynamics of South African culture(s). In short, the category of syncretism perpetuates the message of apartheid to black people: "You are inferior." If this is so, particularly in regard to the one area over which nonelites have modest control through rituals of healing, then the use of syncretism as either descriptive or explanatory must be contested.

In South Africa, religious values and symbols have not declined in spite of white South African society's control of the economy and the land formerly owned by indigenous communities. Instead, indigenous communities enlisted cultural systems such as religion to interpret symbols of ultimate significance and created rituals promoting collective self-identities rooted in political resistance to external domination.

Hence, it is important to note the role that religion plays between antagonistic groups in society. How are social relations imaged by the symbolic universe and ritual practices of St. John's? What analytical concepts uncover the sociopolitical processes responsible for the flow of religious experience in indigenous South African society? Selective conservatism? Or syncretism? In the context of apartheid, religion and politics are entwined by indigenous churches like St. John's into a single cultural complex. Their selective conservatism functions as a metaphoric discourse to delegitimate the power of the white minority as it continues, even in the post-apartheid era, to control the material conditions of life.

Summary

This chapter demonstrates how cultural beliefs and theology were ritually operationalized at St. John's–Guguletu. Members evidenced their belief that God's spirit actively cared for believers in their descriptions of their relationship with Thixo. Their speech about the ways God used Reverend Xaba, worked with their ancestors, and sent a Holy Spirit to heal the sick discloses a theology of God's active intervention in present history. Reverend Xaba's sermons revealed a God who empowered the Holy Spirit to heal people who drank blessed water and performed other ritualized acts. Sermons provided a means for Reverend Xaba to teach members how to live and understand the Bible. In brief, sermons played an important role in the theology of the church and in disciples' lives.

I examined the scholarship of black South African intellectuals in this chapter because it is these scholars who have, as indigenous persons, systematically reflected upon what the theology of St. John's and other independent churches means in the cultural context of South Africa. Selective conservatism is one term that summarizes the theoretical frameworks of these scholars as they interpret the theology of churches such as St. John's and argue against interpretations that they find inappropriate.

CHAPTER 5

Symbols in St. John's Ritual

"It has long been recognized in anthropological literature that ritual symbols are stimuli of emotion."

—Victor W. Turner, *The Forest of Symbols*

"I consider the term 'ritual' to be more fittingly applied to forms of religious behavior associated with social transformations . . ."

—Victor W. Turner, *The Forest of Symbols*

Introduction

Symbols are significant components of ritual action. The symbols and rituals that people create dramatize aspects of their lived reality. Together symbols and ritual action form structures of meaning that are explicitly different from material reduced to text or verbally articulated.

Writing about the function of symbolism used in ritual, Eliade claims that "the most important function of religious symbolism . . . is its capacity for expressing paradoxical situations, or certain structures of ultimate reality, otherwise quite inexpressible" (Eliade 1959:101).

The symbols used at St. John's synthesized the psychosocial and spiritual dimensions of people's lives. Members used symbols such as water, candles, and staffs to dramatize the social, structural, and psychological processes present in their lives and to establish a cultural system that could metaphorically re-create and reconstruct their reality.[1]

The ethnographic profile of St. John's members shows how many resided in townships where violence was customary and frequent, were forced to struggle to find money to care for themselves and their families, and worried about the future of their own and others' children in light of the egregious consequences of apartheid education and their limited financial resources. The liminal social situation in which they lived meant that they looked to the ritual forms at St. John's for resolution of many conflicts. The symbols and rituals created a dialectical process involving continual elevation and leveling that paralleled the flux of South African society. Thus, the symbolization process among members of St. John's created ultimate meaning for them by disclosing an affinity between the unknown and the known. In this way, the symbolization process revealed and linked the psychosocial and spiritual dimensions of their lives.

Symbolic Representations at St. John's

Water

The central element used for healing at St. John's was water. According to St. John's members, water that had been prayed over or blessed provided a cure for many sicknesses. Blessing ordinary water, otherwise an inert medicament, transformed it into a healing agent. The act of ritual prayer over the water connected members to a belief system that psychologically and spiritually provided a cosmic power able to restore health. At St. John's, water represented renewed life and health.[2] Frequently, different elements such as ash and salt were blended into the water to form a mixture called *isiwasho,* thus incorporating indigenous healing medicines into ritual action. Many members said that they were given isiwasho to make them vomit, to bathe in, and to use in administering enemas. Isiwasho was also used for baptisms and as a medication for purification.

Before each healing service, members helped Reverend Xaba prepare for the ritual. I wrote the following passage after observing a healing ritual at St. John's–Guguletu. My description shows the significance of proper preparation and the use of water for cleansing and healing:

One of the men brought out a teapot and water basin. Another man unrolled a large rectangular cloth that was white with a blue border. This blue-and-white cloth matched the uniforms that members were wearing. Six people, three on each side, held the edges of the sheet in the air so that a canopy was formed. Reverend Xaba came down from the pulpit and walked over to the containers of water. While holding his sacred staff, he stretched his hands over the water and said a prayer to bless it. Then he walked to the man who had the teapot of water. The man poured water over Reverend Xaba's hands, enacting a ritual of cleansing. Mama Xaba followed next in having her hands cleaned with the water. Then I followed in this ritual drama. My hands, too, were washed with this mysterious water. I stood with Reverend and Mama Xaba under the canopy. Mama Ntiliti, the evangelist, followed. Her hands were washed, and then she stood under the canopy. The people in the congregation formed a line. Each person was given a little cup of water to drink. Some people drank two cups of the water, as though they needed an extra source of healing. Each person, which included little children and adults, walked under the canopy, and the four who had their hands washed in the sacred water laid hands upon and blessed them. After all the members walked under the canopy, Reverend Xaba took a cup of the water and drank it. The rest of us followed and repeated his ritual action. We returned to the pulpit while the congregation sang, "*Seteng Seliba Samadi,*" which means "There is a Lake of Blood."

This ritual drama demonstrates the ways in which St. John's used water in the healing services.[3] The blessing ritual transformed the water into a powerful, life-giving substance that when used produced a spiritual power that maintained and restored health to members of the community. The water served as a symbol of absolution, standing for the removal of pollution and the strengthening of the community.[4] On Sunday, 8 December 1991, Reverend Xaba preached a sermon about the Spirit's power to transform ordinary water into a healing medium: "I give thanks to God for the way in which I was healed. . . . People who drink the water survive when difficulties are encountered."

Another member exclaimed during a testimony, "I used to suffer in this world and I got a bottle of water. . . . The Spirit of God has brought me into this place." For this person, the "bottle of water" and the "Spirit of God" created the means to relieve suffering. The same adherent continued, "I remember how I was penniless, without work, food, and even clothes to wear, and God brought me here. He wanted to work through me." When I asked another member what the water symbolized, she responded, "It means that we will be healed. We believe that it heals. If you drink the water while you have pains in your body, you feel healthy."

Many people who attended the St. John's festival in Newcastle in August 1991 brought containers of water to be blessed by Archbishop Njobe.[5] These containers were placed in a ritual space (*ichibi*) outside the sanctuary. Archbishop Njobe explained why people brought containers of water for blessing: "The faith healer prays for the water and then that water can be used for any sickness. It is like a remedy. That is why everyone brings his own bottle full of water. If you come with tap water in a bottle, it is put in the place where we pray for the water [ichibi]. It's obvious that there's nothing in the bottle except water. So many people have been healed by drinking that water." In the St. John's community, the symbolization process transformed water into a healing element that could disengage members from physical maladies or oppressive societal issues. Belief and ritual action brought demonstrable change to the lives of St. John's community members.

Members did not explain to me why they thought blessed water was used for vomiting and enemas. However, they associated water with cleansing and purification with healing; living in a sinful state resulted in impurity and dirtiness.[6] They saw the use of water for vomiting, enemas, and bathing as ritual acts that cleansed internally and externally. Mama Mazibula talked about how she used water at St. John's for cleansing and purification: "I go to church on Thursday and Friday during the week. I go and help the people there to give enemas and to give water. All those who have belts help to give enemas, and to bathe other sick people. On Wednesday, Saturday, and Sunday the sick people vomit from 10:00 A.M. to 10:30 A.M. The enemas are given on the same three days. Those who need a bath get a bath. Those who are supposed to get an enema, get an enema, and those who are supposed to vomit are given water to vomit." Thus, the ritual use of water purified that which was associated with dirt and washed away that which might generate sickness. Purification rituals were formal and were performed by specialists who wore belts to signify both St. John's membership and a personal experience of having been healed by these same rituals.

Candles as Symbols

Candles had symbolic significance in St. John's rituals. Candles burned day and night in the sanctuary.[7] Members of the church brought candles as an offering during worship and were responsible for keeping them lit at all times. My description of the use of candles provides a sense of their connection with *umoya,* or Spirit: "The first time I worshiped at St. John's, I was struck by the presence of white candles burning in every area of the church. My first glimpse of a burning candle occurred when Mama Ntiliti escorted me into a room adjacent to the sanctuary where we waited to enter the worship service. It was a very small room and in the corner was a candle burning softly and flickering gently. This lone candle cast a glow that gave the room a welcoming presence. Mama Ntiliti got on her knees to pray when we entered the room. I did the same."

"After we entered the sanctuary, I saw seven candles burning in a candelabrum. They burned throughout the entire service. When a candle burned to a low point, one of the members inserted a new one in its place."

The significance of the lighted candles lay in the flame's energetic motion and its light. Flickering candles embodied the closeness and the movement of the Spirit that gave power. The light of the candles accorded additional significance to ritual actions taking place in the space where they burned. According to Kiernan: "The candle, once blessed, becomes mystically empowered to dispel the works of darkness and to protect a person against evil spirits and their debilitating effects" (Kiernan 1972:214). Light was associated with honorable behavior, good health, and good fortune. One of the bishops of St. John's said to me, "Candles and water are the main things at St. John's. We must always have candles so that we can see what we are doing." In other words, candles provided power for members to heal.

In a sermon given on 10 November 1991, Reverend Xaba, drawing on imagery found in Revelation 3, explained to the congregation the significance of candles: "The book [Revelation 3] says there are seven candles.[8] When you see the seven candles that we use when we make a sacrifice, know that it is those seven stars [from Revelation]. Those are your stars. Your candles are seven. The book says so." Reverend Xaba's sermon equated the seven stars in Revelation 3 with the seven candles that continually burned in the sanctuary. When people came to St. John's to be healed, they often brought a gift of seven candles to be used in the church. As the stars in Revelation 3 provided light, the ever-burning candles at St. John's provided closeness to the Spirit.

The Staff as Symbol

Mama Mazibula articulated the symbolic importance of the staff. When asked what symbols were important for St. John's Church, she responded: "Did you see that stick that Reverend Xaba has in his hand when he goes to church? That stick is very important in our church . . . you can't do the prophets if you haven't got that stick. He uses it a lot. . . . It gives power to somebody who's carrying the stick; to feel the power of God . . . when we pray for the people, we use the stick most of the time."

The stick was called *indonga yokuphilisa,* and members often mentioned its importance when asked about healing.[9] Reverend Xaba's ability to divine, prophet, or heal came from its use. Thus, indonga yokuphilisa was an authoritative symbol in the life of St. John's.[10]

Color Symbolism

The symbolic use of color was prominent at St. John's, particularly in relation to healing and caring for sick persons.[11] St. John's members made a direct correlation between healing and the ritual use of belts and cords of particular colors. They believed that wrapping a colored cord around an ailing part of the body immediately medicated that part. Mama Mazibula explained how and why belts of various colors were used for healing: "Even the belt—they give a belt to you to put on. The color they give makes you have good health. But you don't just get belts, you get them when it is necessary. The belts are blue, white, red, and green. The red covers you from outside enemies. Blue and white are very good colors so that you don't see terrible things at night. You can dream very good. You can have nice dreams. You can see everything in your dreams and even in visions. Green also protects you from outside enemies. It's the same as red."[12]

Mama Mazibula's outline of a color classification system for healing suggests that in St. John's cosmology spiritual power was manifested through material objects such as colored belts. Hence, St. John's members chose material objects for their healing rituals on the basis of color coding and the power associated with particular colors.[13]

During rituals, healers were required to wear blue and white, the colors about which Mother Christinah Mokutuli Nku had a vision before she established St. John's Apostolic Faith Mission Church in 1938. The colors were used with great reverence because of their sacred healing power. Bishop Njobe explained how Mother Nku chose the colors used by the church: "The white stands for purity, and the blue stands for a special peace. These colors are part of the ritual. Mrs. Nku had a vision of these colors that was quite scriptural. The apostles used to take yards of material and sleep on it. The people who touched the material or who were bound to the material would get well. Mother Nku felt that her method was to bless all who passed under the material. Those who passed under the material with these colors were healed." People who were healed at St. John's offered testimonies about the ways the church helped them, always while wearing blue and white. During a sermon, Reverend Xaba pointed to the white coat he wore and spoke about the promise in Revelation 3 that God "will bless you in a white garment. When you came out of water during baptism you were given new clothes." He continued, "White clothes . . . say that you have overcome."

Baptism was the ritual required to become a member of St. John's. Only after baptism could a person wear the blue-and-white uniform. One informant said, "When I was baptized, they gave me my uniform." Another explained, "today, I am putting on the white coat as a person who is a believer."

All St. John's members wore blue (*luhlaza*). Women wore a blue shirt and belt along with a blue cape draped over their shoulders. Men wore a blue belt across a white coat. On Sunday, 27 October 1991, Mr. Ndongeni became a member and was robed by Reverend Xaba in a white coat and blue and white belt. During the robing ritual, Reverend Xaba addressed Mr.

Ndongeni about the significance of the belt, particularly its healing power. Reverend Xaba stressed that the blue-and-white belt must be used exclusively for healing rituals at St. John's and was not to be worn cavalierly: "This belt is not for decoration. It is a belt of power. You are being given this belt in order that you can heal people. If you serve us the water, you must use this belt. If anyone is ill, you must pray for that person with this belt on. . . . This is not an ornamental belt. This blue and white cannot be worn in town. This blue-and-white uniform is for the lake. This belt is for sick people."

Mama Mazibula explained the meaning of the blue belt this way: "The blue belt means that you are a full Apostolic. It means you must work. If anyone comes here and is very sick, you must do something, because you have the power of God with this belt." Thus, the color blue signifies God's power at work through a human source to heal others.

White (*mhlophe*) represented cleanliness, purity, and virtue. White was related to light and drew forth all that strengthened life.[14] During a worship service Reverend Xaba said: "It is the miracle of the laying on of hands and water that has swelled our ranks so that today, we see so many white uniforms. The prophets who came before us worked for the great numbers we have today." The people of St. John's saw the increased membership of the church as evidence that healing changed people's lives.

On 12–14 October 1991, a St. John's congregation in Cofimvaba, Transkei, held a festival attended by representatives from St. John's churches all over the country.[15] Such festivals were an occasion for a church to celebrate its accomplishments and receive financial gifts from sister churches. Reverend Xaba presided at the festival's Friday evening service and, as a woman was taking the vows of membership, said: "With how many people have I shared the miracle of the prophets' healing, the miracle of being healed by the laying of hands? That is why I thank the God of Mother Shenxane, who picked me up in Cape Town. I thank Father Masango, who sent God's person so that today, I am putting a white coat on a person who appears to be a believer. That is why I am here. I have come to be empowered here. . . . I have come to put my light on this new believer." The white coat symbolized a new life of empowerment given by former prophets. Mother Shenxane was the woman who healed Reverend Xaba before he became a minister in St. John's. Father Masango was the archbishop who led a branch of the church after its initial split.

Thus, the wearing of white uniforms, the laying on of hands, and the use of water and certain spiritually powerful colors constituted the recipe for healing at St. John's. Mother Nku was the church's greatest prophet because she had instructed the church in the use of the colors. People were healed through the symbolic power of the colors, and the colors also served as symbols to outsiders. For instance, the blue-and-white uniforms represented the church, indicating that members had chosen to live in a spiritual way (Kiernan 1974).

The Eucharist as Symbol

The Eucharist was conducted at quarterly festivals as well as at festivals hosted by local churches.[16] On the rare occasions it was conducted at St. John's–Guguletu, it was celebrated in the evening, to replicate the time of day when Jesus served the disciples, according to biblical Scripture. The service began with foot washing, to reenact Jesus' washing the feet of the twelve disciples and thus symbolically becoming a servant in his community (see Kiernan 1980b). Then, bread and wine, symbolizing the body and blood of Christ, were blessed and distributed to those who were full members of the church. Full membership included only those who were baptized. Members prepared themselves for the Eucharist by fasting, praying, and reconciling strained relationships.

At the Friday night service in Cofimvaba, Transkei, after the Eucharist, Reverend Xaba said:

> There is one word I heard, a word that talks about this evening, where it is said that Jesus took the bread and blessed it and gave it to his disciples. He took the cup, prayed and blessed it and gave it to his disciples saying that they should drink. . . . I am disturbed by the evening when Christ did this and commanded that this be done by us. After tears, after sweating and praying in Gethsemane, Jesus performed a task. He was going to live with his disciples even though he would soon be hung on the cross.
>
> I thank God for my presence here tonight. I wish that God may plead on my behalf as he does for his disciples. I give thanks to the angel of Father Masango and Mother Anna, people who respected God. We too are helped by giving respect to God. I too will descend in prayer.

Reverend Xaba remembered Father Masango and Mother Anna, two deceased prophets of St. John's. The Eucharist was an occasion to remember the believers who had died in the promise of eternal life.

All of the symbols used at St. John's Apostolic Faith Mission–Guguletu were essential components of the ritual drama created during healing services.

Through the ritual use of symbols, members dramatized ambiguous life situations within a cultural context that included belief in supernatural powers able to augment healing in members' lives. The dynamic deployment of symbols (that is, water, candles, cloth, and staffs) synthesized the psychosocial and spiritual dimensions of members' way of life. Symbolic representation, moreover, expressed in a fundamental fashion a certain cosmology of ultimate reality inexpressible in verbal discourse or written texts.

CHAPTER 6

St. John's Health Care System

"What good is your medicine if you can't tell me why I got sick?"
—John J. Pilch, "The Health Care System in Matthew"

Overview of Medical Anthropology

Medical anthropology examines the beliefs and procedures associated with sickness, particularly as those practices are related to local cultures that do not depend solely upon biomedical theoretical frameworks. Medical anthropology also explores ways in which communities of people maintain health and understand the causes of illness. The totality of health-related behavioral patterns equals a cultural system that can be analyzed by using data from participants.

Biomedicine, one approach within the subfield of medical anthropology, places primary emphasis on biological indicators of illness, factors that may or may not be known to the patient. Through modern scientific development, biomedicine has come to dominate medical understanding and treatment, often to the exclusion of other strategies. Although information and knowledge possessed by the patient and the patient's sociocultural behavior patterns are not central to biomedical diagnosis and treatment, these areas of inquiry nevertheless offer significant definitions and explanations of human health problems. The popular and the folk systems of health care (the nonbiomedical) and the biomedical approaches to health stand in counterdistinction to each other. Yet human beings in cultures around the globe are known to employ all three approaches. It is not coincidental that poor people more often than not specifically choose the contextual healing of popular and folk practitioners over those associated with biomedicine.

Clearly, national political and economic forces set the stage, influence, and eventually determine the kind of health care a community of people will receive. The political economy of a nation determines the distribution of sickness and death, because macrolevel decisions related to the social costs of production determine the microcategories of who will live and who will die (Feierman 1985:73–74). The social costs of production—such things as the expense of supporting laborers and their relatives, sustaining fit labor conditions, and supporting retired workers—are viewed primarily as "factors of production" (Feierman 1985:93). Whether or not national funding is provided for health care, literacy, or family maintenance ultimately determines which segments of a nation's population have access to a healthful life (Feierman 1985:93). An understanding of this macrolevel context is essential for valid anthropological analysis of healing rituals among members of St. John's Church–Guguletu.[1]

Social Costs of Production and Health Care in South Africa

The social costs of production in South Africa during the apartheid era affected adversely the cost of health care for black South Africans. Steven Feierman comments on the social costs of production in South Africa and the relationship of those costs to health care: "South Africa's decision to use a migrant labor workforce has had significant consequences for health within the country and the southern Africa region. The costs of caring for ailments, the costs of old age support, child rearing, and food for workers' families, are borne to the greatest extent possible by the workers and their families" (Feierman 1985:95). The migrant labor workforce in apartheid South Africa was composed primarily of African men who left their family households in order to secure income from work in other localities. However, income earned by these men was typically inadequate to sustain even themselves, and there was rarely any excess to be returned to family members at home. This separation of African men from their families had a disastrous effect on African women and other family members. The South African apartheid government used the absence of African men from their homes to define the work of African women as confined entirely to "the domestic sphere," thus legally separating their work from the recognized workplace and from society in general. This resulted in African women's work, which included everything from household care to subsistence farming in rural areas, being considered neither as labor nor as production but almost exclusively as "reproductive activity" (Feierman 1985:95). The differentiated valuation of the labor of men and women produced an unequal system of health services and a vast differential in the health care available to "workers" as compared to that available to African women and other family members. No national funds were allocated for women's work, which meant there were few available resources for the health care and maintenance of family members left behind by male migrants. There was a clear and direct correlation between the system of using male migrant laborers and the absence of health care for women and children in communities (Kistner 1990). Cross-cultural studies show an equally clear correlation between the lack of income from migrant laborer–fathers and the malnutrition of their children (Feierman 1985:92;101; Thomas 1981:553).

Fifteen members of St. John's–Guguletu migrated from the Transkei and Ciskei. Of these fifteen, three were single women who lived with their children in a one-room shack at the church. With the abolition of the Influx Control Law in 1986, many black South Africans migrated from rural areas, where the majority of black South Africans lived during the apartheid era, to urban areas, occupying any vacant land that was available (Cook 1991:26–42). These migrants, called informal settlers, hoped to find a better way of life in the cities (Lemon 1991:114–15; Crush, Jeeves, and Yudelman 1991). African children living in the city had better access to health care and food because of their proximity to resources from local clinics and hospitals and to neighborhood networks in the townships (Feierman 1985:92,103). The women at St. John's who worked as domestics and raised children without the presence of fathers developed a network that supported the care and nutritional development of their children.[2]

Emic and Etic Approaches to Health Care

To appreciate fully approaches to health care in the context of South Africa, the anthropologist's dichotomy of "emic," an insider's view, and "etic," an outsider's view, is useful. The emic perspective can be seen in a healer who assesses a patient's chronic headaches and identifies herbs that may bring relief. Significantly, the healer gives credence to the patient's report that she did not dedicate her last child to a deceased maternal aunt who was childless. This constitutes an emic approach because the healer lives in the same cultural microlevel system as the patient. Biomedicine, on the other hand, might use laboratory tests to assess the biological cause of the headaches. Within the anthropological framework, this constitutes the etic approach, because many specialties in biomedicine do not necessarily consider the social situation in which a patient lives. The biomedical strategy may view the patient as merely a body with a malady and may consider social relations to be inconsequential. In other words, the body may be separated from the social relations (Feierman 1985:109; Helman 1990:89).[3] For the most part, biomedical strategies do not take seriously the popular and folk methods of healing (Kleinman 1980:31–33; Kleinman and Sung 1979).

My greatest challenge in this anthropological study of healing rituals at St. John's has been to find the meaning(s) of the emic health care discourse within St. John's–Guguletu. More important, the challenge has been for me to engage St. John's participants in culturally appropriate ways so that they articulate their own meanings for health and healing and thereby construct their own sociocultural context for these phenomena. This examination therefore moves from "etic to emic and back to etic again" (Malina 1981b:1307) and in so doing makes the experiences of members of St. John's understandable to those who do not participate in the rituals.

Before we can adequately examine the internal dynamics of the healing rituals at St. John's and their meaning, we must clarify these activities from a biomedical perspective with regard to issues of sickness, disease, and illness. For this purpose, Arthur Kleinman's critique and model are helpful.

Kleinman's Model of Health Care as a Cultural System

Arthur Kleinman suggests that medical anthropology often views sickness singularly, as a way to explain a particular reality, and treats disease and illness as explanatory ideas for understanding that single reality (Kleinman 1980:72). Disease is a biomedical construct that explains abnormalities in the structure and function of organs. These pathological abnormalities may or may not be culturally acknowledged (Pilch 1985:143). A disease may affect the body of an individual, and the treatment offered is generally to the individual. From a biomedical perspective, the "sickness" of a married woman who is unable to become pregnant may not be caused by a disease and could proceed as an untreatable incident.

Kleinman offers a critique of medical anthropology's etic focus on the healer as a separate entity, suggesting that "The overwhelming distortion in medical anthropology . . . has been one in which healers were studied in isolation as the central component of medicine in society" (Kleinman 1980:205). Kleinman suggests a more inclusive health care model, one that sees a local health care system as a *total* model with three intersecting areas: professional, popular, and folk.[4]

1. The Professional Sector: The professional sector consists of all organized healing professions, including the indigenous professionalized healers (Kleinman 1980:53–59).
2. The Popular Sector: Included in the popular sector model are the lay, nonprofessional, and nonspecialist practitioners. Usually, this sector has the largest number of practitioners. There is great potential for transcending limitations of biomedical anthropology by exploring the popular sector (Kleinman 1980:50–53).

3. The Folk Sector: This sector includes nonprofessional specialists who are not connected with formal institutions. While folk medicine is associated with many different dimensions of culture, it is most closely identified with the popular sector and
overlaps with the intersection of the professional and popular sectors (Kleinman
1980:59–60).

Patients and healers comprise the cultural system of Kleinman's health care
model, and any analysis of healing must begin with both groups. Healing takes
place through the cultural system as a whole and not simply through the
agency of the healer (Kleinman 1980:72).

A model of the system is a map to guide our understanding of human
behavior within that system as it relates to health care. More specifically, use
of the model helps to point out the ways in which a given group of people
think about health and what actions they take to use their sociocultural system
of care. The actions of group members are generated by beliefs that in turn
reflect cultural assumptions.

One can say that a health care system is cultural, yet it is not limited to
culture. It is also societal in orientation, design, purpose, and relevance
(Kleinman 1980:27). Stated succinctly, "the health care system is created by a
collective view and shared pattern of usage operating on a local level, but seen
and used somewhat differently by different social groups, families and individuals" (Kleinman 1980:39). The anthropological study of a health care system, therefore, may be from either a macrolevel or whole-society approach or
from a micro- or local-settings approach. We move now to the microlevel perspective, examining the biblical theology used at St. John's for healing.

Biblical Theology as a Foundation for Ritual Healing

How can this framework shed light on the biblical texts used by and for St.
John's members? Interviews with members reflect commitment to biblical
tradition and allegiance to rituals initiated by St. John's founder, Mother
Nku.

The Old and New Testaments of the Bible provided the people of St.
John's Church with a solid biblical theology for their ritual activity. The Bible
served as a key source by which people reflected upon their lives. The majority of the eighteen people interviewed owned Bibles and indicated that the
Bible was a source of inspiration and revelation and was a tool with which to
reflect upon life. Indeed, the Bible was the source from which all testimony
emanated during worship services, and it was the only resource used for
preaching. When Mama Mazibula was asked, "Why do you have a Bible?" she
said: "I'm supposed to have a Bible because I'm a Christian. Once we go to the

church, we are asked to open our Bible. Then we read it. I have to know what is in the Bible." When asked, "How does the Bible guide your life?" she responded: "The Bible leads you to the Spirit of God and also to the love of God. It leads you. I have never seen God, but the Bible leads you to love your neighbors and to love the people you see on the streets. That means anybody; your family, your brother, anybody." Thobeka asserted that she had a Bible "because I'm a Christian. I must have a Bible. We believe in the Bible. If we didn't need the Bible, we wouldn't be Christian." Finally, Mama Joxo claimed, "I must have a Bible. How can I go to my church without a Bible?"

When a sick person came to him, Reverend Xaba used the Bible to find out the nature of his or her life. During an interview, Reverend Xaba reported: "The way that I find out about a person is to open the Bible and to see what God's word speaks to me. I can always depend on the Bible to tell me what I need to know and how to instruct the person. The Bible leads me to the truth about the person's illness." Hence, the Bible provided Reverend Xaba with a source through which to heal and a means by which to understand the sickness of adherents. It likewise provided members a way of knowing about God. As Nonceba stated, "I want to know the knowledge of the Bible." Thus the members of St. John's understood that being Christian meant knowing the Bible.

Moreover, the members of St. John's responded to the Bible with commitment, because it was a source by which people came to understand healing and to experience a renewed life. For instance, the powerful God revealed in Exodus 15:26 who says, "I am the Lord, your healer" was understood literally by St. John's members.

Drawing from the themes found in the Hebrew Scriptures,[5] members believed that an essential ingredient in a recipe for healing was "right living," which meant living a life as free of sin as possible. Sickness could be caused by uncleanliness or deviation from the way of God. To illustrate St. John's focus on righteous living, I wrote the following description in my field notes after I went to Reverend Xaba about my personal experience of sickness:

> When I sought counsel from Reverend Xaba about a health problem, a series of ritualized events occurred over a three-week period. During my first meeting with him, he gave me his Bible and asked me to read Leviticus 5. This chapter is about how a person sins, becomes ceremonially unclean, or is guilty of wrongdoing. The writer of Leviticus outlines in great detail the ways in which a person may enter a disfavored relationship with God. Silence regarding knowledge of a private matter that should become publicly known is a sin (v. 1); a person may enter a ceremonially unclean state through various actions: for example, by touching the carcasses of unclean animals (v. 2) or by touch-

ing a human being who is in an unclean state (v. 3); or a person is guilty if an oath is taken thoughtlessly (v. 4). If a person is guilty of any of these acts then he/she must confess his/her sin and make an appropriate offering, such as a lamb or goat. The priest is an intermediary and makes atonement on behalf of the person (vv. 5–6). The sinner is to bring an offering that is affordable (v. 11).

After reading Leviticus 5, Reverend Xaba and I had a discussion about the scripture. He suggested that something concerning my health was out of order because my ancestors, specifically my parents, were unhappy with me because I was not acknowledging them. My health could be restored by honoring them with a sacrifice. He explained that while the scripture suggested that a lamb or goat be offered, the founder of the church, Mother Nku, understood that most people affiliated with St. John's were poor and could not afford to buy a lamb or goat or even a pigeon. The church therefore permitted people to make a monetary gift that ritualistically represented a "cow or lamb or goat." A cow was R40, a lamb was R20, and a goat was R10. He stressed that each person had to decide for him/herself what was affordable.

I told Reverend Xaba that where I lived people did not believe in the ancestors. Gazing at me with disbelieving eyes, Reverend Xaba slowly stood up and walked around the small living room. After a pregnant silence, he responded, "How can you people not believe in the ancestors? They are in the Bible. The Bible tells us about Abraham, and his wife, Sarah. It tells us about Isaac and Rebecca. There are many others. Even Jesus. How can you say there are no ancestors?" Looking with eyes fixed downward, I realized that Reverend Xaba offered an interpretation of ancestor that I had not known before. Because I had esteem for the Bible as a book of faith, I decided then and there that ancestors were a reality for me. Moreover, I was in a culture where ancestors were as real as people who were alive. I also realized that I was a long way from home and I missed by deceased parents very much. Perhaps it was fitting to honor them now that I was on African soil. I gave Reverend Xaba R10, signifying that I wanted to make a sacrifice to honor my parents and to have my health restored. Having made that decision, I immediately felt relief.

This field note gives some indication of how biblical theology, belief, and personal economics were woven together in the healing process. The Bible provided the theological foundation for the ritual activity that St. John's members performed and hence God was the healer of people who were desperate for restoration. Ritual action was the unfolding drama that moved members from a state of being out of control in their social environment into a shared community context in which Reverend Xaba, who represented the sacred, restored security, harmony, and order within the sacred space of the church. St. John's members were bombarded by a constant state of chaos, often represented by violence, that was a way of life. While it may be an overstatement to say that the chaos and violence, products of the macro social system perpetuated by the structures of apartheid, caused illness among poor populations like the community at St. John's, it is not an exaggeration to suggest, as Ramphele does, that apartheid "affects people's sense of well being that goes along a continuum."[6] The formula that produced the healing of individuals at St. John's was the combination of the ritual use of biblical texts and the belief of the community of faith in the power of healing, the sacred power bestowed upon Reverend Xaba, and the church's specialized ritual activities.

John 5: An Essential Biblical Text for Healing at St. John's

Drawing on resources from the New Testament, members of St. John's used John 5 as the central Scripture for healing rituals. Reverend Xaba explained that Mother Nku made this passage the foundation of healing in the church because it is about a man being healed at the pool in Bethesda. Reverend Xaba always stressed the importance of this text for the history and healing ministry of the church. He explained that the water that was prayed over symbolized the water described in John 5, and therefore water that had been blessed was the central healing element at St. John's Church.

John 5 is about a disabled man who sat at a pool of water that was known to be a source of miraculous healing, in a town called Bethesda. The man sat by the pool for many years, desperately hoping that someone would help him into the water. While passing through Bethesda, Jesus came to this pool and asked the man if he wanted to be healed. The man explained that he had no one to help him get into the pool when the water was stirred. Jesus said to him, "Get up! Pick up your mat and walk." At once the man stood up, picked up his mat, and walked.

The importance of this story for the St. John's community was twofold. First, the disabled man, like the St. John's community, believed that the water in the pool had healing properties because many had immersed their bodies in it and been restored. Thus this story established that water was used as an agent of healing during biblical times. Second, the story reinforces Jesus' role as a popular healer. In the passage immediately before John 5, Jesus healed an official's son (John 4:43–54). Jesus usually began a healing by asking the ailing person whether she or he wanted to be healed. When he asked the disabled man at the pool this question, he received a positive response. However, Jesus healed him, not by using water from the pool, but by using his sacred power,

which consequently amplified his own role as a popular healer. Since water
and popular healing were central elements in the rituals, the impact of this
Scripture on the theology and ministry of St. John's Church was significant.
The water for healing at St. John's parallels the pool in Bethesda, and Reverend
Xaba's role as priest-healer parallels Jesus' role as a popular healer. In the same
way that the New Testament biblical community believed that water and Jesus
could heal, so the St. John's community believed that blessed water and
Reverend Xaba could heal.

The service of healing was the last segment of the Sunday morning worship service. As described in chapters 4 and 5, the water was blessed and given
to people to drink in small cups. Nozipo, who lost three children to illnesses
before becoming a member of St. John's, explained to me that since she and
her last-born child, Thembisa, had become part of St. John's and begun to
drink the water, neither she nor her daughter had been sick again. The women
who lived in the shack at the church with their children said that they mar-
veled at the health of their children, who had been drinking the blessed water
at least once a week.

St. John's members, on a microlevel, interfaced with the larger macrolevel
South African culture. The microlevel of St. John's health care rituals had several components: social networks, the family, and worship services. These
components led to particular practices and categorizations of sickness.

Social Networks

Kinship, biological or fictive, and other social networks were present as formal
social institutions in the St. John's–Guguletu congregation. These social networks played a significant role in the popular sector of the health care system
and were manifested in various ways.

The congregation of St. John's was a close-knit group. While the official membership was forty-eight, attendance at the four daily worship services fluctu-
ated, with the 11 A.M. Sunday worship service having the highest
attendance. Attendance at other services was smaller (ten or fewer) and more
intimate, having the effect of building tight network groups among those in
attendance. For example, there was a network of older women members who
were not employed outside their homes and who assisted Reverend Xaba with
the healing rituals. Members of this group lived in their own homes in
Guguletu, had an in-depth knowledge of the theology and rituals of the
church, and usually had experienced healing personally. Women in this network formed a stable and committed social group within the congregation,
and Reverend Xaba could always rely upon them to assist with the sick. They

were also the women who attended the Thursday afternoon worship service for "mothers," or mature married women.

Male members who had their own homes in Guguletu or an adjacent township also formed a small social network. Most of these men were employed and therefore unable to assist Reverend Xaba with the sick during the week. They were present at Sunday worship services and actively participated in testifying, lighting candles, and reading the Scriptures.

There was a third network among men and women who lived in the shacks on the church's premises. Those in this network were sick and unemployed, or well but unemployed, or employed but too sick to work, or well and employed, and they included both members and nonmember adherents. The nonmember adherents were usually new arrivals who came to St. John's to be healed or because they did not have a place to live. Those who were well and employed usually had experienced being healed at St. John's. One member in this group, having been restored to health, looked for a place to live in the township. Two shacks next to the church were transitional living quarters established for individuals who were recovering from various kinds of maladies.

The unifying factor among all the networks was that each looked after the welfare of all members of the church. For instance, the older women gave ritual baths and enemas to the infirm, who usually lived in the shacks; and this latter group had an elaborate system of care among themselves. Those who did not work looked after the children of those who worked. Those who worked, in turn, shared food and money with those who did not. When the unemployed managed to acquire a job, or when the sick regained their health and were once again working, they shared with those who were ailing or unemployed or both.

Thus, a ritualized circle was formed of those who were healed and those who found work sharing with others who were sick and unemployed. Those who lived in the shacks were in general less economically stable than homeowners, and they often experienced difficulty finding a permanent place of residence. They had usually experienced healing fairly recently, in contrast to the group of older women who assisted Reverend Xaba. Members who were in good health were usually quite willing to assist with the sick, because someone had cared for and attended them when they first came to the church. Thus, the networks replenished themselves as new arrivals became members and helped with the healing rituals. There were also members of the church who were less active; that is, they did not attend services regularly or assist Reverend Xaba with the sick. Those who lived in the shacks, the women who assisted with the healing rituals, and the men who participated on Sunday mornings were the most active. Women's networks differed from men's only in that women pensioners made more time available to be at the church and to assist than men did. The networks of those women who lived in the shacks functioned essentially in the same manner as the networks of men who were shack dwellers.

Family

The church provided health care for families who were associated with St. John's adherents. During an interview, Reverend and Mama Mjoli talked about an illness Mama Mjoli manifested before they were members of St. John's. Reverend Mjoli originally became a member of the church as a result of the healer's expectation that he would actively participate in his wife's healing process. Mama Mjoli spoke of her illness: "I was very sick when I came to St. John's; that was the only problem. I was suffering. There was a burning sensation between my shoulders. I heard from somebody that there was a woman called Mama Shenxane in Woodstock. So I went to Woodstock. When we met, she said that she could not tell me anything unless I took the Bible and I started to prophet through the Bible." Mama Mjoli explained how she was healed by Mama Shenxane: "She prayed for me and she always put her hand on me. She prayed for the water and gave me a bottle. She told me that I must always have this bottle at home and that I must pray at home. She also gave me water so that I could vomit. I also had an enema. I was healed in 1954." Reverend Mjoli talked about how Mama Shenxane insisted that he come to the church if Mama Mjoli was to be treated. He explained: "Mama Shenxane said to my wife, 'I will not start your healing process unless you come with your husband.' What I liked most about Mama Shenxane is that she didn't just take my wife and work only with my wife. She also called me as a husband because she was unwilling to do anything without me."

In this case, Mama Mjoli was clearly the individual with the illness. However, her family, represented by her husband, had to be involved in order for her to receive treatment. In effect, the life of the whole household shifted, because both husband and wife became part of St. John's community, and subsequently Mr. Mjoli became a minister of the church.

Taxonomy of Sickness

Each part of the health care system formulates its own clinical reality, which consists of beliefs, hopes, standards, actions, and disclosures related to sickness, health care seeking, practitioner-patient relationships, healing activities, and evaluation of results (Kleinman 1980:42).

Since illness is socioculturally constructed, the ways in which people talk about their sickness give insight into how they view the world. The following interview provides an example of an illness caused by spiritual forces, "Xhosa illness," which was frequently reported to me.

LT: Tell me about your illness.

XX: I was sick because I had Xhosa sickness to be a diviner. . . . I was sick from 1985 up to 1989.

LT: What did you do as a diviner?

XX: When you're sleeping, you see your ancestors, and they tell you what you must do. They want to put beads on your arms, and then they tell you if you want to be healed, you do this. They show you these beads. . . . And while you are sick (that kind of sickness of being a diviner), some times you look like a mad person. Sometimes the people don't like you because of your actions and you sometimes like to stay alone without anybody; even a radio. When they switch on a radio, you don't like it. It just makes you mad. And you feel that you can stay alone where you are. And then after that, you have to get somebody who can treat you right.

Illnesses caused by spiritual forces were not the only pathologies that were diagnosed at the church. The following transcript came from a woman who had asthma. She described what happened when she came to the church:

LT: Tell me, how did you decide to become a member of St. John's?

XX: It was through ill-health.

LT: What was your illness?

XX: It was asthma.

LT: What happened when you came to St. John's?

XX: Asthma was troubling me more often, but when I came to St. John's I got treatment.

LT: What was the treatment?

XX: I used to have some water to drink, a tot or glass to drink. Sometimes we have a vomit or an enema.

LT: What happened when you drank the water and had the enema?

XX: When I vomited, I used to vomit very dirty things; the terrible ones.

LT: When did your healing come?

XX: About three years.

LT: Tell me about the healing. What happened?

XX: There was nothing else but the water, the vomiting, the faith. As I received the treatment, I became better and better. . . . So I carried on with the treatment, till I felt that I was 100 percent better.

Infertility was another prevalent disorder. Here are two examples:

LT: How did you become a member of St. John's?

XX: I was looking for children. When I asked for children, then I got them.

LT: What do you mean that you were looking for children?

XX: I couldn't get children, then I started to come to St. John's.

LT: And what happened when you came to St. John's?

XX: Then I got children.

LT: What did they do to help you get children?

XX: They were praying together with me and they were praying for me, so that I could have children. They used to give me water . . . the prayed water. . . . Then I did all the rituals with the water and they prayed for me and I got children.

Another woman who was infertile told how St. John's helped her with its rituals:

LT: How did you decide to become a member of St. John's?

XX: I didn't get children when I was married.

LT: What happened when you went to St. John's?

XX: Then I got a baby.

LT: What did the people at St. John's do to help you to get a baby?

XX: They just did all the work they do.

LT: What is the work that they do?

XX: They gave me enema and they gave me water to vomit and they also bathed me.

LT: How long after these treatments did you have a baby?

XX: I didn't have any problem after I took all that. Then I just fell pregnant. I had my baby.

LT: How long did it take you to conceive after starting the treatments at St. John's?

XX: When I went to my husband in Welkom, . . . he was already in St. John's. He took me to his church and explained to the people that I didn't get babies. From that time they started to do all their work. They started to give me enemas and those three things. It was not a month before I fell pregnant.

Ndsilibe talked about how he became a Christian through his encounter with healing at St. John's. He described an illness related to bad spirits:

I became a Christian because I was pulling hard even when I was growing up. It was very bad because I was sick all the time. So, although I was sick, I was healed in this church. That's why I decided to become a Christian in St. John's. I used to dream terrible things—evil things. I dreamed like this: sometimes if I was walking on the street, I saw people who wanted to do something bad to me. So I decided to go to St. John's when I saw all these things that were happening to me. Once in St. John's, they started by giving me water to vomit. They also gave me water so that I could use it at home. Then they prayed for me. They put their hands on my head and they prayed for me. That is why I decided to come to this church, because I could see that it healed me. Before I attended St. John's, even before they helped me to vomit, I took medicine. I also went to the diviner. The medicine and the diviner never helped me. I got help in St. John's. I could see the difference, so I believed. I feel in my heart that I believe in this church. This church is my shepherd which will look after my life.

Categories of illness that emerge from these transcripts are bad spirits, infertility, affliction by outside spirit forces, and respiratory disease. George Foster's ethnomedical work in Mexico prompted him to conclude that health care systems could be classified and based on etiology. He divided the causes of disease into personalistic (intervention from human or divine beings) and naturalistic (organic disorders). While people tended to prefer one or the other as the cause of their sickness, the categories were not mutually exclusive (Foster 1976:54).

The speech of St. John's members indicates that the church's health care system dealt with both personalistic and naturalistic etiologies and that the personalistic category provoked concern about what forces were responsible for an illness and why it affected a person. About these Foster writes, "In personalistic systems, illness is but a special case in the explanation of all misfortune" (Foster 1976:776). Peter Worsley adds an important point: "We are not dealing with illness but with misfortune and the prevention of misfortune" (Worsley 1982:327).

St. John's members reported episodes of illness by using emic explanations that described a dimension of the sociocultural construction of their lives. They thought that some illnesses involved incorporeal forces, and they sought to understand the ways those forces acted.

Healing, as reported in these examples from the popular sector of the health care system, was more than self-care. The sick went to a practitioner for healing in a community context. More specifically, they went for healing to a priest-healer affiliated with a church.

Worship Services

The worship services at St. John's were free-flowing, expressive performances whose echoing movements helped members experience a reprieve from turmoil and obtain a sense of hope. All services included a cappella renditions with stylized rhythmic hand clapping. A portion of the worship service was devoted to community testimony in which people talked about their lives and made specific requests to God.[7] Additionally, the Bible was read, and those who wished to do so expounded upon Scriptures. Prayer was interspersed throughout the service. All services were begun by lay men or women. The minister usually entered the sanctuary while testimonies were being given.

The ritualized testimonies were known as the time to "ask of God" (*Siyacela Kuwe, Jehovah*).[8] In one testimony given at St. John's–Guguletu, a woman talked about her own health and made an appeal to God for her husband to find employment. "I felt that I should come because I feel down. My body is not well. . . . I want to ask for my husband that he may get a job." On another Sunday in October 1991, a woman said: "I thank God for giving me a job. I used to be unfortunate—whites would not even open their doors for me when I went about asking for a job because I was despicable. But, because of the prayers I received here, things have changed. I used to be pressurized by means of medicine. Someone working his magic on me. I prayed and God showed his presence."

Both testimonies show women who were concerned about their own and their families' livelihoods. Many of the members lived with unemployment as a daily reality. The instability that unemployment caused in their lives was an issue that these women chose to lift in testimony for God and the community to hear. The church was a place where they could talk about their concerns and be understood and supported. The support was immediate in that after each "asking," those present said a prayer for the specific petitions that were requested.

Reverend Xaba and the members of the church formed a vibrant healing community. St. John's therapeutic healing community had some parallels to the one John Janzen discusses in his book on healing in the Kongo (Janzen 1978). Janzen's work led him to conclude that at the onset of sickness, a network of people gathered to support the ailing person and to influence the type of care that was provided. Janzen called this circle of people a "therapy managing group" (Janzen 1978). The networks at St. John's at times resembled Janzen's therapy-management groups in their care for the infirm. For instance, a sick person usually came to St. John's because of the personal testimony of another person, because the sick person heard about the healing ministry of the church, or because a St. John's member brought him or her to the church. The first person whom sick people usually met was Reverend Xaba, who commenced therapeutic care immediately in that initial encounter. Typically, Reverend Xaba asked the sick person, "Why have you come here? Do you want to be healed?" During all his years in ministry, Reverend Xaba could not recall a time that a person came to him and declined to be healed. Reverend Xaba propheted the person and in so doing found out more about the individual and her or his circumstances. Next, Reverend Xaba called on the network of women members who administered ritual baths, enemas, and vomiting. These congregants were essentially a therapeutic health care group that managed the care of the person, believed that the infirm person would be rehabilitated, and helped the person through the stages of healing. For instance, food was prepared for the person, accommodations arranged, and assistance provided for getting to the church services if necessary. Thus, the members of St. John's formed therapeutic management groups as they were deemed necessary to care for the sick.

Priest-Healer

Reverend Xaba operated in an environment in which many other healers were called upon to make diagnoses and perform healing rites. The other healers worked in secular contexts; that is, their work was not grounded in Christianity, and thus their healing powers did not arise from a belief in the Bible and the power of the Holy Spirit as witnessed in biblical tradition.

How was the priest-healer effective in the St. John's community? Many members called upon Reverend Xaba in his capacity as priest-healer, a role that revealed the power of the sacred. The priestly role identified Reverend Xaba with God and the church. The role as healer identified him with the sacred power that restored health. Following are some examples of the ways that people referred to Reverend Xaba. Yoliswa said:

> I went to St. John's because I was sick. I came specifically to Cape Town because of St. John's. My sickness was like this. I was asleep and when I woke up I couldn't turn and look on the other side. Since I was ill, I decided to go to Tata Xaba. When I went to him, he put his hand on my head and prayed. He gave me water to drink. He gave me a string of twine to put on around my legs. He also gave me twine to put around my head and around my waist. I told him about my dreams. My dreams were just pushing me to this church. As I followed the rules of the church, they prayed for me. Then I decided to join the church. Up to now, this is

how I live. I believe that since I decided to join St. John's, the way I live is different. We are different from the other churches. I do not know other churches that put hands on people and pray. We give the water to drink for healing. We also have special times to pray. I go to church on Sundays, but at other times I pray in my house, because the church is very far away to go at other times.

This passage highlights Reverend Xaba's role as healer. Tata Xaba, as healer, made contact with Yoliswa, the patient, by touch; he spoke to a holy power on her behalf; and he gave remedies that, in his mind as healer, were the means to her recovery. Healing not only restored physical health but also reestablished the means to a livelihood. Yoliswa told me what she liked most about St. John's and about how she found work:

I like the symbols at St. John's. When I started St. John's, I was sick and not working. I stayed with Mama Xaba and Tata Xaba at the church. They told me that I must sit down and not look for a job. They said that while I stayed in the church, I would find a job. They were right. Really, I did get a job. I am working for a white family (white people don't like some people; they do funny things). Sometimes I stay at their house for two weeks. But, if I stay there two weeks, before I go, I drink the blessed water and I spray myself with the water. I go straight to work, and they accept me. If I ask something from them, they give it to me. They make me like their child.

The other thing that I like about St. John's is that people come to this house of God because they are sick. We pray for them. We give them the water and they are healed. It is a miracle for them. They don't know how the healing happens.

Living in the sacred space of the church along with Mama and Tata Xaba and receiving direction from them changed Yoliswa's life. She found a job in the home of a white family that she believed treated her decently, and she also believed that the water helped her relationship with the white family. Thus, water healed not only physical sickness but also social distress.

At the end of interviews, it was customary for me to ask if there were any questions that the person wanted to ask me. One man showed his ardent belief in the abilities of Reverend Xaba, the priest-healer, by inquiring if I had not already asked Reverend Xaba all the queries that I had just put to him. This brief exchange illustrates the confidence that this man had in Tata Xaba's authority in all matters relating to the church and its ministry.

LT: Do you have any other questions to ask me?
XX: Yes, I want to ask you about the answers you got about the cloth

[canopy] we put up when we go to the lake on Sundays. I'm definitely
sure that before you came to us, you talked to our minister. I want to
know what Tata Xaba said to you, because I can't tell you. I want to
know what he said and why you want to know from me now?

LT: Oh, . . . when I talked with Father Xaba, I asked him many things, but
I did not ask him about the cloth yet. When he comes back from Pretoria,
I will talk with him again.

Finally, Mama Mazibula described how she began to go to St. John's and
her encounter with Reverend Xaba:

Before I joined the church, I just went to see what was going on inside there. I
took a long time. Then after a while I signed my name and they took me to be
baptized. When I was baptized, they gave me my uniform. I got sick again, but
it didn't take long for me to heal after I went to St. John's. When you are sick,
you go to St. John's and the first thing that happens is they take you to Tata
Xaba. Then Tata Xaba tells you everything, all your problems. He takes the
Bible and looks at the Bible and tells you everything—all that is happening to
you and what's going to happen, too. Then after that, he tells you what you
must do. He tells you that you must come to the church. When you come, the
members give you some water to drink so that you can vomit, and then after
that they give you water for an enema. The next time they give you a bath and
then some water to take home so that you can spray your house. You also drink
the water at home.

This passage describes the powers of Reverend Xaba. If a person wanted
to go to Reverend Xaba, usually a member of the church took the person to
him. By visually examining and talking to the patient, Reverend Xaba was able
to discern the sickness or malady and to recommend the standard treatment
of using blessed water for drinking, vomiting, enemas, and bathing. These
treatments emerged as a response to decades of neglected health services for
black South Africans. South Africa's failure to provide adequate health care for
the majority of its population influenced microlevel social relations like those
found at St. John's–Guguletu.

In Guguletu, health services available to the community included a day
clinic staffed by biomedical professionals. In the greater Cape Town area,
there were several hospitals with full professional staffs. While these hospitals
were open to all people regardless of race during the time this research was
conducted, many of them previously had a history of being only for white
South Africans. It was not possible to ascertain how the change in apartheid
policy affected black people's behavior. That is, even though these hospitals

had recently opened their doors to all races, it is difficult to determine whether those who were once forbidden their use felt comfortable enough to utilize them (Kistner 1990:2). Members of St. John's visited the day clinic in Guguletu, and some members used the hospitals in Cape Town. However, all members had an association with the healing system at St. John's. Thus, members blended health care systems, by utilizing the biomedical and popular/folk models. Members did not often explicitly mention their use of the biomedical system in interviews, and their references to doctors were usually implicit. For example, Nyawuza mentioned that he had taken medicine received from the clinic, but when he did not get relief, he went to Reverend Xaba. He then acknowledged that the cord that Reverend Xaba had given him to put around his neck had eased his pain.

The treatment of disease at St. John's Church consisted of five key ritual acts that used prayed water: drinking the blessed water, inducing vomiting, administering enemas, bathing with the water, and spraying blessed water to remove evil spirits. Harriet Ngubane's research among Zulu-speaking black South Africans in Natal indicates that some Zulu- and Xhosa-speaking peoples in Natal used similar procedures to relieve disorders. For example, Zulu-speaking people used liquid herbal medicine for enemas because they believed that it would draw harmful substances from internal abdominal organs. They also treated painful menstruation and barrenness in this manner, using specific roots for each condition (Ngubane 1977:107–8). St. John's members used water and ash for a similar purpose.

The presentation of sickness at St. John's initiated a decisive course of treatment. Ngubane provides data about the way in which Zulu-speaking people used popular healing to relieve disorders without utilizing the formal institutions of biomedicine or its representatives. The members of St. John's used similar techniques for all sicknesses, thus creating a health care system that incorporated religious ritual procedures to restore health to the sick. A comparison of Ngubane's work among Zulu healers and my work with St. John's members shows that similar rituals are used by secular healers and those who work within the church. It also demonstrates that St. John's members use African religion and African cultural features in their cosmology even as their rituals stand within a Christian framework.

In this chapter I have investigated critically the relation between health care and South African indigenous approaches to illness and well-being during the apartheid and immediate post-apartheid eras. While St. John's Apostolic Faith Mission Church members employed both medicine based on biological indicators and that based on indigenous treatments for illness and healing relative to environmental and religious factors, it is the latter approach that permeated the worldview and practical ritual remedies of poor black South African members of St. John's. Therefore I have argued that an analysis of the sickness-health dynamic for nonelites in South Africa has to take seriously the pervasive reliance upon nonbiomedical ways of life, especially the symbolic and repetitive deployment of religious rituals as the site of both resistance against the macromeanings of apartheid and the creation of "spiritual" space conducive to the well-being of the most marginalized sectors of South African society.

CHAPTER 7

Conclusions

The principal goal of this book was to examine the relationship between the daily lives of poor black South Africans who are members of St. John's Apostolic Faith Mission Church and the rituals they perform in order to survive in the historical context of apartheid and post-apartheid South Africa. The study focused on healing in microlevel social relations and its transformative role in the daily lives of St. John's members; these rituals empowered them to persevere in macrolevel apartheid space. I have drawn several major conclusions from the fieldwork.

First, South African history reveals that the macrostructures that developed to give advantage to white South Africans are the same macrostructures that guaranteed the underdevelopment of African, Asian, and Colored communities in South Africa, and that these macrostructures are a direct outgrowth of the culture, bias, and history that white South Africans brought with them from their European origins. From the time these Europeans set foot upon southern African soil and encountered indigenous peoples, they promoted dependence among them, which served to limit the development of black South Africans. Successive South African governments dictated that economic profits from the labor of exploited black South Africans should be diverted to benefit the country's privileged and developed minority—white South Africans.[1] Of the many consequences of underdevelopment that black South Africans suffered, perhaps the most extreme were in the area of health care. Comaroff and Comaroff write about the role of black South Africans in the global economy and the renaming of symbolic meaning: "Our own evidence shows that the incorporation of black South Africans into a world economy did not simply erode difference or spawn rationalized, homogenous worlds. Money and commodities, literacy and Christendom challenged local symbols, threatening to convert them into a universal currency. But precisely because the cross, the book, and the coin were such saturated signs, they were variously and ingeniously redeployed to bear a host of new meanings as non-

Western peoples, . . . [black South Africans] fashioned their own visions of modernity" (Comaroff and Comaroff 1992:5).

Macrolevel events influenced microlevel cultural forms in South Africa. Years of social, political, and economic dynamics laid the foundation for local communities of black South Africans to create meaning for their lives by developing their own cultural forms. St. John's Church is one expression of the way black South Africans redeployed signs and created their own local histories (Comaroff and Comaroff 1992:5). St. John's represents a particular microlevel expression that helped black South Africans negotiate the material social process in which they were entrenched.

Second, poor black South Africans have developed healing rituals to reorient, and, in a sense, reinvent their social reality. The history and effects of apartheid have restrained the black population, the poor in particular. The transformative nature of healing rituals has influenced whether the effects of apartheid replicated or transformed social relations. A tension exists between replication and transformation (Jean Comaroff 1985:6). St. John's adherents, as social beings, moved back and forth between acceptance of the hegemonic apartheid system and its legacy of abusive racial discrimination on the one hand and, on the other, resistance to that system. Transformation and replication are not static categories but are in fact active historical processes. Thus, the healing rituals of St. John's represented, in sacred and healing space, the processes of negotiation and renegotiation. In this way, nonelites or subordinates used the sacred space available to them to reshape secular history. Poor black people thus created a new order of social relations that permitted them to cope with a fragmented and hostile secular world.

Third, rituals of healing performed in sacred space empowered people when they entered secular space. The healing rituals utilized symbols that served as hermeneutical text to understand the world in which members lived their lives.

It is important to ask how the symbols used in St. John's rituals interfaced with the social structures and psychological processes of members' lived reality. A symbol may have many meanings; moreover, these meanings emerge from the context in which it is used, as well as from the goals of its users (V. Turner 1967:21). St. John's symbols and their meanings in macro- and microstructures are an example of oppressed people redeploying symbolic meaning to generate power on the microlevel, in spite of nearly overwhelming exterior macroforces (Comaroff and Comaroff 1992:5; Scott 1990:136–201; Chidester 1989; Kertzer 1988:17,102–24,178). The symbols, as a means for reordering social reality for St. John's members, were produced not only from the life experiences of St. John's members but also, and equally importantly, from the interaction of

116

South African ideological/intellectual, political/economic, psycho/social, and sacred/secular macrosystems.

As St. John's members entered the liminal period created by ritual and reflected in the social reality of their lives, they participated in a drama that transformed categories of domination imposed by the macrostructure into microlevel factors of existence that were life enhancing. While the macrolevel created and maintained an apartheid ideology that controlled cultural meaning on the national level, the microlevel of St. John's created rituals that contested those meanings in sacred space and negotiated new meanings that could be lived out in secular space.[2] This transformative drama used common but essential elements: water, candles, and colored fabric that protected members' bodies; and a Eucharist that protected their spiritual lives. These elements were enhanced by *umoya*, the powerful Spirit providing continuity with the past. The use of the Eucharist also reenacted acceptance of imported Christianity's symbol of a suffering Jesus, who after death was transformed into the living Christ. This powerful symbol of the suffering Jesus and resurrected Christ provided an avenue for the renewal of a suffering people in spite of life's hardships. As one St. John's member disclosed, "I used to suffer in this world and I got the bottle of water. . . . I remember how I was penniless, without food and even clothes to wear, and God brought me here."

What did the bottle of water represent for this member? Was the water a means of connection to a community of people who gave him life's physical necessities: food, clothing, and shelter? What other meaning lay in these symbols? Did the umoya-enhanced candles and staff give poor black Africans the strength to face obstacles? Were they buttressed against the life-thwarting macrolevel social structure? Indeed, the symbols employed in the rituals at St. John's expressed the paradox of life in South Africa for those who lived with the harsh realities of physical sickness and pollution of their national body, a body whose structures further impeded already difficult lives.

Healing Rituals

People who exhibited various sicknesses were usually restored by healing rituals. When people participated in the healing rituals at St. John's, they became part of a communal mutual-care network. As people personally experienced healing of physical ailments or relief from circumstances such as unemployment, they customarily became active in attending worship services, reading the Bible, attending St. John's festivals, and helping others who came to the church for healing. Thus, adherents were transformed from vulnerable individuals into members of a community through which they were healed. This movement from sickness to health took place in the sacred space of St. John's

Church. Hence, the liberating process of healing in a communal context brought the infirm person into community and provided all things necessary for the person's physical and emotional livelihood. During the span of my fieldwork, no persons left the community because they were unhappy or uncomfortable with the community context. All members whom I interviewed articulated satisfaction with the role the church had taken in their life.

The priest-healer played an important role that had liberating features for the congregation. Healers had special skills mediated through supernatural means and were therefore elevated and esteemed by the church community (Oosthuizen 1992:22–72). The relationship between healer and patient reflected a strong bond providing an ambiance conducive to the expectation that healing not only could but would occur.

The healing rituals, however, also contained confining features related to the cultural-historical reality in which St. John's members found themselves as they interacted in the secular space of apartheid. First, St. John's adherents were black and poor and had been restricted to an elementary level of education. Forced to live in African townships where violence was rampant, health care minimal, and economic demise expected, St. John's members lived on the edge of life and yet attempted to conduct themselves with dignity and esteem for self and others. Even so, their acceptance of the social limitations caused by apartheid's brutal structural castration of poor, black, and minimally educated South Africans had an acute effect on their self-image (Fanon 1966:169–70; Biko 1986:29). Some members attested in interviews that their relationships with white employers, and with white people generally, were strained. These members believed that although the devastating violence in African townships was perpetrated by blacks, ultimate responsibility for the violence lay with the whites who initiated and financed it. As one informant said, "Behind every black man who commits a crime is a white man with money."

In response to the cultural-historical reality of their lives, St. John's members developed ways to reorient life despite the externally imposed limitations. Thus, through healing rituals, they transformed the disordered environment into a purposeful and unified atmosphere at the personal and communal level. One can only admire the mastery and flexibility that engendered such ingenious responses. The community's healing rituals provided people with something for which to live.

Communal Survival Strategies Resulting from Healing Rituals

St. John's members, as "liminal personae" living in apartheid culture, were constantly at risk. Whether through chronic violence or unemployment, their sense of well-being was regularly compromised and jeopardized. Apartheid precipitated a state of uncleanliness (Douglas 1966:7–28) that was frequently manifested in sickness, violence, and systemic deprivation of those things to which white South Africans had virtually automatic access, such as land, quality housing, health care, education, and employment. The rituals of healing propelled St. John's members toward transformation and restructuralization. In a sense, the congregation represented "communitas" (Turner 1969:97), a microcosm of society that rises to oppose accommodating patterns of behavior actualized by people who are oppressed by macrolevel structures. In this instance, members contested the shared knowledge that was articulated, distributed, and controlled by apartheid society and refashioned it into a meaning system that made singular sense to them as marginalized persons. The ritual actions of Reverend Xaba, the priest-healer, and the congregation created new meaning structures as their roles represented status elevation and reversal (Turner 1969:172).[3] The healing rituals formed the core of a contesting religious movement initiated by grassroots people to protest symbolically against apartheid and empower poor people to survive in a system intended to destroy their sense of self through separate and unequal development based on race.

More specifically, the rituals provided a means for poor black South Africans to turn to a comforting community and to a respected holy leader when sickness (*ukugula*) surfaced. The healer, who lived in the same local context as the patient, provided support that could not be duplicated by an outsider (Oosthuizen 1992:70–72). When a sickness was acute, members went to clinics and hospitals, but in most cases they consulted initially with Reverend Xaba and followed his prescribed healing applications.

Another form of resistance in St. John's dissenting religion was support networks. Ramphele notes that a communal survival strategy among hostel dwellers was an "economy of affection" that included relatives, "home-people" (*amakhaya*), and acquaintances (Ramphele 1991:456). In like fashion, St. John's members developed an "economy of affection" at the church. For instance, when people were too sick to work, those who had been healed and had jobs shared their income, food, and services. Those who were well but unemployed cared for the children of those who worked. Thus, the sharing of resources, material and spiritual, was a communal benefit.

An additional survival strategy among St. John's members was the sharing of stories for strength and renewal. Since potential initiates usually came to the church in crisis, members regularly talked about the reasons they joined St. John's and their experiences of healing. Those who had been healed helped those who were inexperienced in the ways of St. John's; newcomers in crisis participated in a variety of activities that facilitated their healing process, including ritual baths, enemas, vomiting, worship services, and baptism.[4] St.

John's minimized individualism by quickly incorporating people into a community of love and support. Members believed themselves to be a transformed community because of their relationship with a liberating supernatural source. Through shared ritual activity they overcame the devastating effects of ill health and societal conditions. In so doing, members created an emancipatory space in which to exist.

Healing rituals at St. John's–Guguletu were "dialectic in a double sense" (Jean Comaroff 1985:252). First, the cultural-historical design of apartheid constructed a hegemonic system of dominance to enforce the subordination of blacks. Second, St. John's healing rituals created interaction between micro- and macrostructures of apartheid and social relations among poor black South Africans, resulting in the empowerment of St. John's members. The dynamic interplay among these factors show why St. John's founders and members rewrote and reconstructed the social expectations and symbols of the missionaries into categories meaningful to their own human experience and historical worldview; this redeployment was essential to their spiritual, psychological, and perhaps even physical survival.

St. John's healing rituals were a product of synchronous parallelism and transformation, a process that began when indigenous African beliefs first collided with expanding European colonialism (Jean Comaroff 1985:252). European colonialism initiated an apartheid culture when the newly arrived English began to dominate the colonists of Dutch descent in 1795. The Afrikaners, the descendants of the Dutch, bitterly resented English domination, and in time, when the Afrikaners came to power in 1948, they moved swiftly to oppress the majority of the population (i.e., black South Africans). They built an economic base that relied upon the wage labor of black South Africans to provide the means of production. St. John's members lived with the tyranny of this unjust economic system manufactured at the macrolevel of society.

The initial encounter between European and American missionaries and indigenous African people precipitated interaction between at least two divergent worldviews with different systems of symbolic meaning. The worldview of the indigenous African peoples in southern Africa, being more open and fluid than the European (Setiloane 1986:9–11; Gray 1990:81–84), was able to condone and absorb the symbols of the missionaries, while the missionaries tolerated and accepted little of African symbolism. However, interacting worldviews influenced each other. Missionaries came to southern Africa carrying their colonial attitudes as well as their material goods; they established a dominating presence by force and imposed religious and secular symbol systems on African peoples. The condensation of symbols, or "bricolage," depicted a boundless redeployment of signs and practice determined by people in local contexts that both created new meanings and replicated traditional meanings (Lévi-Strauss 1966:16–30; Jean Comaroff 1985:253).

St. John's Church, by indigenizing symbols received from missionaries, contesting the expected norms of imported religion, and incorporating indigenous symbols in healing rituals, "signaled dissent" when it transposed the meanings generated in the impossible social contradictions inherent in apartheid. As Jean Comaroff writes:

> The purposive act of reconstruction, on the part of the nonelite, focuses mainly on the attempt to heal dislocations at the level of experience, dislocations which derive from the failure of the prevailing sign system to provide a model for their subjectivity, for their meaningful and material being. Their existence is increasingly dominated by generalized media of exchange—money, the written word, linear time and the universal God—which fail to capture a recognizable self-image. These media circulate through communicative processes which themselves appear to marginalize peoples at the periphery; hence the major vehicles of value have come to elude their grasp. In these circumstances, efforts are made to restructure activity so as to regain a sense of control. (Jean Comaroff 1985:253)

Thus, St. John's and other African indigenous churches are a form of dissenting Christianity that redesigned the signs of orthodox Christianity and the industrial world system (Jean Comaroff 1985:253). The meaning systems reconstituted by Africans for themselves in their own sacred space allowed value to return to their lives, despite the daily devaluation they experienced in secular apartheid space.

St. John's, then, symbolized dissenting Christianity that empowered its members in sacred space so they could live emboldened lives in secular space. St. John's cosmology was a ritualized midpoint between the local order and the macrolevel world of apartheid, which drained resources and energy. The ritualized space, betwixt and between worlds, served to rejuvenate people. While the healing rituals did not reverse the powerful formal and informal structures of the apartheid macrosystem as a sociocultural form, they empowered poor black South Africans, the most vulnerable within the system, to live as liberated a life as possible under the press of the macrostructure.[5] The establishment of an institution that was independent of colonial control was an act of resistance. African peoples created a new cosmology in separate sacred space to practice religion on their own terms. Indeed, the microlevel symbolic order of St. John's healing rituals stood in stark contrast to the entrenched patterns of the macrolevel. As such, the micro-order symbols worked to disempower apartheid structures, assisted marginalized persons to assert their own self-determined religious identity, and created order in a chaotic macroworld.

St. John's and the Politics of Resistance

Were healing rituals the opiate of St. John's members? Did they pacify people, lulling them to accept lives of poverty, subservience, and oppression, in a sense permitting the macrosystem to function like a giant mother rocking its baby to sleep? Or were St. John's and other African indigenous churches firmly grounded in a *politique* of resistance, with the genius of subliminality working against the forces of apartheid, perhaps in a disguised form?[6] St. John's instilled pride in people to the point that they infrequently utilized hospitals and medical personnel. When a sickness started, members began with diagnosis and treatment by their own trusted priest-healer, an act of protest and defiance against an apartheid health care system (Kistner 1990; *Race Relations Survey* 1992:109–66). Such acts of resistance did not directly challenge the hegemonic force of the macrosystem; yet they contested and prevented the polluted system's invasion into the sacred space of St. John's.

This type of resistance cannot be discounted, although it is tacit. While apartheid affected St. John's members' perceptions of themselves as black people, it did not prevent them from creating a symbolic reality that empowered them on the microlevel and provided the tenacity for them to function in the macroworld. St. John's members had a consciousness about their race and the ways in which white people used color to determine dominance. They saw clearly and understood the mechanisms of the dominance exercised by white people. They also had a sense of the power of their rituals to transform their own lives. Thus, they created a counterhegemonic force through the use of rituals of healing.

Methodology

Henceforth, neither the experience nor the interpretive activity of the scientific researcher can be considered innocent. It becomes necessary to conceive ethnography, not as the experience and interpretation of a circumscribed "other" reality, but rather as a constructive negotiation involving at least two, and usually more, conscious, politically significant subjects. Paradigms of experience and interpretation are yielding to paradigms of discourse, of dialogue and polyphony.

— James Clifford, "On Ethnographic Authority"

Introduction

Current literature on ethnographic research methods debates the appropriateness of using "traditional" paradigms in conducting fieldwork. The issue that is most contested is the relationship between the knowledge and power of the researcher and those being studied. Who has authority over the subject matter pursued and the way it is collected and interpreted? Some scholars argue that it is necessary to examine not only the methods of inquiry, but also the elaborate social networks of power that emerge while doing research (Marcus 1986:165–93; Marcus and Fischer 1986:33–44; Clifford 1983; 1988:21–54; Clifford and Marcus 1986; Keesing (1987); Rosaldo 1989:25–45; Ramphele 1990:1–15; Comaroff and Comaroff 1992). Moreover, contemporary scholarship concerns itself with the "subject" and the politics of identity as societies include subjects who not only share histories but also are affected by race and ethnic affiliations as well as gender and class constructions (e.g., Faubion 1995; Turner 1994; Sider 1993; cf. Ashcroft, Griffiths, and Tiffin 1995).

One of the principal questions raised by these debates is: How much will the observed participate in the design, implementation, and conduct of the research of which they are the subject (Ramphele 1990)? This is a difficult question for every ethnographer, including myself. In my own case, my interest in the church in South Africa was stimulated when I visited the country in 1985 under the auspices of the Methodist Church of Southern Africa. Since my research project was with members of African indigenous churches, when I returned to South Africa in 1991, I arranged several sessions with informants, who provided invaluable input for my research design, which integrated local knowledge and the categories articulated by members of independent churches. While all informants were fluent in English, conversations with those in the Cape region were conducted in their mother tongue, Xhosa. These conversations were facilitated by my research assistant, Mrs. Barbara Mantata, an indigenous Xhosa speaker who lived in the African township of New Crossroads and who previously had done extensive fieldwork in African townships in Cape Town with Mamphela Ramphele of the University of Cape Town. Mrs. Mantata accompanied me to all informal and structured interviews. Her translations were verified by a second Xhosa-speaking research assistant, Mr. Percival Mbulelo Bhoqo, who lived in a rural Xhosa-speaking area in the Orange Free State. Mr. Bhoqo moved to Cape Town for the duration of my research.

Another forum that greatly influenced my research design was a symposium on the African indigenous church held at the Witwatersrand University, 3–5 July 1991. The research unit New Religious Movements and Indigenous Churches, sponsored by the Human Sciences Research Council under the auspices of the University of Zululand, was responsible for bringing together members and ministers of African independent churches, as well as scholars. Since this symposium was held two weeks after my arrival, I used it as an opportunity to do informal interviews to develop a schedule of questions to ask during structured interviews with members of St. John's Apostolic Faith Mission Church. The symposium accorded me a rare opportunity to meet indigenous church members and leaders as well as scholars from all over Southern Africa. It also provided a means to get input from ideas presented in papers and to have conversations with participants.

Methods Used

There are several units of analysis in this study. I used various methods so that the data base would be substantial. Thus, the data collection included:

- structured interviews/life histories of eighteen St. John's members
- an audit of the physical environment of the homes of eighteen interviewees
- a literature review of detailed material that pertained to the townships at the local government level and from the private sector

- group discussions
- observation of ritual and worship

Structured Interviews

Open-ended structured interviews were conducted in the space in which people lived. Some interviews were held in private homes, and others were held in one-room shacks located at St. John's Apostolic Faith Mission Church–Guguletu. Interviews were conducted with adherents who were available and willing to participate. I began by interviewing Reverend Xaba, the priest-healer, so that he would know the kinds of questions that I would ask members of the church. I also hoped that by interviewing him first, others might be less reluctant to be interviewed.

Interviews were set up by talking with people after Sunday worship. The times of the interview were determined by the interviewee's schedule. Often interviews had to be rescheduled because of unforeseen circumstances arising in member's lives. Since the majority of interviewees did not have telephones, I would find that an interview had been canceled only after I arrived at the designated time. All discussions were conducted in Xhosa with the aid of a research assistant.

Narratives

Interviews were conducted with eighteen members in individual and group settings. Texts from the life stories are thematically woven throughout the book, and tables that present demographic data on all eighteen appear on pages 129–132. The interviews, which utilized open-ended questions, provided information about the member's social background. This social information was added to the data on rituals in which I observed members participating. The questions attempted to bring time depth to the field of knowledge about the person; that is, I asked people to talk about their earliest memories, the people who raised them, the traditions that were part of their families of origin, experiences of births and deaths, and the religious beliefs and practices of the people who surrounded them in their early years. The life histories encouraged people to talk about what motivated them to become members of St. John's and to tell about their illness and the healing process. Interviewees were also asked to give a running commentary of a typical day in their lives— what time they got up; how they used their mornings, afternoons, and evenings; what kind of food they ate and how they obtained and prepared it, etc. (Ramphele 1991:35). Finally, I asked questions about the changes occurring in South Africa and their hopes for the future.

Appendix 1

Group Discussions

Interviews with people who lived in the one-room shacks located on church property were conducted in small groups of four to six persons. During the group interviews, I asked questions and observed the interaction among participants (Bennett and McAvity 1985). Mrs. Barbara Mantata, my research assistant, was present for all group interviews.

Observation of Living Space

Each interview included questions about other household members as well as about the physical space in which the individual lived. Generally, these questions were about the number of rooms in the house and whether there was running water and a toilet.

Search for Literature Dealing with Specific Information Related to Townships

I gathered as much information as possible about the demographics of the African townships in Cape Town. I also attempted to uncover plans for the future, projected population, unemployment figures, and so on. These data came from the city council of Cape Town, the South Africa Research Unit (SALDU) at the University of Cape Town, the Urban Foundation, and the South African Institute on Race Relations (SAIRR).

Protection of Study Participants

The political situation in South Africa, on both macro- and microlevels was quite volatile. Before each interview I read a statement of my research aims to interviewees and explained that if they wished not to participate, it was their privilege to refuse. All interviews were confidential; my research assistants were asked to abide by the code of confidentiality as well. Pseudonyms are used throughout the text for members of St. John's–Guguletu.

Analysis of Data

The data collected were subjected to qualitative analyses. The analysis employed a dialogical and polyphonic method in order to have a dialogical authorial voice (Clifford 1988:133). The "original speech"[1] included in the text was translated by Barbara Mantata and verified by Percival Mbulelo Bhoqo. As a researcher, I attempted not to be the singular voice of authority who interpreted data; instead, I used an approach that gives the voice of the informants a major role so that readers may interpret the data for themselves. I used Clifford's approach as a corrective to the limitations of interpreting culture as "text" and to take into account the "subjectivities and specific contextual overtone" (Clifford 1988:42) in data that were collected during a period of South

African history in which the laws supporting apartheid were repealed while the ideological, political, and economic structures of apartheid remained firmly entrenched in the culture.

My examination of ritual data included the analysis of symbolization on an exegetical level in light of members' interpretation. I examined symbols on an operational level, specifying how they were used ritualistically. Finally, symbols were examined in relation to other symbols to discern any emergent patterns (V. Turner 1967:51).

Data collected from structured interviews and life histories have been integrated to fill out other data. In July and August 1992, I reinterviewed several informants, repeating many of the questions asked in the period of June 1991 through January 1992. All the previously collected data were verified in the second interviews.

Theoretically speaking, my analysis used the categories of ideological/intellectual, political/economic, psycho/social, and sacred/secular space. The events that affected the lives of St. John's members never escaped the ideology of apartheid, which saturated South African society to the point that it was a deeply ingrained condition of life that was not discussed (Bourdieu 1977:87, 188; Comaroff 1985:5). Members' lives were constantly affected by the political/economic sphere of national and local concerns. The psycho/social and sacred/secular space were the dimensions over which the adherents had the most control and through which the rituals of healing were appropriated.

The use of the categories "microlevel" and "macrolevel" is of great importance in the analysis of data. Public events related to the social lives of St. John's members are examined from the microlevel.

As I conducted interviews in the homes of members in Guguletu and the adjacent townships of Crossroads, Nyanga, New Crossroads, and Langa, I became familiar not only with microlevel issues that affected the lives of people but also with macrolevel issues. The leading macrolevel issue was the level of violence in the townships of Crossroads, New Crossroads, and Nyanga. Two primary factors were catalysts for the violence. The first was the high unemployment rate and its corollary effects of lack of food, shelter, and health care. The second was the taxi war, which claimed the lives of black South Africans daily. Apartheid separated the living space of the designated "race" groups to such an extent that the taxi war was basically confined to African townships. Taxis were the means the African population used to commute to Cape Town proper. Thus, on a daily basis, people's lives were at risk as they traveled to and from work. The war had a devastating effect on the economy and the psychology of many black inhabitants of the townships.[2]

Walter Pitts's technique of the ritual frame was used to obtain "snap-shots" of the stages of ritual in action (Pitts 1989:283–285). My methodological approach to worship services was to examine the order and the parts of the service, observe the participants, and record their activities. I recorded songs and words used in rituals. I chronicled what God was called and how God was described. I also noted the kind of theology that was espoused and the way in which operational symbols, such as the Bible, water, candles, and colors were used. An analysis of operational and other symbols is presented in chapter 4.

All the services at St. John's–Guguletu were conducted in Xhosa. Church festivals that brought together St. John's members of various ethnic groups and from congregations located throughout the country were multilingual. While many people knew several languages, simultaneous translation was provided during the services.

My Task as Ethnographer

In a general sense, I viewed my task as an ethnographer, studying the lives of members and healing rituals at St. John's within the complex culture of apartheid, as asking two fundamental questions. First, how do members of St. John construct their daily lives? And second, how does the cultural system of healing found at St. John's work and what do the rituals mean to members? In order for the ethnographic enterprise to be successful, the anthropologist must be able to behave appropriately within the object community and "to learn" (Agar 1980:77). Moreover, the effective ethnographer interprets complex sequences of speech and behavior and then restates that understanding to those being studied to confirm the interpretation (Agar 1980:79). Achieving this goal involves participating in the community while remaining outside it. Ethnographers are able to build a theory of events by talking with informants to establish relationships among a series of events (Agar 1980:115). My ultimate goal as an anthropologist is to derive an ethnographic perspective from the interpretation of reality shared by St. John's members.[3] I make a structural analysis of the church in order to discover how it is organized and to observe the connections and conflicts that are ritually represented.[4]

The questions that I asked during structured interviews were designed to learn from St. John's members what various symbols meant and how they related, not only to ritual, but also to other areas of their daily lives.[5] Photography was used to record segments of rituals, and these photographs were used in the interviews to explore the semantic meaning of a particular ritual segment. Interviews included questions that addressed several themes, such as the history of the church, current concerns about South Africa, violence in the townships, the future of South Africa, networks in the local community, and work.

Table 1. Sex, Marital Status, Age, Place of Birth, Number of Surviving Children, Number of Deceased Children

Subject Number	Sex	Marital Status[1]	Age	Place of Birth	Number of Surviving Children	Number of Deceased Children
1	F	M	25	Cape Town	1	0
2	M	M	41	Transkei Willowvale	3	1
3	M	M	25	Transkei Uppper Gwadu	0	0
4	F	W	68	Northern Cape	4	0
5	F	D	56	Transkei Lady Frye	0	4
6	M	S	31	Transkei Ngqamakwe	0	0
7	F	—	—	—	—	—
8	F	W	68	Ciskei–St. Matthew	3	2
9	F	M	30	Ciskei Gxala	2	0
10	M	M	32	Transkei Mabazeal Bhaziya-township	3	0
11	F	M	26	Ciskei Mdatsane	2	0
12	F	M	74	Transkei Qumbui	2	0
13	F	M	65	Transkei Confivaba	4	6
14	F	S	43	Transkei Ngqamakwe	0	1
15	F	S	38	Transkei	2	0
16	F	M	54	Transkei Hange	2	3
17	F	S	19	Transkei	1	0
18	F	W	74	Transkei King Williams Town	4	3
19	F	S	22	Transkei Helshel	N/A	N/A
20	F	M	55	Transkei Tsomo	4	1
21	F	M	31	Transkei Confivaba	1	1

[1] Key for Marital Status: M = Married; D = Divorced; S = Single (Never Married); W = Widow/Widower

Note: Numbers 2 and 21 are married to each other. They have a daughter who was born in 1992 whose name is Songezwa. Songezwa's clan name is Thole (same as her father's).

Note: Numbers 10 and 11 are married to each other. They have a new daughter named Csisanda who was born January 4, 1994.

Table 2. Education, Employment Status, Monthly Income, Current Residence Location, Number of Rooms in Residence

Subject Number	Sex	Marital Status[1]	Education[2]	Employment Status[3]	Monthly Household Income[4]	Current Residence Location	Rooms in Residence
1	F	M	Univ (11)	U	R560	Paarl	4
2	M	M	S5	D	R370	New Crossroad	5
3	M	M	S8	E	R900	Khayalisha	2
4	F	W	S4	P	R222	Guguletu	3
5	F	D	S10	D	R500	Guguletu	4
6	M	S	S7	E	?*	St. John's	1
7	F	—	—	—	—	—	—
8	F	W	S6	P	R715	Guguletu	4
9	F	M	S5	U	R600	Guguletu	4
10	M	M	S7	U	R400*	Nyanga	2
11	F	M	S8	E	R300	Nyanga	2
12	F	M	S6	U	R295	Guguletu	4
13	F	M	S6	P	R1000	Guguletu	3
14	F	S	S5	E	R500	Guguletu	6
15	F	S	S1	E	R440	St. John's	1
16	F	S	S6	E	R560	Crossroad Unati	4
17	F	S	S6	U	0	St. John's	1
18	F	W	S6	P	R295	Guguletu	3
19	F	S	S10	U*	R150	Cape Town	7
20	F	M	S4	U	R600-R00	Crossroad	4
21	F	M	S7	U	R370	New Crossroad	5

[1] Key for Marital Status: M = Married; D = Divorced; S = Single (Never Married); W = Widow/Widower

[2] Key for Education: There are ten levels of education in South Africa called "Standards"; 11 = University.

[3] Key for Employment Status: U = Unemployed; P = Pensioner; E = Employed; D = Disabled; ?* = Income not disclosed; U* = Student

[4] Key for Monthly Household Income: The rate of exchange of South African rand to U.S. dollar in 1991 was approximately R2.8 to $1 U.S.

[5] Income is not guaranteed.

Note: Numbers 2 and 21 are married to each other. The house where they are living does not belong to them. They are living with a new member of St. John's.

Note: Numbers 10 and 11 are married to each other. Number 10 has been unemployed for seven years. The income listed is from informal employment and not guaranteed each month.

Note: Number 19 receives 150R per month from her parents who live in the Transkei.

Note: Number 16 clarified marital status; she is single. The man she was common law married to is with another woman. This happened some time ago although she did not specify when.

Note: There is a decrease in number 16's wages.

Note: The specific area of Cross Roads where number 16 lives is called Unati.

Table 3. Housing Conditions

Subject Number	Sex	Marital Status[1]	Rooms	Bed	Toilet	LISS[2]	Number Sharing Kitchen[3]
1	F	M	4	2	0	4	4
2	M	M	1	2	0	4	N/A*
3	M	M	2	1	0	2	2
4	F	W	3	2	0	4	4
5	F	D	4	4	0	12	12
6	M	S	1	2	0	4	N/A*
7	F	—	—	—	—	—	—
8	F	W	4	1	0	4	4
9	F	M	4	1	0	4	4
10	M	M	2	2	0	4	2
11	F	M	2	2	0	4	2
12	F	M	4	3	0	5	5
13	F	M	4	2	0	6	6
14	F	S	6	3	1	4	4
15	F	S	1	1	0	15	N/A*
16	F	S	4	2	1	4	4
17	F	S	1	1	0	15	N/A*
18	F	W	3	3	0	5	5
19	F	S	7	2	1	3	3
20	F	M	4	2	1	6	6
21	F	M	5	3	1	5	N/A*

[1] Key for Marital Status: M = Married; D = Divorced; S = Single (Never Married); W = Widow/Widower

[2] LISS = Number of people living in the same space

[3] Number connotes individuals sharing the same kitchen. N/A = Not applicable; * = Shack dwellers with no kitchen

Note: Numbers 2 and 21 are married to each other.

Note: Numbers 10 and 11 are married to each other.

Note: Number 16 clarified marital status; she is single. The man she was common law married to is with another woman. This happened some time ago although she did not specify when.

Note: For number 13, in addition to inside rooms, there are three shacks in the back of the house.

Note: For number 20, in addition to inside rooms, there is one shack for a son in the back of the house.

Table 4. Affiliation Prior to St. John's Membership

Subject Number	Sex	Marital Status[1]	Language	Church Affiliation (Prior to membership at St. John's)*
1	F	M	Xhosa	None
2	M	M	Xhosa	None
3	M	M	Xhosa	AME
4	F	W	Setswana	None
5	F	D	Xhosa	Methodist
6	M	S	Xhosa	Methodist
7	F	—	Xhosa	Anglican
8	F	W	Xhosa	Anglican
9	F	M	Xhosa	Old Apostolic Zion
10	M	M	Xhosa	None
11	F	M	Xhosa	Roman Catholic
12	F	M	Xhosa	Anglican
13	F	M	Xhosa	Methodist
14	F	S	Xhosa	Methodist
15	F	S	Xhosa	None
16	F	S	Xhosa	Methodist
17	F	S	Xhosa	None
18	F	W	Xhosa	Presbyterian Church of Africa
19	F	S	Sotho	None
20	F	M	Xhosa	Anglican
21	F	M	Xhosa	Anglican

* All interviewees were members of St. John's at the time interviews were conducted.

[1] Key for Marital Status: M = Married; D = Divorced; S = Single (Never Married); W = Widow/Widower

Note: Numbers 2 and 21 are married to each other.

Note: Number 16 clarified marital status; she is single. The man she was common law married to is with another woman. This happened some time ago although she did not specify when.

APPENDIX 2

Demographic Information

In addition to the eighteen members I interviewed, I also had extensive conversations with two members of the clergy.[1] Of the eighteen members interviewed, fourteen were female and four were male. The total membership of the church as recorded in the official membership ledger was forty-eight, which means that I interviewed 37.5 percent of the congregation. The average church attendance by members for the Sundays for which I collected data was eighteen. My interviews were all with active members who attended church regularly.

The average age of the members interviewed was 43.5 years (see table 1), and their average level of education was 5.7 years (see table 2). Of the eighteen members interviewed, seven were unemployed, five were employed, four were retired with pensions, and one was disabled (see table 2). One female member declined to give demographic data but happily participated in answering open-ended questions about her life in general and about the church specifically.

Seven of those interviewed were married, two were divorced, five were single (never married), and three were widowed. The marital status of one interviewee was not disclosed. All interviewees who had been or were presently married had children, as did some who had never been married (see table 1).

Fifteen of the eighteen members interviewed were born in either the Transkei or the Ciskei, the rural areas from which the overwhelming majority of St. John's congregants originate. One member was born in Cape Town and one in northern Cape Province. Seven individuals born in the Transkei and Ciskei had children who died in these rural areas, while eight born in the Transkei and Ciskei had no deceased children. All of the children of the two members born in Cape Province were living (see table 1).

My data reveal varied histories for religious affiliation. Five women and three men listed St. John's as the only church with which they had ever been affiliated. Three women and one man had been affiliated with the Methodist Church before becoming members of St. John's. Three women had been part of the Anglican Church before affiliating with St. John's. One woman had

133

belonged to the Old Apostolic Zion Church, another had been associated with the Roman Catholic Church, and yet another had been a member of the Presbyterian Church of Africa (see table 4).

Before finalizing a schedule of questions to ask members of St. John's, I conducted a series of informal pilot interviews. During these conversations with black South Africans, I learned that questions about ethnicity or "tribal group" were offensive. One woman stated very forcefully: "Linda, if you want to collect any data, you must not ask about the ethnicity of African people. People do not know you and it has been a government ploy to send people to us to divide black people in South Africa precisely along the lines of ethnicity. They [the government] say we are different because of our ethnicity. Yes, there are cultural differences between African people living in South Africa, but not enough difference to keep us divided from one another politically."

Several others supported this response; therefore, I did not ask a question about ethnicity. I did, however, ask a series of questions about language, since the language a person spoke could possibly tell me something about his or her cultural background. Of the eighteen persons interviewed, seventeen said that Xhosa was their mother tongue, that it was the language they spoke at home, and that it was the language they were most comfortable speaking. One woman who had moved to Cape Town from Bophuthatswana said that she was most comfortable speaking Setswana, the language spoken by Tswana people (see table 4).

With regard to monthly income, thirteen people had incomes from a single source or a combination of sources. These sources included formal employment, informal employment (e.g., sewing, selling goods), pensions, or earnings from family members who worked. Three persons had no monthly income. The highest monthly income was reported by a woman who did sewing for others in her spare time, earning about R310 (U.S. $124) a month; she also received a pension of R250 (U.S. $100) per month. Her husband was formally employed and earned R440 (U.S.$176) per month. This made their monthly income a total of R1000 (U.S.$400). The lowest monthly income was a widow's pension of R222 (U.S.$88.80). All those who had monthly incomes and disclosed them were female. One male who was employed refused to disclose his monthly income (see table 2).

All persons who were interviewed resided in limited physical space with several other persons to reduce expenses (see tables 2 and 3). Sometimes they shared space with family members, sometimes with church members, and sometimes with people who were neither family nor church members. Seven of the people interviewed, three male and four female, lived in one-room shacks on the church property. These shacks each had two beds and no kitchen. The inhabitants cooked on small one-burner gas stoves. Their toilets were outside. Three of the males I interviewed lived in one shack along with two other males who were not involved with this study. Four women and their children lived in another one-room shack, which stood next to the men's shack. This was a low occupancy rate for the women's shack; usually ten women and five children lived there. A married couple lived in a two-room shack in the adjacent township of Nyanga. Their home also lacked indoor plumbing, and they likewise cooked on a gas burner. One woman shared a four-room house with her family in Paarl, a city approximately twenty-five miles from Cape Town. Seven others who were interviewed lived in homes located in Guguletu. All of the homes were small. Four houses had four rooms, and the remaining three had three rooms. Usually these homes had a kitchen and a living room, with the remaining rooms being sleeping areas. All seven houses had outside toilets, and all had two beds in which several people slept, while remaining occupants slept on the floor. One four-room home had twelve occupants. Four to six persons lived in each of the other six houses. Two homes in Guguletu had a shack located in back of the main structure. Usually this was where single males slept.

APPENDIX 3

Schedule of Questions

I am conducting this interview to gather information for a research project that will culminate in a book. Extreme caution will be used to preserve your anonymity. You do not have to answer any questions that make you uncomfortable.

Date of Interview:

Sociological Information

1. Pseudonym
2. Clan Name
3. Gender: female   male
4. Date of Birth
5. Where were you born?
6. Where do you live now?
7. Home language (circle)
   Xhosa
   Zulu
   Sotho
   Tswana
   Venda
   English
   Afrikaans
   English and Afrikaans
   Other
8. What is your mother tongue?
   What language is most comfortable for you to speak?
   What language did/does your mother speak?
   What language did/does your father speak?
9. Marital Status:
   single   1

married   2
living together   3
widow/widower   4
separated   5
divorced   6
10. How many children have you had?
    How many are living?
11. Where is your family living?
    Rural/Urban/Hostel
    Multiple:
    Spouse
    Mother
    Father
    Children
    #1
    #2
    #3
    #4
    #5
12. Employment Status
    Self-employed   1
    Formal Employment   2
    Retrenched (laid off)   3
    Unemployed   4
    Pensioner   5
    Grant   6
    How long in the above status?

136

13. Level of education
- None — 1
- Standard I — 2
- Standard II — 3
- Standard III — 4
- Standard IV — 5
- Standard V — 6
- Standard VI — 7
- Standard VII — 8
- Standard VIII — 9
- Standard IX — 10
- Standard X — 11
- University — 12

14. Name of your church:
15. Religious affiliation before becoming a member of St. John's (circle)
   a. Anglican
   b. New Apostolic
   c. Old Apostolic
   d. Baptist
   e. Congregational
   f. Lutheran
   g. Methodist
   h. Dutch Reformed
   i. Pentecostal
   j. Presbyterian
   k. Roman Catholic
   l. Seventh-Day Adventist
   j. Jehovah's Witness
   k. African traditional religion
   l. Islamic
   m. Hindu
   o. other
16. Who is the founder of your church?
17. Monthly income (family)
   Self   Others
   Formal employment
   Informal sector
   Pensions
   Grants
   Other

Questions Related to Church:

1. How long have you been a Christian?
2. Were your parents Christian? Yes No If no, how would you describe their religious life?
3. What made you become a Christian?
4. Tell me how you decided to become a part of the church that you are now attending.
5. How often do you attend the church (including Sunday worship, mid-week services, prayer meetings, healing services, meetings, Bible classes)?
6. What do you like the most about your church?
7. Is there anything about your church that you do not like? Yes No If yes, please describe what it is.
8. What rituals are used in your church? When are the rituals conducted? What do the rituals mean?
9. What symbols are used in the worship services? What is the meaning of these symbols?
10. Do you do any rituals in your home? Yes No If yes, who participants in them? What are they? When do you do them?
11. Have you had visions?
12. Have you had dreams with messages?
13. Was it occupied by a vision?
14. Was it interpreted by another person?
15. Do you go to any other healers? Yes No If yes, what happened to you?
16. Are there any requirements for being a member of your church? Yes No If yes, what are they?
17. Would you describe yourself as being an active member of your church? Yes No If yes, what makes you describe yourself as such?
18. Are you happy in your church?

19. How is the church responsive to the needs of children, youth, and young adults?
20. What role do women play in the life of the church?
21. Do women feel affirmed in the church?   Yes No
If yes, how?
22. Do you feel affirmed as a woman in the church?   Yes No

Questions about Faith:

1. Does God exist? Yes No
2. What do you call God in Xhosa?
3. How do you think about God? What/Who is God in your life?
4. Does Jesus exist?   Yes No
5. Who is Jesus?
6. What do you call Jesus in Xhosa? By what other names do you call Jesus?
7. How do you think about Jesus?
8. If Jesus died on the cross, how does he live?
9. Do you have a Bible? Yes No
10. If yes, do you read it?
11. In what language is your Bible written?
12. Why do you have a Bible?
13. Does the word of God come to us in ways other than the Bible?   Yes No
If yes, in what other ways?
14. What scriptures are important for your church's ministry? What makes these scriptures important? How are these scriptures applied to your life?
15. What do you know about the Holy Spirit?
16. What have you heard about the Holy Spirit?
17. What can you tell me about being possessed by the Holy Spirit?
18. Have you ever been possessed by the Holy Spirit? Yes No

If yes, what happened?
19. What happens to people when they die?
20. What do you know about the ancestors?
21. How do the ancestors relate to the living?
22. How do the living relate to the ancestors?
23. Do you believe in the ancestors? Yes No
If yes, what do you do to let them know that you believe in them?
24. Do you believe that life continues after death?   Yes No
If yes, how does this belief affect your present life?

Questions about Childhood:

1. Tell me about the community where you lived as a child.
2. What are some of your most vivid memories of your childhood? What are your memories of major events that took place as you were growing up?
3. Did your family have any particular customs? What were they?

Questions about Daily Life/ Work:

1. Tell me how you spend your day. If you are employed, describe your day at work.
2. Tell me about the kind of work that you do. How do you spend your time at work?
3. How many hours do you work a day? How many days a week?
4. What time do you have to be at work?
5. What time do you get up in order to go to work?
6. What time do you leave home in order to get to work?
7. How do you get to work? How do you get home from work?

8. What time do you get home from work?
9. How are your children cared for when you are working?
10. Has the church responded to the child care needs of women who work?

Questions about the Future of South Africa:

1. What did Nelson Mandela's release from prison mean to you?
2. What did President De Klerk's statement on February 11, 1990 mean to you? (This was the day that the ANC and the PAC was unbanned. It is also the day that De Klerk said that Nelson Mandela would be released.)
3. In light of the abolition of apartheid laws, what are your views about the future of South Africa?
4. How would you describe the current situation in South Africa?
5. How do you feel about your country?
6. What is the cause of the violence in the townships?
7. Has the violence affected you or your family directly? Yes No
If yes, how?
8. Should the church play any role in responding to the violence? Yes No
If yes, what should the role be? If no, why not?
9. Who do you expect the next political leader of South Africa to be?

10. How has apartheid affected your life and the life of your family?
11. What does your future hold?
12. What do you hope for the future of your children?
13. Has the church helped you in dealing with the effects of apartheid on a day-to-day basis?
Yes No
If yes, how? If no, should it?
14. Are there any formal/informal societies (e.g., burial societies, etc.) in your community that assist you in any way?
15. What is the cause of the taxi war in Cape Town?
16. Does your church teach anything about politics? Yes No
If yes, what? If no, why not?
17. Do you belong to any political organization (e.g., ANC, PAC, Azapo, or trade union)?
18. How do you view Archbishop Desmond Tutu and his role in the Church?
19. What do you think of feminism?
20. What gives you the stamina to keep going in such difficult circumstances?
21. How do you relax?

Observations about Housing:

1. Is there electricity?
2. Is there indoor plumbing for water?
Yes No
If yes, for how long?
3. Is the toilet inside or outside?

Notes

Introduction

1. "Mama" or "Mother" is a term of respect used to address or refer to a mature or married African woman. In Xhosa and other South African cultures, people are greeted with titles and rarely called by first names only.

2. In Cape Town, the winter rains begin in June and continue through early to mid-August. These heavy rains are accompanied by an often fierce southeastern wind. Because there are no internal heating systems (i.e., furnaces) in homes, this cold, damp season is very chilling and uncomfortable for most visitors.

3. "Taxi rank" is local parlance for depot or station; as in a taxi stop.

4. Fifty rand (R50) was about U.S.$20. A taxi ride to the townships normally cost R2 (U.S.$.80).

5. In a city where violence was rampant, it was notable that the taxi driver assured me that I would be safe. I was quite aware of the crime statistics, particularly crime against women, and my stern response was to signal that I was not naive enough to get into a van with three men unless I felt relatively safe.

6. Details about the Cape Town taxi war may be found in chapter 1, note 26.

7. The phrase "so-called Colored" is used to indicate that the apartheid government created racial categories that separated South Africans who had natural political alliances. Many politically active so-called Coloreds considered themselves "black," because they wanted to be connected to their black ancestry and the struggle for liberation of persons of Colored, Indian, Asian, and black heritage.

8. The Group Areas Act (No. X of 1950), one of the pillars of apartheid, controlled whether a person of a particular race group could own property. It also determined where people could live and what jobs they could occupy on the basis of racial classification. This law, while amended several times by parliament, had far-reaching ramifications as communities of people were legally segregated in all spheres of life. Black Africans were the most severely oppressed, as they were the most subjugated of all the racial groups, which included, white, Coloreds, Asians, and blacks.

9. See Thomas (1997) for more on Mother Nku and the healing of sickness (*ukugula*).

10. The twelve doors represented the twelve tribes in the Hebrew Testament and the twelve disciples in the New Testament.

11. Prospect township was a black urban area located on the Witswatersrand, a geographic area in South Africa's Northern Province (formerly the Transvaal).

12. The eastern Cape of South Africa is home to Xhosa-speakers, a group to which members of St. John-Guguletu's belonged. Beginning in the 1880s, large numbers of Xhosa-speaking people migrated from rural areas of the eastern Cape to Cape Town in search of employment opportunities. See chapter 2 for more details.

13. See Thomas (1997).

14. *Tata* means "father" and is a title of respect and affection that is extended to mature men in Xhosa culture.

15. Transkei is now called the Eastern Cape Province.

16. My research documents the perpetual state of material vulnerability with which St. John's members lived; see appendix 2 for demographic information collected from informants. My data also show that a majority of my informants' expenses far exceeded their income; most risked the destruction of their homes because an open flame was their primary source of energy for light and cooking; and their children's futures were thwarted because of the cycle of poverty exacerbated by a state system established to disempower black South Africans for several generations. For sources that trace the history of poverty among black South Africans, see West (1978), Wilsworth (1980), Wilson and Ramphele (1989), *Key Indicators of Poverty* (1995); and yearly volumes of *South African Township Annual*.

17. See appendix 3 for the schedule of questions used in interviews.

18. See Scott (1990); see also Camoroff (1985).

19. Dr. Mamphela Ramphele uses the constructs "ideological/intellectual, political/economic, and psycho/social" in her study on hostel dwellers in African townships in Cape Town. See Ramphele (1993:3–10).

Chapter 1

1. That African indigenous churches (AICs) attract the socioeconomically poor is well documented. For a definition of what constitutes poverty, see *Key Indicators of Poverty* (1995). Mafeje (1975), drawing on fieldwork conducted in Langa and two rural areas in the Transkei in 1961, points out that members of AICs are invariably at the lower end of the socioeconomic scale. See Kiernan (1977a, 1985, 1994) and West (1975, 1978) for further evidence of poverty among members of AICs. See also Wilson and Mafeje (1973) and Wilsworth (1980) for strategies that poor black South Africans in townships use to survive.

2. "African" refers to black South Africans.

3. See map which appears on page xxiv.

4. African indigenous churches (AICs) are ecclesiastical institutions and denominations initiated and governed by black Africans. These institutions are variously referred to as African independent churches (Sundkler 1961a; 1961b; 1976; H. Turner 1967; West 1975; Du Toit 1980; Mosala 1985, 1989; Pato 1989), churches of the Spirit (Daneel 1989), African-initiated churches (Chidester, Tobler, and Wartten 1997;

Pretorius and Jafta 1997), and African indigenous churches (Kruss 1985; Makhubu 1988; Oosthuizen 1992, Oosthuizen and Hexham 1992). The use of African cultural forms is a distinctive feature of indigenous churches. See Fernandez (1964) for a general description of African religious movements; Beyerhaus (1969) for an approach to AICs; and Hayes (1992) for an examination of the controversy about terminology used to describe these churches.

5. See Dubb (1976) for a detailed study of an AIC in East London (Eastern Cape) founded by evangelist Nicholas B. H. Bhengu in 1950. This study of a Xhosa-speaking community brings an interesting comparison to the present book. See also Mayer (1963) for a discussion of social control and organizational principles of religious "sects" among Xhosa-speaking Africans in East London. Pretorius (1984), drawing on fieldwork conducted around Umtata, documents the historical developments of Zionism in the Transkei and presents biographical sketches of leaders. In Pretorius (1985), he continues work with Transkeian AIC members focusing on church life, beliefs and practices. In Pretorius (1987), he examines eschatological views of Transkeian Zionists. Finally, Pretorius (1993) presents data on three distinctly different Transkeian AICs and examines their social and moral issues. Pretorius argues that while the three churches are dissimilar, all three work with people in difficult social circumstances and play a significant role in the lives of their members.

6. The names of St. John's adherents are pseudonyms.

7. For more on religion as a cultural system, refer to Geertz (1973:87–125).

8. See Motlhabi (1988) and Dubow (1989) for more details about discriminatory practices prior to 1948.

9. These areas were in rural parts of the country, far away from cities, and exclusively for Africans. See Motlhabi (1988:11).

10. For an appraisal by a black South African of the effects of apartheid on the daily lives of black South Africans, see Ngubane (1963).

11. See Dubow (1989:1) for an excellent treatment of the origin of segregation in South Africa from 1919 to1936.

12. See Sundkler (1961a, 1961b, 1976); Verryn (1972); H. Turner (1967, 1977); Kruss (1985); Oosthuizen (1988); and Pauw (1995) for specific sociocultural factors that led to the emergence of indigenous churches. Etherington (1979) notes that it is critical to differentiate between independent churches rather than associate their emergence with "multi-causal" reasons. Pillay (1988) critiques sociological models that explain the emergence of AICs. Applying a missiological analysis of Pentecostalism in South Africa that draws on research among Indians in Durban and Xhosa speakers in Johannesburg, Pillay argues that the rapid growth of Pentecostalism in these communities does not point to social hardship as a casual factor for their growth. In a society in transformation, one must not adopt one theoretical framework for causality. Ranger (1986), drawing on data from over the last century, presents a cogent review of religious movements in sub-Saharan Africa that includes a case study of an AIC in South Africa. Ranger argues that theories that AICs are examples of pure religiosity and "passive false consciousness" are inadequate. A theory that takes seriously culture, religious

ideas, symbols, and ritual in religious movements comprising "counter-societies" must be developed. Moreover, this theory must move beyond "political challenges to colonialism" or Marxist categories of "false consciousness."

13. All scriptural references are from the New International Version of the Bible.

14. Though dated, Lea (1926) offers a perspective about the racially charged attitudes of missionaries toward the emergence of AICs, called the "Native Separatist Church Movement" at the time. Loram (1926) offers a description by an early missionary of the anti-European nature of "separatist churches." According to this missionary's account, the white government was broad minded and progressive toward "Native" churches, and complaints by blacks about racial discrimination were reported to have been overstated. Kiernan (1974) argues that colonial conflict or "race relations" theory is a proper and fitting reason for the formation of AICs. See Majeke (1953); Macmillan (1963); Sillery (1971); Dachs (1972); Beidelman (1982); Templin (1984); Comaroff and Comaroff (1985, 1991); see also John Comaroff (1989) and Gray (1990) for an examination of the relationship between indigenous black peoples and missionaries during the colonial period.

15. Lamola (1988) argues that the repressed history of black religion and AICs in South Africa must be proclaimed. It is a story of a liberatory heritage among black people who protested against white domination and fought zealously for the affirmation of African humanity and selfhood. Lukhaimane (1992) puts the history and development of AICs in the context of colonization, political franchise, and racism within mission churches.

16. Harold Turner has written extensively on African independent churches throughout Africa. See H. Turner (1967, 1977, 1979) and Mitchell and Turner (1966) for further information.

17. See Motlhabi (1988) for a detailed account of the history and work of national liberation movements led by Africans in South Africa.

18. The Transkei is located in the Eastern Cape Province.

19. Thembu is an ethnic subgroup among Xhosa-speaking peoples. For information about ethnic groups among Xhosa speakers, see Bundy (1988).

20. See Chirenje (1987:159) and Wilson and Thompson (1971) for more on the emergence of the African National Congress.

21. For details about the rapid growth of AICs in South Africa, see Oosthuizen (1988); Kritzinger (1993), and Claasen (1995).

22. Dr. G. C. Oosthuizen; interview by author, Durban, Natal, Republic of South Africa, 17 August 1992.

23. Lydia August, the daughter of Mother Nku, has written two unpublished histories about the founding of St. John's. See August (n.d. and 1980?) and Thomas (1997). There are other documents that detail the first split in Mother Nku's church. Petrus Johannes Masango led a group that seceded from St. John's in 1968. See Affidavit to the Supreme Court of South Africa (Transvaal Provincial Division) and Replying Affidavit to the Supreme Court of South Africa for details. Masango later became an archbishop of a branch of St. John's to which the congregation in Guguletu is related.

24. Oosthuizen interview.

25. See tables 1–4 on pages 129–132 for data on educational level, employment status, monthly income, etc. of study participants.

26. The taxi war requires additional explanation. In 1950, the Group Areas Act (No. X of 1950) forced Africans, Coloreds, Asians, and whites to live in segregated residential areas. The practical effect of the Group Areas Act was to force Africans to live the farthest away from the center city, or downtown, often at a considerable distance, while whites lived the closest. The so-called Colored and Asian populations lived in areas between Africans and whites.

Africans supplied part of the labor pool for work in downtown and outlying areas; for instance, African women worked in the homes of white families. To get to and from work, Africans were required to find public transportation. The administration of formal transportation systems was as segregated by race as every other service in South Africa, and the quality of transport services for Africans was quite inferior.

Consequently, there emerged a private, informal transportation system, the "taxis," which are minibuses that comfortably hold up to fifteen passengers. Taxis travel overlapping and alternate routes more frequently and at less cost than buses in the formal sector. Taxis make profits by providing frequent trips along routes and transporting large numbers of passengers.

In African townships in the Western Cape, two taxi companies participated in the informal network. Lagunya, a historically African-run company, originated in the 1960s. Early on, Lagunya established a firm economic base, because it was the only taxi company providing services. In the 1980s, white businessmen financed another taxi company, called Webta, which provided driving jobs for Africans living in the townships. Webta's routes overlapped with those established by Lagunya, and for the first time competition arose in the taxi market.

In 1991, the competition increased to the point that Lagunya began losing profits. Webta, because it was financed by white businessmen, paid their drivers more and put more taxis on the road. As a result of Webta's advantage, a war began between the two companies, with the community caught in the middle. Taxis were attacked by gunfire by unknown people, the homes of drivers were set on fire in the middle of the night, and minivans were often destroyed by fire. The war raged for at least a year, and many passengers were seriously injured. During the first quarter of 1992, the war ended for a brief time when Lagunya and Webta reached a settlement to continue operations in peace.

Thus, the taxi war in the African townships of Cape Town illustrates how poverty and violence were the order of the day for many black South Africans, especially those who depended on the informal transportation system.

27. The "third force," a group responsible for violence, murders, and terrorism in South Africa, apparently dates from 1986, but its activities escalated dramatically after the African National Congress (ANC), the Inkatha Freedom Party (IFP), and the South African government signed the National Peace Accord in 1991. Many suspected the South African government security forces, including the police, of being involved in this violence, along with Chief Mangosuthu Buthelezi and the IFP. The Goldstone

Commission, named after its chair, Justice Richard Goldstone, and established by the parliament a few months after the signing of the peace accord, found substantial evidence to support this suspicion. Commission investigations showed that government police and other security forces recruited, trained, and provided weapons to "hit-men" and instigated violence on trains, in migrant worker hostels, and elsewhere. The government of former President De Klerk, which denied that it instigated violence or supported those who did, was also implicated, at least to the degree that it ignored crimes committed by police and refused to investigate or prosecute such crimes. Third-force violence was apparently random, intended to create an overall climate of terror and conflict in South Africa, and was responsible for tens of thousands of murders every year. The violence corresponded to key political events such as the signing of the peace accord and De Klerk's antisanctions tours, and the group most harmed by the violence was the ANC. Because members and supporters of the ANC were frequent assassination targets, fear led to a decline in open support for the ANC and to lead major obstructions in the ANC of negotiations that would lead to the end of apartheid. The violence primarily benefited the IFP and ultraconservative and right-wing interests. It delayed the peace process and the transition to a democratic government. For more information, see Koshy (1994) and Gastrow (1995).

28. See "Violence Clouds South African Hopes," *Christian Science Monitor* (23 March 1992), sec. 2; David Beresford, "Row Grows in South Africa over Military's Role in Violence," *Guardian* (18 November 1992).

Chapter 2

1. While Africans occupied the Cape Peninsula prior to the 1840s, the arrival of the Dutch settlers in 1652 and the English in 1795, along with a series of frontier wars, pushed them to the Eastern Cape. It would be more accurate to say that in the 1840s they began to reenter the Cape Peninsula. This notion is supported by the work of scholars such as T. R. H. Davenport, who asserts: "The myth, . . . long propagated, that the Bantu-speaking peoples arrived as immigrants on the high veld of the Transvaal at the same time as the Europeans first settled in Table Bay, has been demolished as a consequence of archaeological research" (Davenport 1991:8). See also Marks (1980).

2. See Introduction, note 8, for information on the Group Areas Act.

3. "Kaffir" is a pejorative name for black Africans.

4. *Cape Argus,* 3 June 1943. While the number of unemployed Africans was 40,000, Kinkead-Weekes (1983) notes that 50,000 Africans lived in the Cape Peninsula in 1943.

5. Africans were to have work permits to seek employment in Cape Town. See *Cape Times* 16 May 1947 for details of city council attempts to deal with unemployment and Africans seeking work.

6. See Eiselen (1955). See also Goldin (1984, 1987) for a treatment of Cape Coloured political identity.

7. With the Cape Town city council working in partnership with the South African government, a systematic program was implemented to prevent African immigration and to remove Africans from the Cape Peninsula. All Africans were required to

carry a pass, which documented whether they could reside legally or move around in a particular area. Passes were similar to passports; one could be arrested and sent back to the eastern Cape if this document was not in order.

8. See Muthien (1990) for more on Coloured resistance in the Western Cape between 1939 and 1965.

9. These agencies included the South African Bureau of Race Affairs (SABRA), the Western Cape Committee for Local Native Administration (WCCLNA), and the Technical Advisory Committee (TAC). Kinkead-Weekes (1992:564) points out that WCCLNA and TAC played a surreptitious and unaccountable role in the establishment of the Coloured Labor Preference policy.

10. Deborah Posel (1991:87) notes that in 1951, Verwoerd indicated that the Department of Native Affairs, over which he had jurisdiction, would exercise supplemental constraints on employment of Africans in the Cape Peninsula.

11. See Josette Cole (1987) for the history of the Crossroads squatters camp and the defiance with which Africans fought for their right to live in the Western Cape.

12. A "black spot" was an area targeted by the South African government for demolition. All people who lived there would be forcibly expelled and exiled. See *Cape Times*, 2 October 1957, for a statement about black spots by the chairman of the Housing Committee of the Cape Town city council, Mr. C. Bakker.

13. *Cape Argus*, 26 November 1957.

14. *Pondokkies* are shacks.

15. *Cape Argus*, November 26, 1957.

16. *Cape Times*, 28 May 1958.

17. See West (1983:21) for a comparison of arrest figures in the Western Cape and major urban centers. West 1983:21 n 22 gives source material for figures.

18. See West (1983:25) for examples of procedures used in Langa courts during arrest hearings. In the examples cited, which were compiled from the files of Black Sash (a group of white women activists who worked against apartheid), fines averaged R70 or seventy days in jail.

19. See West 1983, table 4 for data comparing the number of pass arrests of African women in the Cape Peninsula with the number of such arrests in other major urban areas.

20. I am indebted to personal communications with Professors John De Gruchy (University of Cape Town, Department of Religious Studies) and H. Giliomee (University of Cape Town, Department of Political Science) on 25 September 1996, who helped me understand the nature of the Progressive Federal Party and Professor Olivier's contribution to South Africa's political history.

21. Kinkead-Weekes (1992:563–66) argues that Cape Town was a "pioneering city" in relation to the development and growth of influx control.

Chapter 3

1. See map of research area on page xxiv.

2. Tswana is one of several ethnic groups among black South Africans. Large numbers of Tswana people live in the northern part of South Africa.

3. For more detail about amafufunyana, see page 67.

4. Old Crossroads, also known as Crossroads, is a black shantytown adjacent to Guguletu. See Cole (1987) for more details.

5. Two essays explore the ways that members of AICs responded to violence in South African society from 1985 through 1994. Schoffeleers (1988) analyzes the role played by the Zion Christian Church (ZCC) in South African politics, particularly its enthusiastic response to Botha's speech at the1985 annual Easter Vigil. From this ZCC example, the writer asserts two arguments about AICs generally. First, churches that stress healing are politically conservative; and second, Zionist churches symbolize a type of "Black Apartheid" that is a response to "White Apartheid." In conclusion, Schoffeleers claims that the ZCC's rapid growth over the last twenty-five years stems from enlisting people committed to changing the violent climate in South Africa.

For an insightful essay about violence during the transitional post-apartheid era and responses of AIC members in KwaMashu, see Mohr (1991).

6. Kiernan (1977b), on the basis of work in KwaMashu, describes the dangers that AIC members confronted while riding trains between black townships in KwaMashu and central Durban. Zionists held religious services during the train rides to manage risk and tension. Banzi likewise reflects that religious belief helped him to arrive safely at his destinations.

7. The Inkatha Freedom Party existed as early as 1972 as a Zulu cultural group. In 1975, it was revitalized as a political group (Thompson 1990:191; Davenport 1991:377). During the transition period (1991–1994), it was a political rival of the ANC. It is based in Natal Province and is headed by Chief Mangosuthu Buthelezi, who serves as minister of Home Affairs in the ANC government and formerly served as the chief minister of the KwaZulu homeland. In the early 1990s, members of the ANC and the Inkatha Freedom Party clashed violently over national issues. With the release of Nelson Mandela from prison in February 1990, the conflict increased. Disagreements centered around negotiations about democracy and the future direction of South Africa.

8. De Klerk was president of the last apartheid government, which immediately preceded Mandela's presidency. De Klerk is credited with leading the Nationalist Party to end apartheid.

9. For the historical and political background of the taxi war, see chapter 1, note 26.

10. For a history on the reform and repression of Old Crossroads, see Cole (1987).

11. Matriculation is a test that a pupil must take to graduate from high school.

12. Bantustans, or homelands, were an apartheid construction whereby 13.8 percent of the total land of South Africa was set aside for various African groups for self-rule. See Egero (1991) for details.

13. The Transvaal has been renamed the Northern Province.

14. Vrystaat is located in the Orange Free State.

15. A *shebeen* is a bar where people gather to drink alcoholic beverages.

16. To be "propheted" means that a healer performs a divination rite. In Thole's case, Reverend Xaba consulted a biblical scripture, prayed, discerned, and then told Thole about his life and problems.

17. Vomiting was induced by drinking extremely large volumes of water. People

would often literally drink three gallons of water at one time. Because too much water had been ingested, vomiting eventually occurred, thereby cleansing the stomach.

18. Mother Christinah Mokotuli Nku was the founder of St. John's Apostolic Faith Mission Church; Tata Masango became the archbishop of the church after a splinter group seceded in 1968. See respective church constitutions for more details.

19. Newcastle was the district headquarters for St. John's congregations in the Cape Province in 1991. During imgidi, or festivals, members from various congregations gathered for baptisms, Communion, choir vigils, and a time of fellowship.

20. Africans who lived in rural areas were required to have special permission from the apartheid government to travel, visit, or live in cities. Because this woman did not have proper permission, she had to return to the Transkei or risk arrest.

21. Kaffir beer is sometimes called Xhosa beer. It is a home-brewed alcoholic beverage made for special occasions.

22. A "hiding" is a spanking.

23. Many girls were under the strict care of their parents. If the community thought that a girl had too much freedom, she was not respected and was thought by neighbors to be promiscuous.

24. The U.S. equivalent to standard six is the eighth grade.

25. Pass laws restricted the movement of blacks from one area to another without government approval.

26. "Location" is a term used to refer to black townships.

Chapter 4

1. See Williams (1982) and Kiernan (1994) for comparative data on healing among Zionists in Natal in the old and new South Africa.

2. See Kiernan (1990b:103) for a schematic design demonstrating the way Zionist meetings dramatize ritual cycles for issues needing resolution. The rituals create a process that shifts from uncontrol to control; disorder to order. See also Marais (1989) for a description of the relationship between the cosmology of African religion and disease (disorder) as it ties to prophecy and healing (order) in AICs.

3. Peires (1981:72), citing Kaye's manuscript, quotes Ntsikana, the Xhosa Christian prophet: "Nxele [Xhosa prophet during the 1830s] . . . is right in saying that there are two Gods, but they are not *Tayi* and *Mdalidiphu,* but *Thixo* and his son." In Peires (1989:2), Mdalidephu is called "the God of the black man." Thixo is the God of white people, and Tayi is Jesus, whom the whites murdered. According to Soga (1932:150), the pre-Christian Xhosa name for God was *u-Dali* (Creator or Supreme Being), which, Soga claims, is from the same root as *um-Dali.*

4. Drawing upon fieldwork among Zionists in Natal, Kiernan (1976a) explores the leadership of prophets and preachers. Among the Zionists, the prophet bestows specific offerings to individuals in the group. Prophets at St. John's offer spiritual advice (divination).

5. Mahlke (1991) interviews a Zulu Zionist member who is a healer. This essay examines the relationship between the Holy Spirit and the ancestors. The desires of the

ancestors and Zionist members' respect for, and acceptance of, the ancestors are discussed.

6. Reverend Xaba, the priest-healer at St. John's, died suddenly in July 1992. I returned to South Africa for his funeral, which was held on 8 August.

7. The Truth and Reconciliation Commission (TRC) began in 1996 and presented its final report in October 1998. The work of the TRC was done in three areas. The first was hearing the testimony of apartheid victims; the second was consideration of amnesty for former pro-apartheid activists; and the third was consideration of reparations for apartheid victims. While on a year's fellowship leave in South Africa in 1996, I attended a full day's hearing of testimony from apartheid victims.

8. See Matthew 26:36; Mark 14:32–41.

9. See Daneel (1984) for a cogent argument about Christology in AICs, their focus on "redemptive suffering," and the liberation of subjugated persons.

10. See Anderson (1991) for a significant exploration of the work of the Holy Spirit in AICs. AICs are "Spirit-type" churches because of *Moya* (the Holy Spirit). West (1974b) writes about "People of the Spirit" with respect to spirit possession, speaking in tongues, ecstatic dancing, healing, and exorcism. See also Sundkler (1976) for an analysis of Spirit-type churches among Zulu and Swazi groups. See Hammond-Tooke (1989) for a discussion of the "Spirit" in southern Africa.

11. Kiernan (1982), drawing on research conducted among Zulu Zionists in AICs in KwaMashu, Natal, in the late 1960s, describes the religious enthusiasm expressed in Zionist services. Dancing and "violent movement" are documented.

12. Oosthuizen (1992:44–46) describes the way AICs use water. Kiernan (1979) and Becken (1992) provide a detailed analysis of the healing practices of AICs, their use of ashes, and water.

13. Pauw refers to a prayer woman in Mlanjeni, in the Eastern Cape of South Africa, who prays over water used to sustain health (1975:262).

14. See Pauw (1975:270–78) for healing services conducted by priest-healer Mrs. Paul that include the laying on of hands.

15. See Oosthuizen (1992) and Oosthuizen and Hexham (1992) for details about rites of healing, particularly bathing, steaming, vomiting, and purgatives.

16. Daneel (1991b) designates AICs in southern Africa a "mass movement" as well as "liberation movements." In (1991a) Daneel asserts that members of AICs are keepers of the earth because they use African religious practices and enact liberation in their care for the earth. Pauw (1995) also notes that AICs have a positive response to ecological issues. Tshelane (1994) maintains that AICs are based upon a "spirituality of liberation." Kritzinger (1990) asserts that AICs are criticized for noninvolvement in worldview change but acknowledges that they play a role in transformation at the grassroots level.

17. Moripe (1993) stresses that AICs have a commitment of giving and community upliftment.

18. Peires (1981:78) argues that the Xhosa did not passively receive Christianity but chose the parts of it that they wanted and released the remainder.

19. Scholars who Pato and Goba believe have inappropriately linked the emergence of the African indigenous churches with syncretism are Kraemer (1938), Sundkler (1948:297), Luzbetak (1963), Oosthuizen (1968:xiv), Beyerhaus (1969:79), Daneel (1984:67), and Hammond-Tooke (1989:45).

20. The historical development of Christianity has always embraced the ritual practices of indigenous religions that existed prior to the arrival of Christian missionaries. For instance, the apostle Paul adopted Greek culture, and missionaries in Europe employed "pagan" rituals that resulted in celebrating the holy day of Christmas.

21. Makhubu (1988), a leader of the AIC movement, similarly argues that terms such as "sect" are insulting to members of AICs.

Chapter 5

1. According to Kiernan (1979), Zulu Zionists in Natal heal afflictions in their "curing communities" through the healing powers residing in symbols or weapons of Zion. These include special clothing and regalia, staffs, and flags. See also Williams (1982) and Oosthuizen, Edwards, Wessels, and Hexham (1988). In general, Zulu Zionists and members of St. John's have symbols that augment healing through *umoya*. Symbols such as staffs are common in both communities.

2. See Kiernan (1979:13–21), Becken (1992), Oosthuizen (1992), and Oosthuizen and Hesham (1992) for additional information on the use of water by indigenous churches.

3. See Kiernan (1994) for comparative data on healing in the new South Africa among Zulu Zionists in Natal.

4. See Mary Douglas (1966) for notions of purity and pollution.

5. Newcastle is 1,165 miles from Cape Town.

6. See Ndiokwere (1981:10) for more on independent black churches and purification of pollution.

7. For a comparison of candle use by AIC members in the Natal region, see Kiernan (1972:211–12), Ngubane (1977:115), and Dube (1991:11). Each author presents significant data about the use of candles among Zulu Christians.

8. Revelation 3 refers to "seven stars." Reverend Xaba sees the candles as stars and makes it clear, as it later speaks of stars.

9. Oosthuizen (1992:42) describes the use of staffs for healing in independent churches.

10. See Sundkler (1961a) and Kiernan (1980a) for the use of staffs among Zionists.

11. Kiernan (1991) explores the ritual significance of colors used in the religious practices of a Zionist church in Natal. Using his field work and anthropological theory, he notes the therapeutic use of color in Africa and the particular colors chosen by Zionists to express their cosmology, their situation in the world, and their reactions to that situation through healing rituals. See also Williams (1982:128, 151–52, 155–57).

12. For an anthropological study of Zionists in Swaziland for whom the color red is central, see Fogelqvist (1986). This work brings a helpful comparison to the present

study because Swazi Zionists at the Jericho Church associate red garments with mystical power. While red is associated with unresolved anomalies, it has positive attributes at the Jericho Church as well as at St. John's–Guguletu.

13. See V. Turner 1961:21 for his thesis about spiritual power and material matter.

14. The ethnography of other anthropologists who have done fieldwork in southern Africa suggests that the color white represents well-being, courage, peace, grace, and coherence (see V. Turner 1967:57; Ngubane 1977:144).

15. I drove a car to the Transkei, which is about 600 miles from Cape Town. Transportation was thus provided for me, Reverend Xaba, Mrs. Xaba, and my research assistant, Mrs. Barbara Mantata.

16. Kiernan (1980b) documents and refutes inaccuracies in Oosthuizen's earlier works that stated that the Christian Eucharist is absent in AICs. Kiernan draws on West's (1975) work in Soweto AICs, which documents that Communion is celebrated quarterly and at major festivals. As in St. John's celebration of the Eucharist, Kiernan asserts that the "Washing of Feet" precedes the "Holy Meal."

Chapter 6

1. See Mills (1983) for another anthropological perspective on healing in Guguletu. Thomas (1994) writes about healing rituals at St. John's in Guguletu. See also Heap and Ramphele (1991) for an interpretation of health care strategies of residents of hostels in the Western Cape's black townships. Ramphele (1989) analyzes gender relations in the same townships.

2. Jacklyn Cock (1980) has written an extensive text on black South African women domestics. It details macro- and microissues related to the extreme poverty of domestics and white women's role in the continuation of the cycle of economic violence against black women.

3. See Helman (1990:11–30) for an interpretation of culture and the body.

4. See Schoffeleers (1991) for a detailed comparative study of Zionist, biomedical, and traditional healing systems in southern Africa. Each system's relationship to political acquiescence is examined.

5. Oosthuizen (1990) connects the worldview found in the Hebrew Scriptures with the customs and rituals upheld in AICs. Rituals such as sacrifice, circumcision, feasts, and festivals parallel Hebrew Bible codes and practices.

6. Ramphele, personal communication, 12 August 1992.

7. For more details about testimonial requests to God, see Thomas (1997).

8. See Pauw (1975:171–72) and Brandel-Syrier (1962) for descriptions of testimony in independent African church services.

Chapter 7

1. William Roseberry (1991:149) argues that despite conflicting perspectives in dependency literature, there is a correlation between the advancement of some countries and the underdevelopment of other countries. The intention of this systemic

underdevelopment is to limit the growth of economically poor countries. Moreover, advanced countries withdraw surplus from underdeveloped countries, furthering their economic dependency. The correlation between the developed white minority and the struggling black majority in South Africa, particularly during the period of "separate development," is clear.

2. See Roseberry 1991:1–14.

3. A previously cited example from my fieldwork (which noted the way that a young man was revived and transformed by his encounter with the healing powers of the St. John's community and its priest-healer, Reverend Xaba) documents status elevation and reversal. A young, unemployed black man, with no means of economic support, joined St. John's and experienced care and community in sacred space. This experience imbued him with a new sense of self-esteem, reordered his life in a positive manner, and empowered the St. John's community, which witnessed a beneficial change in his life. The community acknowledged and supported this man's elevation and credited his changed life to a supernatural source manifesting its power in their church.

4. When a person was baptized he/she was permitted to wear a blue-and-white uniform.

5. Daneel (1983c) argues that AICs have communicated a message of liberation that is lived out in members' day-to-day lived experience. Evans et al. (1992) offer empirical evidence of the role AICs in Durban play in offering members livelihood, self-sufficiency, and autonomy.

6. The history of slavery in America is replete with examples of slaves using the sung words and phrases of spirituals and blues to serve as signals for escape from bondage (Cone 1972:8–19;133–36; Raboteau 1978:73–74, 246–50; Hopkins 1993:84–130).

Appendix 1

1. This ethnographic category, created by Harold Recinos, is intended to permit the reader to hear the worldview of the informant in his or her own words. The use of such data limits the influence of the ethnographer. Although ethnographic data are not unbiased, a method that uses the words of the informant shifts the power of the ethnographer and provides a way for informants to speak for themselves. See Recinos (1993).

2. I was able to conduct research in the townships only when my research assistant deemed that it was safe to do so. To illustrate the danger: one day as I drove to an interview with my research assistant, a taxi in front of us was attacked by gunfire. The riders in the taxi were hysterical as they fled the van while it was still in motion. I managed to make a U-turn and get out of the line of fire.

3. See Agar (1980:195).

4. See V. Turner (1967:27).

5. See appendix 3.

Appendix 2

1. In St. John's, as in many other churches, clergy are not considered or allowed to be members of local congregations. Rather, they are members of St. John's denominational clergy association.

Bibliography

Aeschliman, Donald R. 1983. "The Independent Churches of the Coloured People of the Cape Flats." Ph.D. diss., University of Cape Town.

Affidavit to the Supreme Court of South Africa (Transvaal Provincial Division). 1970. In the matter between St. John's Apostolic Faith Mission of South Africa, First Applicant, and the Board of Trustees of the St. John's Apostolic Faith Mission of South Africa, Second Applicant, and Johannes Lazarus Nku, Respondent.

African Independent Churches. 1985. *Speaking for Ourselves*. Braamfontein: Institute for Contextual Theology.

Agar, Michael H. 1980. *The Professional Stranger: An Informal Introduction to Ethnography*. Orlando, Fla.: Academic Press.

Anderson, Allan. 1991. *Moya: The Holy Spirit in an African Context*. Pretoria: Institute for Theological Research, University of South Africa.

Ashcroft, Bill, Gareth Griffiths, and Helen Tiffin, eds. 1995. *The Post-Colonial Reader*. New York: Routledge.

August, Lydia. 1980? "A History of Mother Christina Nku and St. John's Apostolic Faith Mission." Photocopy. Johannesburg.

———. N.d. "How St. John's Apostolic Faith Mission Came into Being." Unpublished family records. Evaton, Transvaal.

Barnard, Alan. 1992. *Hunters and Herders of Southern Africa*. Cambridge, England: Cambridge University Press.

Barnes, B. 1988. *The Nature of Power*. Chicago: University of Illinois Press.

Barrett, David B. 1968. *Schism and Renewal in Africa: An Analysis of Six Thousand Contemporary Religious Movements*. Nairobi: Oxford University Press.

Becken, H. J. 1971. "Healing in the African Independent Churches." *Credo* 18 (2): 14–21.

———. 1992. "With Ashes and Water: The Healing Ministry of the African Independent Churches." In *Religion and the Future: Essays in Honour of Prof. G. C. Oosthuizen*. Edited by Gerald J. Pillay. Pretoria: Human Sciences Research Council, 177–203.

Beidelman, T. O. 1982. *Colonial Evangelism*. Bloomington: Indiana University Press.

Bennett, Linda A., and Katharine McAvity. 1985. "Family Research: A Case for Interviewing Couples." In *The Psychosocial Interior of the Family*. 3d ed. Edited by Gerald Handel. New York: Aldine Publishing, 75–94.

Beyerhaus, P. 1969. "An Approach to the African Independent Church Movement." *Ministry*, no. 9: 74–80.

Biko, Steve. 1986. "The Definition of Black Consciousness." South African Students' Organization leadership training paper. In *Steve Biko: I Write What I Like.* Edited by A. Stubbs. San Francisco: Harper and Row, 48–53.

Bodow, Marilyn. 1976. "Urban Squatting in Greater Cape Town, 1939–1948." B.A. thesis, University of Cape Town.

Bourdieu, P. 1977. *Outline of a Theory of Practice.* Translated by R. Nice. Cambridge, England: Cambridge University Press.

Bozzoli, B. 1983. "Marxism, Feminism, and Southern African Studies." *Journal of Southern African Studies* 9 (2): 139–71.

Braaten, C. 1966. *History and Hermeneutics.* Philadelphia: Fortress Press.

Brandel-Syrier, Mia. 1962. *Black Woman in Search of God.* London: Lutterworth Press.

Brown, Karen McCarthy. 1991. *Mama Lola: A Vodou Priestess in Brooklyn.* Berkeley and Los Angeles: University of California Press.

Bundy, Colin. 1988. *The Rise and Fall of the South African Peasantry.* Berkeley and Los Angeles: University of California Press.

Campbell, James T. 1995. *Songs of Zion: The African Methodist Episcopal Church in the United States and South Africa.* New York: Oxford University Press.

Cell, John W. 1982. *The Highest Stage of White Supremacy: The Origins of Segregation in South Africa and the American South.* Cambridge, England: Cambridge University Press.

Chidester, David. 1988. "Religion Alive/Religious Studies Unborn?" *Journal for the Study of Religion* 1 (2): 83–93.

———. 1989. "Worldview Analysis of African Indigenous Churches." *Journal for the Study of Religion* 1 (2): 15–29.

———. 1992. "Independent Churches." In *Religions of South Africa.* London: Routledge. 112–47.

Chidester, David, Judy Tobler, and Darrel Wartten. 1997. *Christianity in South Africa: An Annotated Bibliography.* Westport, Conn.: Greenwood Press.

Chirenje, J. Mutero. 1987. *Ethiopianism and Afro-Americans in Southern Africa, 1883–1916.* Baton Rouge: Louisiana State University Press.

Claasen, Johan W. 1995. "Independents Made Dependents: African Independent Churches and Government Recognition." *Journal of Theology for Southern Africa,* no. 91: 15–34.

Clifford, James. 1983. "On Ethnographic Authority." *Representations* 1 (2): 118–46.

———. 1988. *The Predicament of Culture.* Cambridge, Mass.: Harvard University Press.

Clifford, James, and George Marcus, eds. 1986. *Writing Culture: The Poetics and Politics of Ethnography.* Berkeley and Los Angeles: University of California Press.

Cock, Jacklyn. 1980. *Maids and Madams: A Study in the Politics of Exploitation.* Johannesburg: Ravan Press.

Cole, Josette. 1987. *Crossroads: The Politics of Reform and Repression, 1976–1986.* Johannesburg: Ravan Press.

Comaroff, Jean. 1985. *Body of Power; Spirit of Resistance.* Chicago: University of Chicago Press.

Comaroff, Jean, and John Comaroff. 1985. "Christianity and Colonialism in South Africa." *American Ethnologist*, no. 13: 1–22.

———. 1991. *Of Revelation and Revolution: Christianity, Colonialism, and Consciousness in South Africa.* Vol. 1. Chicago: University of Chicago Press.

———. 1992. *Ethnography and Historical Imagination.* Boulder, Colo.: Westview Press.

Comaroff, John. 1989. "Images of Empire, Contest of Conscience: Models of Colonial Domination in South Africa." *American Ethnologist* 16 (4): 661–85.

Cone, James. 1972. *The Spirituals and the Blues: An Interpretation.* New York: Seabury Press.

———. 1974. "Black Theology and Black Liberation." In *The Challenge of Black Theology in South Africa.* Atlanta: John Knox, 48–57.

The Constitution of St. John's Apostolic Faith Mission. N.d. Masango, Republic of South Africa.

The Constitution of St. John's Apostolic Faith Mission. N.d. Nku, Republic of South Africa.

Cook, G. P. 1991. "Cape Town." In *Homes Apart: South Africa's Segregated Cities.* Edited by Anthony Lemon. Cape Town: David Philip, 26–42.

Crush, J., Alan Jeeves, and David Yudelman. 1991. *South Africa's Labor Empire.* Boulder, Colo.: Westview Press.

Dachs, Anthony J. 1972. "Missionary Imperialism: The Case of Bechuanaland." *Journal of African History* 13: 647–58.

Daneel, M. L. 1970. *Zionism and Faith-Healing in Rhodesia.* The Hague: Mouton.

———. 1983a. "Black Messianism: Corruption or Contextualization?" *Theologia Viatorium* 11 (1): 1–27.

———. 1983b. "Charismatic Healing in African Independent Churches." *Theologia Evangelica* 31 (3): 27–44.

———. 1983c. "Communication and Liberation in African Independent Churches." *Missionalia* 11 (2): 57–93.

———. 1984. "Towards a Theologia Africana? The Contribution of the Independent Churches to African Theology." *Missionalia* 12 (2): 64–89.

———. 1989. *Fambidzano: Ecumenical Movement of Zimbabwean Independent Churches.* Gweru, Zambabwe: Mambo Press.

———. 1991a. "The Liberation of Creation: African Traditional Religions and Independent Church Perspectives." *Missionalia* 19 (2): 99–121.

———. 1991b. "Toward a Sacramental Theology of the Environment in African Independent Churches." *Theologia Evangelica* 24 (2): 99–121.

Davenport, T. R. H. 1991. *South Africa: A Modern History.* London: Macmillan Academic and Professional.

De Coppet, Daniel, ed. 1992. Introduction to *Understanding Rituals.* London: Routledge.

De Gruchy, John. 1986. *The Church Struggle in South Africa.* Grand Rapids, Mich.: Eerdmans.

Douglas, Mary. 1966. *Purity and Danger.* New York: Frederick A. Praeger.

Dubb, Allie A. 1976. *Community of the Saved: An African Revivalist Church in the Eastern Cape.* Johannesburg: University of Witwatersrand Press for African Studies Institute.

Dube, S. W. 1991. "Hierophanies: A Hermeneutic Paradigm for Understanding Zionist Ritual." Paper presented at the New Religious Movements and Independent Churches conference, University of Witswatersrand, Johannesburg.

Dubow, Saul. 1989. *Racial Segregation and the Origins of Apartheid in South Africa, 1919–36.* New York: St. Martin's Press.

Du Toit, Brian M. 1980. "Religion, Ritual, and Healing among Urban Black South Africans." *Urban Anthropology* 9 (1): 21–49.

Egero, Bertil. 1991. *South Africa's Bantustans: From Dumping Grounds to Battlefronts.* Uppsala: Nordiska.

Eiselin, W. 1955. "The Coloured People and the Natives." *Journal of Racial Affairs* 6 (3): 1–19.

Eliade, Mircea. 1959. *The Sacred and the Profane.* New York: Harcourt, Brace and World.

Elphick, Richard. 1977. *Kraal and Castle: Khoikhoi and the Founding of White South Africa.* New Haven: Yale University Press.

Etherington, Norman. 1978. *Preachers, Peasants, and Politics in Southeast Africa, 1835–1880.* London: Royal Historical Society.

———. 1979. "The Historical Sociology of Independent Churches in South East Africa." *Journal of Religion in Africa* 10 (2): 108–26.

Evans, Jeremy et al. 1992. "Prophets for the Poor: African Independent Churches." *Indicator South Africa* 10 (1): 33–40.

Fallers, Lloyd A. 1965. *Bantu Bureaucracy.* Chicago: University of Chicago Press.

———. 1973. *Inequality.* Chicago: University of Chicago Press.

Fanon, Frantz. 1966. *The Wretched of the Earth.* New York: Grove Press.

Fashole-Luke, Edward W. 1974. "Ancestor Veneration and the Communion of Saints." In *New Testament Christianity for Africa and the World.* Edited by Mark E. Glasswell and Edward W. Fashole-Luke. London: Society for Promoting Christian Knowledge, 209–21.

Faubion, James D. 1995. Introduction to *Rethinking the Subject: An Anthology of Contemporary European Thought.* Edited by James D. Faubion. Boulder, Colo.: Westview Press, 1–27.

Feierman, Steven. 1985. "Struggles for Control: The Social Roots of Health and Healing in Modern Africa." *African Studies Review* 28 (2–3): 73–147.

Fernandez, James. 1964. "African Religious Movements: Types and Dynamics." *Journal of Modern African Studies* 2 (4): 531–49.

Fischer, Michael. 1984. *Toward a Third World Poetics: Seeing through Fiction and Film in the Iranian Culture Area.* New York: JAI Press.

Fisher, Miles M. 1953. *Negro Slave Songs in the United States.* New York: Citadel Press.

Fogelqvist, Anders. 1986. *The Red-Dressed Zionists: Symbols of Power in a Swazi*

Independent Church. Uppsala: Uppsala Research Reports in Cultural Anthropology. Vol. 5.

Foster, George. 1976. "Disease Etiologies in Non-Western Medical Systems." *American Anthropologist* 78: 773–82.

Gastrow, Peter. 1995. *Bargaining for Peace: South Africa and the National Peace Accord.* Washington, D.C.: United States Institute for Peace Press.

Geertz, Clifford. 1973. *The Interpretation of Cultures.* New York: Basic Books.

Genovese, Eugene D. 1972. *Roll, Jordan, Roll: The World the Slaves Made.* New York: Pantheon Books.

Giddens, Anthony. 1977. *Studies in Social and Political Theory.* New York: Hutchinson.

———. 1986. *The Constitution of Society.* Cambridge, England: Polity Press.

Giddens, Anthony, and D. Held. 1982. *Classes, Power, and Conflict.* Berkeley and Los Angeles: University of California Press.

Goba, Bonganjalo. 1988. *An Agenda for Black Theology: Hermeneutics for Social Change.* Johannesburg: Skotaville.

Goldin, Ian 1984. "Coloured Preference Politics and the Making of Coloured Political Identity in the Western Cape Region of South Africa, with Particular Reference to the Period 1948–1984" D. Phil. thesis, University of Oxford.

Goldin, Ian 1987. *Making Race: The Politics and Economics of Coloured Identity in South Africa.* London: Longman.

Gordon, Robert J. 1992. *The Bushman Myth: The Making of a Namibian Underclass.* Boulder, Colo.: Westview Press.

Gluckman, Max. 1968. *Politics, Law, and Ritual in Tribal Society.* New York: Mentor Book.

Gramsci, Antonio. 1971. *Selections from the Prison Notebooks.* Edited and translated by Quintin Hoare and Geoffrey N. Smith. New York: International Publishers.

Granelli, R., and R. Levitan. 1977. *Urban Black Housing: A Review of Existing Conditions in the Cape Peninsula with Some Guidelines for Change.* Cape Town: Urban Planning and Research Units.

Gray, Richard. 1990. *Black Christians and White Missionaries.* New Haven: Yale University Press.

Groves, C. P. 1948. *The Planting of Christianity in Africa.* Vol. 1. London: Lutterworth Press.

Hall, Martin. 1990. *Farmers, Kings, and Traders: The People of Southern Africa, 200–1860.* Chicago: University of Chicago Press.

Hammond-Tooke, W. D. 1975. "Xhosa." In *Standard Encyclopaedia of Southern Africa.* Vol. 11. Edited by D. J. Potgieter et al. Johannesburg: Nasou, 550–58.

———. 1989. "The Aetiology of Spirit in Southern Africa." In *Afro-Christian Religion and Healing in Southern Africa.* Edited by G. C. Oosthuizen et al. Lewiston, N.Y.: Edwin Mellen Press, 43–66.

Hannerz, Ulf. 1987. "The World of Creolization." *Africa* 57: 546–59.

Harding, Vincent. 1983. *There Is a River: The Black Struggle for Freedom in America.* New York: Vintage Books.

Hastings, Adrian. 1976. *African Christianity.* New York: Seabury Press.

Hayes, Stephen. 1992. "The African Independent Churches: Judgement through Terminology." *Missionalia* 20 (2): 139–46.

Heap, Marion, and Mamphela Ramphele. 1991. "The Quest for Wholeness: Health Care Strategies among the Residents of Council-Built Hostels in Cape Town." *Social Science Medical* 32 (2): 117–26.

Helman, Cecil. 1990. *Culture, Health, and Illness.* London: Wright.

Herskovits, Melville J. 1967. *The Myth of the Negro Past.* Boston: Beacon Press.

Hexham, Irving. 1981. *The Irony of Apartheid: The Struggle for National Independence of Calvinism against British Imperialism.* New York: Edwin Mellen Press.

Hirsch, E. D. 1976. *The Aims of Interpretation.* Chicago: University of Chicago Press.

Hobsbawm, Eric. 1983. "Introduction: Inventing Traditions." In *The Invention of Tradition.* Edited by Eric Hobsbawm and Terence Ranger. Cambridge, England: Cambridge University Press, 1–14.

Hobsbawm, Eric, and Terence Ranger, eds. 1983. *The Invention of Tradition.* Cambridge, England: Cambridge University Press.

Hodgson, Janet. 1982. *The God of the Xhosa.* Cape Town: Oxford University Press.

Hollenweger, Walter J. 1972. *The Pentecostals: The Charismatic Movement in the Churches.* Minneapolis: Augsburg Publishing House.

Hopkins, Dwight N. 1993. *Shoes That Fit Our Feet: Sources of a Constructive Black Theology.* Maryknoll, N.Y.: Orbis Books.

Horrell, M. 1954. *Survey of Race Relations, 1954–55.* Johannesburg: South African Institute of Race Relations.

———. 1957. *Survey of Race Relations, 1956–1957.* Johannesburg: South African Institute of Race Relations.

———. 1978. *Laws Affecting Race Relations in South Africa, 1948–1976.* Johannesburg: South African Institute of Race Relations.

———, comp. 1978. *Laws Affecting Race Relations in South Africa (1948–1976).* Johannesburg: South African Institute of Race Relations.

Inskeep, R. R. 1978. *The Peopling of Southern Africa.* Cape Town: David Philip.

Janzen, John M. 1977. "The Tradition of Renewal in Kongo Religion." In *African Religions.* Edited by Newell S. Booth. New York: NOK Publishers International, 69–116.

———. 1978. "The Comparative Study of Medical Systems as Changing Social Systems." *Social Science and Medicine* 12 (2B): 121–29.

Karis, Thomas G., and Gail M. Gerhart. 1977. *Challenge and Violence, 1953–1964.* Vol. 3 of *From Protest to Challenge: A Documentary History of African Politics in South Africa, 1882–1964.* Edited by Thomas G. Karis and Gwendolen M. Carter. Stanford: Hoover Institution Press.

Kealotswe, O. N. O. 1991. "Spiritual Healing and Traditional Medicine in Botswana." In *Afro-Christian Religion in Southern Africa.* Edited by G. C. Oosthuizen and Irving Hexham. Lewiston, N.Y.: Edwin Mellen Press, 184–90.

Keesing, Roger. 1987. "Anthropology as Interpretive Quest." *Current Anthropology* 28 (2): 161–74.

Kertzer, David I. 1988. *Ritual, Politics, and Power*. New Haven: Yale University Press.

Kiernan, James P. 1972. "Preachers, Prophets and Women in Zion: A Study of Leadership and Social Control in Some Zionist Sects in a South African Township." Ph.D. diss., University of Manchester.

———. 1974. "Where Zionists Draw the Line: A Study of Religious Exclusiveness in an African Township." *African Studies* 33 (2): 79–90.

———. 1976a. "Prophet and Preacher: An Essential Partnership in the Work of Zion." *Man* 11 (3): 356–66.

———. 1976b. "The Work of Zion: An Analysis of an African Zionist Ritual." *Africa*, no. 46: 340–56.

———. 1977a. "Poor and Puritan: An Attempt to View Zionists as a Collective Response to Urban Poverty." *African Studies* 36 (1): 31–41.

———. 1977b. "Public Transport and Private Risk: Zionism and Black Commuters in South Africa." *Journal of Anthropological Research* 33: 214–26.

———. 1979. "Salt Water and Ashes: Instruments of Curing among Zulu Zionists." *Journal of Religion in Africa* 10 (1): 13–21.

———. 1980a. "The Weapons of Zion." *Journal of Religion in Africa* 11 (2): 124–33.

———. 1980b. "Zionist Communion." *Journal of Religion in Africa* 9 (2): 124–36.

———. 1982. "Authority and Enthusiasm: The Organization of Religious Experience in Zulu Zionist Churches." In *Religious Organization and Religious Experience*. Edited by J. Davis. New York: Academic Press, 169–79.

———. 1984. "A Cesspool of Sorcery: How Zionists Visualize and Respond to the City." *Urban Anthropology* 13 (2–3) : 219–36.

———. 1985. "The New Zion." *Leadership South Africa* 4 (3): 90–98.

———. 1990a. "African and Christian: From Opposition to Mutual Accommodation." In *Christianity amidst Apartheid*. Edited by Martin Prozesky. New York: St. Martin's Press, 9–27.

———. 1990b. *The Production and Management of Therapeutic Power in Zionist Churches within a Zulu City*. Lewiston, .

———. 1990c. "Zionist Ritual." In *The Production and Management of Therapeutic Power in Zionist Churches within a Zulu City*. Lewiston, N.Y.: Edwin Mellen Press, 75–103.

———. 1991. "Wear 'n' Tear and Repair: The Colour Coding of Mystical Mending in Zulu Zionist Churches." *Africa* 61 (1): 26–39.

———. 1994. "The Healing Community and the Future of the Urban Working Class." *Journal for the Study of Religion* 7 (1): 49–64.

———. 1995. "African Independent Churches." In *Living Faiths in South Africa*. Edited by Martin Prozesky and John De Gruchy. Cape Town: David Philip, 116–28.

Kinkead-Weekes, B. 1983. "The Solution of the African Squatter Problem in the 1950s." Unpublished paper presented at the Fourth Cape Town History Workshop, University of Cape Town, June.

———. 1992. "Africans in Cape Town: State Policy and Popular Resistance, 1936–73." Ph.D. thesis, University of Cape Town.

Kistner, Ulrike. 1990. "The Role of Health in the Making of Apartheid." Paper presented at the Africa Seminar at the Centre for African Studies, University of Cape Town.

Kleinman, Arthur. 1980. *Patients and Healers in the Context of Culture.* Berkeley and Los Angeles: University of California Press.

Kleinman, Arthur, and L. H. Sung. 1979. "Why Do Indigenous Practitioners Successfully Heal?" *Social Science and Medicine,* 13B: 7–26.

Kluckhohn, Clyde. 1942. "Myths and Rituals: A General Theory." *Harvard Theological Review* 35: 45–79.

Koshy, N. 1994. "'Third Force' in South Africa." *Economic and Political Weekly* 29 (15): 847–48.

Kraak, G. 1984. *Financing of African Worker Accommodation in Cape Town.* Saldru Working Paper 164. Cape Town: Southern Africa Labour and Development Research Unit.

Kraemer, Henry. 1938. *The Christian Message in a Non-Christian World.* New York: Harper and Brothers.

Kritzinger, J. J. 1990. "African Independent Churches and Development." *Skrif en Kerk* 1 (1): 48–65.

———. 1993. "The Numbers Game: Independent Churches." *Africa Insight* 23 (4): 246–49.

Kruss, Glenda. 1985. "Religion, Class, and Culture: Indigenous Churches in South Africa, with Special Reference to Zionist-Apostolics." M.A. thesis, University of Cape Town.

Lamola, J. M. 1988. "Towards a Black Church: A Historical Investigation of the African Independent Churches as a Model." *Journal of Black Theology in South Africa* 2 (1): 5–14.

Lea, Allen. 1926. *The Native Separatist Church Movement in South Africa.* Cape Town: Juta.

Lears, T. J. Jackson. 1985. "The Concept of Cultural Hegemony: Problems and Possibilities." *American Historical Review* 90 (3): 567–93.

Lemon, Anthony, ed. 1991. *Homes Apart: South Africa's Segregated Cities.* Cape Town: David Philip.

Levine, Larry. 1977. *Black Culture and Black Consciousness.* New York: Oxford University Press.

Lévi-Strauss, Claude. 1966. *The Savage Mind.* London: Weidenfeld and Nicolson.

Lienhardt, R. G. 1961. *Divinity and Experience.* Oxford: Clarendon Press.

Lipschitz, M. 1984. *Housing and Health.* Carnegie Conference Paper 164. Cape Town.

Loram, C. T. 1926. "The Separatist Church Movement." *International Review of Missions* 15: 476–82.

Lukhaimane, E. K. 1992. "In Defence of the African Separatist and Independent Movements in South Africa." Paper presented at the Conference on People, Power, and Culture: The History of Christianity in South Africa, 1792–1992. University of the Western Cape, 12–15 August.

Luzbetak, Louis. 1963. *The Church and Cultures.* Techny, Ill.: Divine Word Publications.

Macmillan, William Miller. 1963. *Bantu, Boer, and Briton.* Westport, Conn.: Greenwood Press.

Maduro, Otto. 1982. *Religion and Social Conflict.* Maryknoll, N.Y.: Orbis Books.

Mafeje, Archie. 1975. "Religion, Class, and Ideology in South Africa." In *Religion and Social Change in Southern Africa.* Edited by M. G. Whisson and M. E. West. Cape Town: David Philip, 164–84.

Mahlke, Reiner. 1991. "'The Ancestors Have Hold on Us': An Interview with a Zulu Zionist Church Leader." *Africana Marburgensia* 24 (1): 67–71.

Majeke, Nositho. 1953. *The Role of the Missionaries in Conquest.* Johannesburg: Society of Young Africa.

Makhubu, Paul. 1988. *Who Are the Independent Churches?* Johannesburg: Skotaville.

Makosana, Solomon Victor. 1988. "Aspects of the Historical Development of Guguletu, 1958–1987, with Special Reference to Housing and Education." B.A. thesis, University of Cape Town.

Malina, Bruce. 1981. *The New Testament World: Insights from Cultural Anthropology.* Atlanta: John Knox Press.

Marais, M. 1989. "Christian Worship Movements in Africa: The Emergence of New Styles of Worship in the African Independent, Mainline, and Mission Churches." *Theologica Viatorium* 19: 93–101.

Marcus, George E. 1986. "Contemporary Problems of Ethnography in the Modern World System." In *Writing Culture: The Poetics and Politics of Ethnography.* Edited by James Clifford and George E. Marcus. Berkeley and Los Angeles: University of California Press, 165–93.

Marcus, George E., and M. Fischer. 1986. *Anthropology as Cultural Critique: An Experimental Moment in the Human Sciences.* Chicago: University of Chicago Press.

Marks, Shula. 1980. "South Africa: The Myth of the Empty Land." *History Today* 30 (1): 7–12.

Marquard, Leo. 1960. *The Peoples and Policies of South Africa.* Cape Town: Oxford University Press.

Martin, M. L. 1975. *Kimbangu: An African Prophet and His Church.* Oxford: Basil Blackwell.

Mayer, Philip. 1963. "Some Forms of Religious Organisation among Africans in a South African City." In *Urbanisation in African Social Change.* Edited by K. Little. Edinburgh: University of Edinburgh Press, 113–26.

Maylam, Paul. 1986. *A History of the African People of South Africa: From Early Iron Age to the 1970s.* Cape Town: David Philip.

Mayoral Minutes. 1898. Cape Town: City of Cape Town.

Mays, Benjamin. 1938. *The Negro's God.* New York: Atheneum.

McLaughlin, James L. 1981. "Historical Setting." In *South Africa: A Country Study.* Edited by Harold D. Nelson. Washington, D.C.: U.S. Government Printing Office, 1–62.

McVeigh, Malcolm J. 1974. *God in Africa: Conceptions of God in African Traditional Religion and Christianity.* Cape Cod, Mass.: Claude Stark.

Mills, Janet. 1983. "Health, Healing and Dis-ease in a South African Township." M.A. thesis, University of Cape Town.

Ministry in the Office of the President. *Key Indicators of Poverty in South Africa.* 1995. Reconstruction and Development Programme, October.

Mitchell, R. C., and H. W. Turner. 1966. *A Bibliography of Modern African Religious Movements.* Evanston, Ill.: Northwestern University Press.

Mohr, Matthias. 1991. "'Walking the Tightrope': Zionist Responses to a Climate of Violence." *Africana Marburgensia* 24 (1): 47–60.

Moripe, S. 1993. "The Notion of Independence and Rendering of Service to the African Independent/Indigenous Churches." *Hervormde Teologiese Studies* 49: 862–69.

Mosala, Itumeleng. 1985. "African Independent Churches: A Study in Socio-Theological Protest." In *Resistance and Hope: South African Essays in Honour of Beyers Naude.* Grand Rapids, Mich.: Eerdmans, 103–11.

———. 1989. *Race, Class, and Gender as Hermeneutical Factors in the African Independent Churches' Appropriation of the Bible: A Final Report to the Human Sciences Research Council.* Pretoria: Human Sciences Research Council, South Africa.

Motjuwadi, Stan. 1984. "Bishop Masango: From Groom to Rich Guru." *Drum Magazine,* April: 57–58.

Motlhabi, Mokgethi. 1988. *Challenge to Apartheid: Toward a Moral National Resistance.* Grand Rapids: Eerdmans.

Muthien, Yvonne. 1990. "Protest and Resistance in Cape Town, 1939–65." In *Repression and Resistance: Insider Accounts of Apartheid.* London: Hans Zell Publishers. 52–85.

Muzorewa, Gwinyai H. 1985. *The Origins and Development of African Theology.* Maryknoll, N.Y.: Orbis Books.

Nelson, Harold D., ed. 1981. *South Africa: A Country Sudy.* Washington, D.C.: U.S. Government Printing Office.

New International Version of the Holy Bible. 1978. Grand Rapids, Mich.: Zondervan Bible Publishers, 1978.

Ndiokwere, N. I. 1981. *Prophecy and Revelation: The Role of Prophets in the Independent African Churches and in Biblical Tradition.* London: Society for Promoting Christian Knowledge.

Ngubane, Harriet. 1976. "Some Notions of 'Purity' and 'Impurity' among the Zulu." *Africa* 46: 274–84.

———. 1977. *Body and Mind in Zulu Medicine: An Ethnography of Health and Disease in Nyuswa-Zulu Thought and Practice.* New York: Academic Press.

———. 1981. "Aspects of Clinical Practice and Traditional Organization of Indigenous Healers in South Africa." *Social Science Medicine* 15B: 361–65.

———. 1986. "The Predicament of the Sinister Healer." In *The Professionalisation of African Medicine.* Edited by Murray Last and G. L. Chavunduka. Manchester, England: Manchester University Press.

Ngubane, Jordan K. 1963. *An African Explains Apartheid.* New York: Frederick A. Praeger.

Omoyajowo, Joseph Akinyele. 1973. "Human Destiny, Personal Rites, and Sacrifices in African Traditional Religion." *Journal of Religious Thought* 30 (Spring-Summer): 5–15.

Oosthuizen, G. C. 1968. *Post-Christianity in Africa: A Theological and Anthropological Study.* London: Hurst.

———. 1979. *Afro-Christian Religions.* Leiden: E. J. Brill.

———. 1988. "Interpretation of Demonic Powers in Southern African Independent Churches." *Missiology* 16 (1): 3–23.

———. 1990. "Hebraic-Judaistic Tenets in the African Independent Churches (AICs) and Religious Movements in South Africa." In *South African Association of Jewish Studies: Proceedings of the Eleventh Annual Conference, 4–7 September 1988.* Durban: South African Association of Jewish Studies, 1–25.

———. 1991. "The Place of Traditional Religion in Contemporary Southern Africa." In *Afro-Christian Religion at the Grassroots in Southern Africa.* Lewiston, N.Y.: Edwin Mellen Press, 14–34.

———. 1992. *The Healer-Prophet in Afro-Christian Churches.* Leiden: E. J. Brill.

———, ed. 1986. *Religion Alive: Studies in the New Religious Movements and Indigenous Churches in Southern Africa.* Johannesburg: Hodder and Stoughton.

Oosthuizen, G. C., and Irving Hexham, eds. 1991. *Afro-Christian Religion at the Grassroots in Southern Africa.* Lewiston, N.Y.: Edwin Mellen Press.

———. 1992. *Empirical Studies of African Independent/Indigenous Churches.* Lewiston, N.Y.: Edwin Mellen Press.

Oosthuizen, G. C. et al., eds. 1988. *Afro-Christian Religion and Healing in Southern Africa.* Lewiston, N.Y.: Edwin Mellen Press.

Parkin, David. 1992. "Ritual as Spatial Direction and Bodily Division." In *Understanding Ritual.* Edited by Daniel de Coppet. London: Routledge, 11–25.

Pato, Luke. 1989. "An Authentic African Christianity: Some Methodological Considerations." In *Towards an Authentic African Christianity.* Edited by Luke Pato. Umtata: University of the Transkei, 25–36.

———. 1990. "The African Independent Churches: A Socio-Cultural Approach." *Journal of Theology for Southern Africa* 72: 24–35.

Pauw, B. A. 1974. "The Influence of Christianity." In *The Bantu-Speaking Peoples of Southern Africa.* Edited by W. H. Hammond-Tooke. London: Routledge and Kegan Paul, 415–40.

———. 1975. *Christianity and Xhosa Tradition: Belief and Ritual among Xhosa-Speaking Christians.* New York: Oxford University Press.

———. 1995. "African Independent Churches as a 'People's Response' to the Christian Message." *Journal for the Study of Religion in Southern Africa* 8 (1): 3–25.

Peires, Jeffrey B. 1981. *The House of Phalo: A History of the Xhosa People in the Days of Their Independence.* Johannesburg: Ravan Press.

———. 1989. *The Dead Will Arise: Nongqawuse and the Great Xhosa Cattle-Killing Movement of 1856–57.* Johannesburg: Ravan Press.

Pilch, John J. 1985. "Healing in Mark: A Social Science Analysis." *Biblical Theology Bulletin* 15: 142–50.

———. 1986. "The Health Care System in Matthew: A Social Science Analysis." *Biblical Theology Bulletin* 16: 102–6.

Pillay, Gerald J. 1988. "The Use of Functional-Type Theories in the Study of Independent Christian Movements: A Critique." *Neue Zeitschrift fur Misionwissenschaft* 44 (1): 125–35.

Pitts, Walter. 1989. "If You Caint Get the Boat, Take a Log: Cultural Reinterpretation in the Afro-Baptist Ritual." *American Ethnology* 16 (2): 279–93.

Posel, Deborah. 1991. *The Making of Apartheid, 1948–1961: Conflict and Compromise.* Oxford: Oxford University Press.

Pretorius, H. L. 1984. "Historical Trends in Transkeian Zionism." *Missionalia* 12 (1): 7–12.

———. 1985. *Sound the Trumpet.* Pretoria: Iswen.

———. 1987. "The New Jerusalem: Eschatological Perspectives in African Indigenous Churches." *Missionalia* 15 (1): 31–41.

———. 1993. *Ethiopia Stretches out Her Hands unto God: Aspects of Transkeian Indigenous Churches.* Pretoria: Institute for Missiological Research, University of Pretoria.

Pretorius, H., and L. Jafta. 1997. "'A Branch Springs Out': African Initiated Churches." In *Christianity in South Africa.* Edited by Richard Elphick and Rodney Davenport. Berkeley and Los Angeles: University of California Press, 211–26.

Raboteau, Albert J. 1978. *Slave Religion.* New York: Oxford University Press.

Race Relations Survey 1989/90. 1990. Johannesburg: South African Institute of Race Relations.

Race Relations Survey 1991/92. 1992. Johannesburg: South African Institute of Race Relations.

Ramphele, Mamphela Altetta. 1989. "The Dynamics of Gender Politics in the Hostels of Cape Town: Another Legacy of the South African Migrant Labour System." *Journal of Southern African Studies* 15 (3): 393–414.

———. 1990. "Participatory Research: The Myths and Realities." *Social Dynamics* 16 (2): 1–15.

———. 1991. "The Politics of Space: Life in the Migrant Labour Hostels of the Western Cape." Ph. D. diss., University of Cape Town.

———. 1993. *A Bed Called Home: Life in the Migrant Labour Hostels of Cape Town.* Athens: Ohio University Press.

Ranger, Terence. 1983. "The Invention of Tradition in Colonial Africa." In *The Invention of Tradition.* Edited by Eric Hobsbawm and Terence Ranger. Cambridge, England: Cambridge University Press, 211–62.

———. 1986. "Religious Movements and Politics in Sub-Saharan Africa." *African Studies Review* 29 (1): 1–69.

Ray, Benjamin C. 1976. "Independent Christianity." In *African Religions: Symbol, Ritual, and Community.* Englewood Cliffs, N.J.: Prentice-Hall, 192–217.

Recinos, Harold. 1993. "The Politics of Salvadorian Refugee Popular Religion." Ph.D. diss., American University.

Replying affidavit to the Supreme Court of South Africa (Transvaal Provincial Division). 1970. In the matter between St. John's Apostolic Faith Mission of South Africa, First Applicant, and the Board of Trustees of the St. John's Apostolic Faith Mission of South Africa, Second Applicant and Johannes Lazarus Nku, Respondent.

Rosaldo, Renato. 1989. *Culture and Truth: The Remaking of Social Analysis.* Boston: Beacon Press.

Roseberry, William. 1988. "Political Economy." *Annual Review of Anthropology* 17: 161–85.

———. 1989. *Anthropologies and Histories.* New Brunswick, N.J.: Rutgers University Press.

Sahliyeh, Emile, ed. 1990. *Religious Resurgence and Politics in the Contemporary World.* Albany: State University of New York Press.

Sargent, Carolyn Fishel. 1982. *The Cultural Context of Therapeutic Choice.* Dordrecht: D. Reidel Publishing.

Saunders, C. C. 1970. "Tile and the Thembu Church: Politics and Independency on the Cape Eastern Frontier in the Late Nineteenth Century." *Journal of African History* 11 (4): 553–70.

Schoffeleers, Matthew. 1988. "The Zion Christian Church and the Apartheid Regime." *Leidschrift*, no. 3: 42–57.

———. 1991. "Ritual Healing and Political Acquiescence: The Case of the Zionist Churches in Southern Africa." *Africa* 60 (1): 1–24.

Scott, James C. 1990. *Domination and the Arts of Resistance: Hidden Transcripts.* New Haven: Yale University Press.

Segar, J. 1988. "Living in Anonymity: Life in the Hostels of Cape Town." Paper presented at the annual conference of Anthropologists of Southern Africa. Rhodes University, Grahamstown.

Setiloane, Gabriel M. 1986. *African Theology: An Introduction.* Johannesburg: Skotaville.

Shorter, Aylward. 1974a. *African Culture and the Christian Church.* Maryknoll, N.Y.: Orbis Books.

———. 1974b. *Prayer in the Religious Traditions of Africa.* New York: Oxford University Press.

Sider, Gerald. 1993. *Lumee Indian Histories: Race, Ethnicity, and Indian Identity in the Southern United States.* Cambridge, England: Cambridge University Press.

Sillery, Anthony. 1971. *John Mackenzie of Bechuanaland, 1835–1899: A Study of Humanitarian Imperialism.* Cape Town: A. A. Balkema.

Soga, John Henderson. 1932. *The Ama-Xosa: Life and Customs.* Lovedale: Lovedale Press.

South African Township Annual. 1992. Rivonia: Industrial Relations Research Survey.

Stewart, Charles, and Rosalind Shaw, eds. 1994. *Syncretism/Anti-Syncretism: The Politics of Religious Synthesis.* New York: Routledge.

Stocking, George W., ed. 1983. *Observers Observed: Essays on Ethnographic Fieldwork.* Madison: University of Wisconsin Press.

Stoler, Ann Laura. 1991. "Carnal Knowledge and Imperial Power: Gender, Race, and Morality in Colonial Asia." In *Gender at the Crossroads of Knowledge: Feminism in the Postmodern Era.* Edited by Micaela Di Leonardo. Berkeley and Los Angeles: University of California Press, 51–101.

Sundkler, B. G. M. 1948. *Bantu Prophets in South Africa.* London: Lutterworth.

———. 1961a. *Bantu Prophets in South Africa.* 2d ed. London: Oxford University Press.

———. 1961b. "The Concept of Christianity in the African Independent Churches." *African Studies* 20: 203–13.

———. 1976. *Zulu Zion and Some Swazi Zionists.* London: Oxford University Press.

Templin, J. Alton. 1984. *Ideology on a Frontier.* Westport, Conn.: Greenwood Press.

Thomas, C. 1987. "Conflicts and Their Resolution in Guguletu Migrant Hostels: A Study of the Role of the Western Cape Hostel Dwellers Association." B.A. thesis, University of Cape Town.

Thomas, G. C. 1981. "The Social Background of Childhood Nutrition in the Ciskei." *Social Science Medical* 15A: 551–55.

Thomas, Linda E. 1994. "African Indigenous Churches as a Source of Socio-Political Transformation in South Africa." *Africa Today* 41 (1): 39–56.

———. 1997. "Christina Nku: A Woman at the Center of Healing Her Nation." In *Embracing the Spirit: Womanist Perspectives on Hope, Salvation, and Transformation.* Edited by Emilie Townes. Maryknoll, N.Y.: Orbis Books, 57–71.

Thompson, Leonard. 1990. *A History of South Africa.* New Haven: Yale University Press.

Thornton, R. 1988. "Culture." In *South African Keywords.* Edited by E. Boonzaier and John Sharp. Cape Town: David Philip, 17–28.

Tshelane, Sipho. 1994. "The Witness of the African Indigenous Churches in South Africa." *International Review of Missions* 83: 173–78.

Turner, Harold. 1967. *African Independent Churches.* Vols. 1 and 2. Oxford: Clarendon Press.

———. 1977. "Independent Churches of African Origin and Form." *Concilium* 106: 105–11.

———. 1979. *Religious Innovation in Africa.* Boston: G. K. Hall.

Turner, Terence. 1994. "Anthropology and Multiculturalism." *Cultural Anthropology,* no. 8: 411–29.

Turner, Victor W. 1961. *Ndembu Divination: Its Symbolism & Techniques.* Manchester: Rhodes-Livingstone Institute, Manchester University; New York: Humanities Press.

———. 1967. *The Forest of Symbols: Aspects of Ndembu Ritual.* Ithaca: Cornell University Press.

———. 1968. *The Drums of Affliction.* Oxford: Clarendon Press.

———. 1969. *The Ritual Process.* London: Routledge and Kegan Paul.

————. 1974 *Dramas, Fields, and Metaphors: Symbolic Action in Human Society.* Ithaca: Cornell University Press.

————. 1982. "Dramatic Ritual/Ritual Drama: Performative and Reflexive Anthropology." In *A Crack in the Mirror.* Edited by Jay Rubin. Philadelphia: University of Pennsylvania Press, 83–97.

Van Jaarsveld, F. A. 1975. *From Van Riebeeck to Vorster, 1652–1974.* Johannesburg: Perskor Publishers.

Verryn, Trevor D. 1972. *A History of the Order of Ethiopia.* Cleveland, Ohio: Central Mission Press.

Vilakazi, Absolom. 1962. *Zulu Transformations.* Pietermaritzburg: University of Natal Press.

————. 1986. *Shembe: The Revitalization of African Society.* Johannesburg: Skotaville.

Villa-Vicencio, Charles. 1988. *Trapped in Apartheid.* Maryknoll, N.Y.: Orbis Books.

Weber, Max. 1947. *The Theory of Economic and Social Organization.* Edited by T. Parsons. New York: Oxford University Press.

West, Martin E. 1974a. "Independence and Unity: Problems of Co-operation between African Independent Church Leaders in Soweto." *African Studies* 33 (2): 121–29.

————. 1974b. "People of the Spirit: The Charismatic Movement among African Independent Churches." *Journal of Theology for Southern Africa* 7: 23–29.

————. 1975. *Bishops and Prophets in a Black City.* Cape Town: David Philip.

————. 1978. "Poverty and Relative Deprivation in African Independent Churches." In *Affluence, Poverty, and the Word of God.* Edited by K. Nurnberger. Durban: Lutheran Publishing House, 241–46.

————. 1983. "Influx Control in the Cape Peninsula." South African Labour and Development Research Unit Work Paper 50. Cape Town, Saldru: 15–36.

————. 1988. "Confusing Categories: Population Groups, National States and Citizenship." In *South African Key Words.* Edited by E. Boonzaier and John Sharp. Cape Town: David Philip, 100–110.

Western, John. 1996. *Outcast Cape Town.* Berkeley and Los Angeles: University of California Press.

Williams, Charles S. 1982. "Ritual Healing and Holistic Medicine among Zulu Zionists." Ph.D. diss., American University.

Wilson, Francis, and Mamphela Altetta Ramphele. 1989. *Uprooting Poverty: The South African Challenge.* Cape Town: David Philip.

Wilson, Monica Hunter. 1961. *Reaction to Conquest.* London: Oxford University Press.

Wilson, Monica. 1969. "Co-operation and Conflict: The Eastern Cape Frontier." In *The Oxford History of South Africa.* Vol. 1. Edited by Monica Wilson and Leonard Thompson. London: Oxford University Press, 233–71.

————. 1971. *Religion and the Transformation of Society.* Cambridge, England: Cambridge University Press.

Wilson, Monica, and Archie Mafeje. 1973. *Langa: A Study of Social Groups in an African Township.* Cape Town: Oxford University Press.

Wilson, Monica, and Leonard Thompson, eds. 1969. *The Oxford History of South Africa*. Vol. 1. London: Oxford University Press.

———. 1971. *The Oxford History of South Africa*. Vol. 2. London: Oxford University Press.

Wilsworth, Mercia Joan. 1980. *Strategies for Survival: Transcending the Culture of Poverty in a Black South African Township*. Occasional Paper 24. Institute of Social and Economic Research, Rhodes University, Grahamstown.

Worsley, Peter. 1982. "Non-Western Medical Systems." *Annual Review of Anthropology* 11: 315–48.

Index

African indigenous churches (AICs), 1, 13, 14, 15, 16–20, 32, 35, 68, 69, 78, 79, 80–85, 122, 124, 142n. 1, 142n. 4, 143n. 5, 143n. 12, 144n.14, 144n. 15, 144n. 16, 144n. 22, 148n. 5, 148n. 6, 149n.2, 150n. 9, 150n. 10, 150n. 11, 150n. 12, 150n. 16, 151n. 19, 151n. 21, 152n. 5, 153n. 5

African National Congress, 19, 27, 33, 42, 68, 144n. 20

African nationalism, 18, 19

African townships: Blouvlei, 26; Crossroads, 11, 23, 127, 147n. 11; Guguletu, 1, 2, 3, 4, 6, 11, 13, 15, 20, 22–32, 34, 36, 37, 48, 53, 64, 103, 104, 112, 113, 127, 135, 144n. 23; Khayelitsha, 11, 23, 30, 32, 40, 42; Langa, 3, 11, 23, 24, 27, 28, 29, 31, 37, 41, 127, 147n. 18; Ndabeni, 23; New Crossroads, 11, 23, 124, 127; Nyanga, 11, 23, 26, 27, 28, 37, 42, 135; Old Crossroads, 37, 40, 41; Uitvlugt, 23; Windermere, 26, 27

Amafufunyana, 36, 67,

ancestors, 6, 7, 9, 35, 54, 55–57, 59, 64, 65, 66–67, 85, 101, 106, 138, 149n. 5

animal sacrifice, 6, 9, 56, 58, 67

Anna, Mother, 93

antiapartheid movement, 14

apartheid, 7, 8, 9, 13, 14

August, Lydia, 69, 79

Bantustan policy, 42, 148n. 12. See also homelands; reserves

Banzi, 36, 38, 39, 40, 42, 43, 44, 59

baptized, baptism, 6, 16, 49, 87, 91, 93, 112, 119, 149n. 19, 153n. 4

bath, 50, 51, 52, 53, 54, 75, 76, 87, 89, 104, 107, 110, 112–13, 119

Becken, H. J., 81

Beliqoco, Ndsilibe, 37

Beliqoco, Yoliswa, 37

Bethesda, 102–3

Bhoqo, Percival Mbulelo, 124, 126

Bible, 50, 51, 56, 64, 65, 72, 77, 80, 85, 99–103, 105, 109, 110, 112, 117, 128, 137, 138

black spots 26, 147n. 13. See also forced removals

burial association, 57

candles, 51, 86, 89–90, 94, 104, 117, 128, 151n. 7, 151n. 8

canopy, 6, 8, 15, 55, 61, 75, 87, 88–90, 112

Cape Colored Preference Policy, 24–26, 30, 32

Cell, John W., 17

Chidester, David, 82

children, 6, 7, 8, 20, 26, 27, 31, 34, 37, 40, 41, 42, 44, 45, 46, 49, 50, 51, 52, 54, 55, 57–58, 59, 61, 68–69, 76, 86, 88, 97, 103, 104, 107, 119, 133, 138, 139; housing, 45; schools, 20, 40

circumcision, 58

Ciskei, 24, 27, 31, 37, 97, 133

civil rights movement, 9

clan, 7, 27, 38, 66

color symbolism, 90–93, 151n. 11, 151n. 12, 152n. 14

Comaroff, Jean, 7, 120, 121

Comaroff, Jean and John, 115

Communion (Eucharist), 6, 55, 93, 117, 149n. 19

De Gruchy, John, 19, 147n. 20
De Klerk 39, 43, 139, 148n. 8
divination, diviner, 9, 36, 49, 64, 65, 66, 90, 100, 106, 108, 112
domestic, domestic worker, 33, 37, 44, 45, 50, 58, 76, 97
dreams, 54, 56, 57, 67, 91, 108, 110, 137
Dubow, Saul, 17, 143n. 8, 143n. 11

Easter, 69
education, 7, 19, 20, 37, 40, 41, 58, 59, 86, 118, 119, 133
Eliade, M., 86
emergency camps, 27, 32
employment, 20, 22, 24, 25, 26, 29, 31, 32, 33, 35, 37, 38, 40, 41, 42, 43–46, 49, 76, 79, 104, 109, 111, 119, 133, 134, 136, 138, 146n. 5. *See also* labor conditions
enema, 51, 52, 53, 55, 75, 76, 87, 89, 104, 105, 106, 107, 110, 112, 113, 119
Ethiopian Church, 19
Eucharist, 93–94, 117, 152n.16. *See also* Communion
evangelist, 37
evil spirits, 54, 56, 67, 76, 90, 107, 113
exile(s), 43

family, families, 8, 16, 21, 26, 31, 38, 41, 44, 45, 46, 47, 53, 56, 57–58, 60, 66, 67, 68, 76, 86, 96, 100, 105, 109, 125, 134, 136
festivals, 6, 51, 52, 69, 92, 93, 117, 128
forced removals, 22, 23, 25, 26–27, 32
Foster, George, 108
future, 39, 41, 59–61, 65, 68–69, 86, 125, 126, 139

Golden, Ian, 26
Group Areas Act, 4, 22, 24, 26, 38, 141n. 8

Hastings, Adrian, 80
healing process, 35, 50–59, 87–89
Hexham, Irving, 19
homelands, 11, 33. *See also* Bantustan policy; reserves

Horrell, M., 26
hostel, 29, 37, 39, 119

Ibandla LaseTiyopiya. *See* Ethiopian Church
imigidi, 51. *See also* umgidi
Indongo yokuphilisa, 90
infertility, 6, 50, 107, 108
influx control, 11, 22, 23–24, 25, 26–27, 30–31, 32, 97
initiation rites, 12, 27, 35, 58
Inkatha, 39, 148n. 7
Isiwasho, 87

Janzen, John, 109
Jesus, 7, 17, 64, 68–71, 74, 75, 93, 102–3, 117, 138
Johannesburg, 38, 43, 52
Joxo, 40, 43, 44, 45, 46, 48–49, 53–54, 56, 58, 66, 100

Kiernan, James, 90, 144n. 14
Kleinman, Arthur, 98–99

labor conditions, 42, 43–46, 115, 120, 138; strike, 39; surplus, 33, 43; trade unions, 80, 139; wages, 31, 32, 33, 39, 41, 43, 44, 45, 120
lake (ichibi), 54, 55, 74, 88, 92, 112
liquor outlets, 29
liturgical, 5, 51, 52, 63, 80

Madlebe, Mr., 27
Makosana, Solomon, 26
Mama Ntiliti, 4, 36
Manata, Barbara, 11, 124, 126
Mandela, Nelson, 20, 33, 34, 39, 42–43, 61, 139
Mantolo, 67
Masango, Petrus Johannes, 6, 49, 51, 55, 92, 93, 144n. 23, 149n. 18
Mazibula, 38, 39, 44, 45, 48, 55, 56–57, 72, 89, 90, 91, 92, 99, 112
migrant workers, 21, 28, 29, 36, 39, 96
mines, 36, 39, 43, 96–97

misfortune, 49–50, 65, 108
mission churches, 1, 70, 81
missionaries (emissaries), 17–20, 64, 83, 120–21, 144n. 14
missionary movement, 17–20
Mjoli, Mama, 72, 105
Mjoli, Tata (Reverend), 66, 72, 76, 105
Mjolis, 72, 105
Mokone, Mangena Moses, 19
Molo, 77
Mthetheleli, 37
Myria, 36

Ndongeni, 91–92
Ndsilibe, 9, 71, 107
Newcastle, 51, 52, 88
Ngubane, Harriet, 113
Njobe, 88, 91
Nku, Christina Mokotuli, 5, 6, 20, 51, 69, 81, 91, 93, 99, 101, 102, 141n. 9, 144n. 23, 149n. 18
Nonceba, 37, 73, 100
Nozipo, 39, 40, 41, 42, 44, 45, 46, 59, 60, 68, 103
Ntili, 70–71
Ntiliti, 4, 48, 49, 50, 51–3, 58, 65, 75, 88, 89
Nyawuza, 36, 65, 113

Olivier, Nicolaas J. J., 30–31
Oothuizen, G. C., 19, 80

passes and pass laws, 17, 25, 26, 42, 53, 58, 146n. 7, 149n. 25
Pato, Luke, 83–84
personal challenges, 46–47
political prisoners, 43
pondokkies, 26–27, 28
poverty, 6, 7, 8, 9, 10–11, 13, 14, 15, 20, 21, 22, 31, 32, 33, 34, 35, 39, 40, 41, 42, 44, 45, 46, 48, 55, 58, 59, 60, 61, 64, 68, 70, 79, 81, 82, 83, 86, 95, 96, 97,101, 102, 104, 114, 115, 116, 117,118, 119, 120, 121, 122, 142n. 1, n. 16, 152n. 2
power, 7, 15, 19, 49, 50, 51, 52, 56, 59, 61,
63, 64, 65, 66, 69, 70, 71, 73, 74, 75, 76, 78, 79, 82, 83, 84, 85, 87, 88, 90, 91, 92, 93, 94, 100, 102, 110, 111, 112, 116, 117, 120, 121, 122, 123, 153n. 3
pray, prayer, 6, 8, 38, 42, 45, 48, 49, 50, 51, 52, 53, 54, 55, 59, 60, 64, 67, 68, 71, 75, 77, 78, 80, 87, 88, 90, 92, 93, 102, 105, 107, 108, 109, 110, 111
priest-healer, 110, 114, 118, 119, 122, 125
prophet, prophecy, propheting, 50, 65–66, 73, 77, 90, 92, 93, 105, 110, 148n. 16, 149n. 2, 149n. 4
purification, 35, 75, 76, 87, 89

race relations, 16–20, 144n. 14, 21, 24–26, 38–42, 42–43, 44, 46, 81, 112, 127, 143n. 10, 143n. 11, 144n. 14, 144n. 15
racial discrimination, 9, 14, 15, 16–20, 24–26, 30, 31, 32, 80, 81, 96–97, 112, 116, 143n. 8, 143n. 10, 143n. 11, 144n. 14, 144n. 15. *See also* race relations; underdevelopment
racial segregation, 4, 16–20, 39, 40, 46, 112, 127, 143n. 11, 144n. 14.; examples of, 39; open universities, 43; separate development policies, 7, 46, 68. *See also* race relations; underdevelopment
racism, 9, 14, 17. *See also* race relations; racial discrimination; racial segregation
Ramphele, Mamphela, 11, 15, 102, 119, 124, 142n. 19, 152n. 6
Ranger, Terence, 143n. 12
reasons for coming to St. John's, 35, 47–50
reserves, 16. *See also* Bantustan policy
revelation, 65–66
ritual, 9, 10, 12, 13, 14, 18, 19, 21, 32, 35, 49, 50–59, 62–85, 86–94, 98, 99–102, 103, 104, 107, 109, 113, 114, 115, 116, 117–22, 125, 127, 128, 137, 149n. 2, 151n. 20, 152n. 1, 152n. 5

salt, 51, 54, 55, 87
selective conservatism, 80–82, 83, 85
sermons, 13, 74, 77–80, 85, 90, 91

Shenxane, 8, 36, 53, 92, 105

soap, 53

social networks, 103–5

South African Native Congress. *See* African National Congress

spirit (umoya), 6, 16, 54, 61, 64, 69, 71–74, 75, 78, 79, 80, 85, 88, 89–90, 100, 110, 117, 138, 149n. 5, 150n. 10

spirit possession, 9, 71–74

staff, 56, 86, 87, 90, 94, 117, 151n. 10

symbols, 5, 10, 13, 16, 17, 55, 59, 63, 70, 75, 81, 82, 83, 86–94, 111, 114, 115, 116–17, 119, 120–21, 127, 137, 144n. 12, 151n. 1

syncretism, 13, 82–85

taxi, 3, 42, 45, 48, 127, 141n.3, n.5

taxi war, 3, 20, 21, 35, 40, 42, 127, 139, 141n. 6, 145n. 26

taxonomy of sickness, 105–8

testimony, 8, 16, 51, 67, 88, 91, 99, 104, 109–10, 152n. 7

Thembisa, 37, 103

Thembu National Church, 18

third force, 21, 145n. 27

Thixo, 64, 85

Thobeka, 36, 74, 76, 100

Thole, 36, 48, 50–51, 65, 75

Thozama, 37, 76

Tile, Nehemiah, 18

Transkei, 8, 18, 24, 27, 31, 36, 37, 46, 50, 53, 57, 92, 93, 97, 133, 142n. 15, 144n. 18, 152n. 15

Truth and Reconciliation Commission, 68, 150n. 7

Tshawe, 35

tuberculosis, 29

Turner, Harold, 18, 144n. 16

Tutu, Desmond, 42, 68, 139

Urban Areas Consolidation Act, 28

Ubuntu, 7

Ukugula, 6, 8, 15, 34, 36, 38, 47–50, 52, 55, 62, 119, 141n. 9

umgidi, 6, 8, 51. *See also* festival; imigidi

underdevelopment, 7, 28, 40, 44, 46, 68, 115, 119, 152n. 1

unemployment, 6, 16, 24–26, 32, 33, 34, 37, 43–46, 49, 79, 104, 109, 111, 117, 118, 119, 126, 127, 133, 146n. 4, 145n. 5

Vilakazi, Absolom, 18

violence, 6, 8, 11, 33, 34, 35, 36, 37, 38–42, 43, 46, 59, 60, 64, 68–69, 70, 71, 78, 79, 86, 102, 118, 119, 127, 128, 139, 141n. 5, 146n. 28, 148n. 5, 148n. 6, 153n. 2

vision, 56, 57, 73, 91

vomit, 51, 53, 54, 75, 76, 87, 89, 105, 106, 107, 108, 110, 112, 113, 119, 148n. 17

water, 8, 45, 46, 52, 53, 54, 55, 75, 76, 86, 87–9, 92, 93, 94, 102–3, 105, 106, 107, 108, 110, 111, 112, 113, 117, 128, 150n. 13, 151n. 2; blessed, 9, 50, 55, 61, 74, 75, 76, 85, 87, 103, 111, 112, 113; prayed, 6, 8, 9, 55, 61, 76, 87, 113

West, Martin, 84

Wilson, Monica, 80–82, 84

women, 2, 4, 6, 25, 26, 27, 28, 30, 34, 37, 42, 44, 45, 46, 47, 49, 51, 53, 55, 66, 71, 91, 96–97, 103, 104, 105, 109, 110, 133, 138

worship services, 6, 9, 16, 27, 35, 55, 71, 77, 89, 92, 99, 103, 104, 109–110, 117, 119, 125, 128

Worsley, Peter, 108

Xaba, Mama, 1, 2, 5, 8, 11, 41, 42, 48, 75, 87–88, 111

Xaba, Tata (Reverend), 1, 2, 5, 8, 16, 35, 36, 48, 49, 50, 51, 52, 53, 65, 72, 74, 75, 76, 77–79, 85, 87–88, 90, 91–92, 93, 100–103, 104, 109–14, 119, 125, 150n. 6

Xhosa beer, 54, 56, 149n. 21

Xhosa religion, 63–65

Xhosa sickness (illness), 9, 49, 106

Xolisa, 37

Yoliswa, 110–11